Music in American Life

A list of books in the series appears
at the end of this volume.

Voices of the Jazz Age

Voices of the Jazz Age

Profiles of Eight Vintage Jazzmen

Chip Deffaa

University of Illinois Press
Urbana and Chicago

Manufactured in the United States of America
C 5 4 3 2 1

This book is printed on acid-free paper.

Library of Congress Cataloging-in-Publication Data

Deffaa, Chip, 1951–
Voices of the Jazz Age : profiles of eight vintage jazzmen / Chip Deffaa.
p. cm.—(Music in American life)
Includes bibliographical references.
ISBN 0-252-01681-5 (alk. paper)
1. Jazz musicians—United States—Biography. I. Title.
II. Series.
ML395.D44 1990
781.65'092'273—dc20
[B] 89-5242
CIP
MN

To P.R.F.

Contents

Acknowledgments

I am particularly indebted to the Institute of Jazz Studies at Rutgers University, to its director, Dan Morgenstern (who has always been so generous with his time and knowledge), and to his associates, Ed Berger and Vincent Pelote. I have drawn extensively upon the institute's collections of jazz clippings, reference books, and oral histories. I am grateful for the encouragement and general advice that has always been provided to me by Richard Sudhalter and Frank Driggs, and by Leslie Johnson, editor of the *Mississippi Rag,* which has published shorter versions of these profiles (except for the one on Beiderbecke).

I appreciate, too, the assistance in various ways of Stan Hester (who supplied copies of some rare Beiderbecke letters), Vince Giordano, Alan Roberts, Randy Sandke, Chuck Creasy, George T. Simon, Bill Priestley, Charles Smith, C. A. Tripp, Avery Sherry, Rudy Leuthauser, Jack Howe, Irving Dilliard, Rich Conaty, Joe Franklin, Joe Boughton, Nancy Miller Elliott, Ed Shanaphy, Tari Miller, Lorraine Gordon, Frank Reuter, Phil Evans, Herb Sanford, Edith Rothman, Duncan Schiedt, Michel Bastide, S. Ailin Coffee, Will Friedwald, Theodore Peterson, Nathan W. Pearson, Jr., and Judith McCulloh. Frank Jolliffe prepared the index. My special thanks to Theresa L. Sears for her conscientious copyediting.

Introduction: Three Days in New York

"Last Night in This Location" announces the sign in front of Eddie Condon's Club on Fifty-fourth Street in New York. At a quarter to six on July 31, 1985, Condon's—that famous, venerable base for traditional jazz—is already jam-packed. The patrons suspect that, despite the optimistic slant of "last night *in this location,*" this will be the last night for Condon's, period. They have gathered to mark the end of an era. Jimmy Ryan's Club, up the street, which was just as venerable as Condon's and which likewise featured older styles of jazz, lost its lease not long ago; the management found it economically impossible to reopen. Ed Polcer, one of Condon's co-owners, is telling TV and newspaper reporters his lease has run out and he hopes to reopen elsewhere at some future date. The wrecking ball will be here any day—a skyscraper is going up on the site—and he hasn't been able to find another suitable spot.

I work my way in through the mob, greeting musicians and other friends. Condon's is more than just another nightspot; it's a club where people with an interest in older jazz can gather. In spirit, it seems something of a descendant of the speakeasies; a touch of the 1920s lingers about the place. Some of those here tonight clearly *are* old enough to remember the 1920s, when Eddie Condon and his brash young jazz cohorts first descended upon New York from Chicago. Others probably recall listening to hot jazz at Condon's first club, some forty years ago. And those of us who weren't even born then have picked up the heritage from recordings and older musicians.

Leading the band is Jimmy McPartland. His style hasn't changed all that much since the jazz age. When he picks up his cornet, you can hear in his phrasing echoes of long-gone contemporaries such as Bix Beiderbecke and Red Nichols. Without fanfare, he leads his musicians crisply into "Sugar." He first recorded that number, along with Condon, Red McKenzie, and others, back in 1927. Sometimes you think of these standard jazz tunes as having been around forever; yet some of the originators, the people who first played them, are still with us. There are even some working musicians who were born before the term "jazz" came into use. The whole history of jazz has taken place within their lifetimes.

McPartland doesn't bother telling the crowd about when he first played "Sugar" or any of the other tunes he is playing. The reporters may not know, but the faithful gathered here know who he is, know the music he plays. When he offers one of Bix's tunes, they know what it is, and they know Bix was his friend. A TV crew from one of the network affiliates has begun taping.

Someone tugs at the back of my shirt and I turn around. "Hi! How's your mom?" I ask. "She's working tonight at the Ninety-second Street 'Y'! First time she's worked since getting out of the hospital," answers Paula Morris. I smile. Her mother is famed jazz singer Maxine Sullivan, who has been ill with pneumonia.

The music here is relentlessly upbeat. I'm reminded of those New Orleans jazz funerals, where they would bury somebody and head back into town playing the most joyous, uninhibited stuff they could come up with. A cartoonist from the *New York Daily News* is trying to capture the feeling of this night on his sketchpad. Polcer is telling a reporter how many clubs once throve in this part of town.

My eye spots the trombone, mounted on the wall, of the great Vic Dickenson, recently deceased. So many jazz veterans have died in the last few years. The real pioneers are almost gone. I step outside for some air. Condon's is a last, tenuous link to the music of the 1920s, and it's beginning to feel too much like a funeral in there. What other club in New York would even present Jimmy McPartland?

It's a warm evening, but I realize that, if I hurry, I can walk the forty blocks to the Ninety-second Street "Y" and hear some of Sullivan's set. I do just that, picking up dinner along the way from a Central Park hot dog vendor. There's no living singer I enjoy more than Sullivan, who is now seventy-four; in fact, with each passing year, I appreciate her presence more. Her voice is a bit shaky tonight, as if she hasn't quite gotten over her bout with pneumonia.

I cut out at the intermission, so I can see how the eleven o'clock news covers Condon's closing. Channel 2 shows a clip of Jimmy Mc-

Partland playing "Sugar," taped while I was there. Channel 4, broadcasting live from the club, catches a glimpse of Benny Goodman, who came to New York in the 1920s about the same time as Condon and McPartland and has dropped in for this final night.

The next evening I attend a re-creation of Paul Whiteman's 1924 Aeolian Hall concert. Jazz re-creations have become fairly commonplace in New York. Ten years ago a concert like this would have included several Whiteman alumni in the orchestra. Even last year the organizers were able to come up with one member of Whiteman's 1924 orchestra. But tonight, I note, there are only younger musicians on stage.

The following morning, Friday, I'm back to my usual work schedule as a jazz writer, putting into shape an article on jazz pioneer Sam Wooding. Back in the 1920s Wooding took the first black jazz orchestra to continental Europe. He's been telling me a hell of a story, most of which has never been printed. For years he had been saving it all for his own book, but he has spoken with me freely—having realized, no doubt, that he will never see his own book published. He recently turned ninety and his health has been failing.

I telephone Wooding's apartment to ask his wife if I can borrow some photos for the article. "Sam passed," she tells me simply. There's a pause. It takes a moment for me to understand her meaning. "He passed yesterday," she says. "We'll have the viewing tomorrow and the funeral on Sunday."

This book, a collection of profiles of jazzmen who came up during the 1920s, began crystallizing during those three days in New York. It was as if, with the closing of Eddie Condon's one day and the passing of Sam Wooding the next, I could see some last links to the jazz age fading before my eyes. I made a list of older jazzmen I had long wanted to interview properly—the real veterans—and told myself not to put it off any longer, that I was racing against time. I wanted to hear their stories personally. Talking with them would help me connect with those earlier years, and collectively their profiles would create a kind of window onto that period in jazz. I rearranged my priorities over the next two years, spending much less time writing and much more time tape-recording the reminiscences of older players, both for this book and for a companion volume on swing era survivors.

Within two weeks of Wooding's passing I was at the Long Island home of Jimmy McPartland, whose recollections would be worth preserving for posterity if he had done nothing more than play lead horn on those famed sides of the Austin High Gang in the late 1920s. His former wife, Marian, had cautioned me that he was apt to be forgetful, and that day he did, in fact, repeat some of his stories as if unaware he had already told them to me. But with each retelling he would include different details and I was glad for every nugget of jazz history he was sharing.

That same week I visited with Freddie Moore, who recalls an era when jazz and entertainment were closely linked. His past includes street parades, touring black minstrel shows, King Oliver's Jazz Band, and countless club gigs. Today, at eighty-eight, he is still performing regularly in a New York club.

Two weeks later I connected with Bud Freeman, who was, along with Coleman Hawkins, one of the most influential tenor sax men to emerge in the 1920s. Like McPartland, Freeman is an Austin High Gang alumnus, and their combined recollections constitute a definitive account of the origin of that group. Freeman also happens to be one of my all-time favorite players, one of the few musicians I'd drive 500 miles to hear—which I did, to the Conneaut Lake (Pennsylvania) Jazz Festival. Besides being a unique sax stylist, he's also a lively and witty raconteur.

I caught up with Jabbo Smith in New York in the fall of 1985. I had seen him about a half dozen years earlier in the stage show *One Mo' Time,* playing trumpet and singing; occasionally I would spot him in the audience at the Village Vanguard, but I had never interviewed him. A blazing comet of the late 1920s, Smith wound up spending most of the rest of his life in puzzling obscurity, until his re-emergence in the 1970s. I last saw him perform in 1987, backed by avant-garde trumpeter Don Cherry and company, at the Vanguard. He sang some inimitable wordless vocals that swung like nothing else I've heard in years.

Joe Tarto, who died on August 24, 1986, a year and a half after I profiled him for the *Mississippi Rag,* was one of the last survivors of the 1920s New York crowd associated with Red Nichols, and I had long loved the jaunty music they made. He had also been associated somewhat with Bix Beiderbecke, as, of course, had McPartland and Freeman.

The prominence of Beiderbecke in their world prompted me to add his profile to this book. The recollections of arranger Bill Challis, a close associate of Beiderbecke's whom I interviewed in 1986 at his home in Harvey's Lake, Pennsylvania, were particularly valuable to me. Even though others—most notably Richard Sudhalter and Philip Evans—have written about Beiderbecke, I wanted to offer my own synthesis; he just seemed too important a piece in the puzzle to be left out. The Beiderbecke profile accompanied, in somewhat modified form, a limited-edition boxed set of his complete recorded works, released in September 1988 by Sunbeam. Since then I've obtained copies of several letters he wrote in the last months of his life and summarize their contents here for the first time.

Because Benny Waters is an expatriate who has lived in Paris since 1952, our meeting had to wait until he visited the United States in 1987. It was well worth it, since he is unusually open and outspoken and is a direct link to Harlem's glory years, when white society types—and white jazzmen—were making their way nightly to clubs like Smalls's Paradise. Waters burned his candle at both ends then but somehow managed to outlast nearly all of his contemporaries. At age eighty-seven, he still works a lot.

The eight jazzmen profiled here were all born at least eighty years ago. They were contemporaries; they came up when jazz was new. The hot music that was played in New Orleans brothels in the mid-teens found its way, in diluted and popularized forms, into countless speakeasies and dance halls all across the country by the early 1920s, thanks in no small part to the growing popularity—and improved technology—of records. Sheet music conveyed melodies as their composers had written them, but records could capture improvisations created by jazz musicians.

The first jazz records appeared in 1917 and helped take jazz into every backwater town in the country. (Rudimentary forms of jazz may have been played in New Orleans as early as the turn of the century; but before there were records and radio, new developments in music could remain confined to localized areas.) By the 1920s, phonographs and records were in nearly every home; in 1927 Americans bought nearly 100 million records. Initially, record companies recorded more white than black jazz artists. Then, in the early 1920s, they began recording a number of black blues singers, and in 1923 they recorded, for the first time, King Oliver's potent Creole Jazz Band, which made the white bands they had recorded earlier sound like mere pretenders. The second half of the decade constituted a kind of golden age of jazz recording, as Louis Armstrong, Bix Beiderbecke, Red Nichols, Duke Ellington, Fletcher Henderson, the Chicagoans, and others came into full flower.

The growth of radio also helped in the dissemination of jazz. The first regularly scheduled radio broadcasts began in 1920. A few bands (such as Coon-Sanders—"radio's aces") exploited the medium in the early twenties, enabling people in the sticks to hear jazzy sounds live from distant cities. Later in the decade, remote broadcasts became a significant factor in popularizing bands. In the 1930s, as radio reached full strength, network remote broadcasts became commonplace. Radio played a crucial role in the popularization of such bands as Duke Ellington's and Benny Goodman's.

The jazz age was a time of national high spirits. Prohibition was widely flouted. Sexual mores were loosening. And if some conservative elders thought the younger generation was running wild, jazz musicians were happy to supply the beat. Leopold Stokowski aptly noted: "Jazz has come to stay because it is an expression of the times, of the breathless, energetic, superactive times in which we are living."[1] Not all jazzmen of that era were alike, however, and any reader coming to this book with that assumption will be disappointed. The eight musicians profiled here may recall the same years, but they do so from varying perspectives.

To begin with, four of the jazzmen in this book are white, four are black. During the 1920s the music world was officially segregated, with whites and blacks belonging to separate unions and playing in separate bands. The terms "white jazz" and "black jazz" were used commonly by musicians—even those whose worlds overlapped: after-hours jam sessions, exchanges of musical ideas, and some degree of socializing. Black musicians and white musicians in those days experienced considerably different realities.

That point noted, the reader should not assume that all black (or white) jazzmen who came up in the 1920s are alike. For one thing, life isn't that simple. Freddie Moore and Sam Wooding are both black, but Moore—who grew up in the rural South, started in carnivals and minstrel shows and forever combined music with clowning—was far different from the rather sophisticated Wooding, who wanted an orchestra that would be as respected as Paul Whiteman's. Bud Freeman and Bix Beiderbecke are both white midwesterners, but Freeman is avidly interested in all of the arts, while Beiderbecke was so obsessively focused on music that it's impossible to imagine him doing anything else. Joe Tarto worked at music in the same methodical way many people work at whatever jobs they happen to have; he is, in fact, one of the journeymen musicians who so rarely get written about but without whom we'd never have so many great jazz records.

These eight individual stories, which overlap at times, collectively cover a surprising amount of jazz history. I asked these veterans (with the exception of Beiderbecke, of course) not just about their early years but about their entire lives. I wanted to trace the full arcs of their careers, to find out what became of those who did not maintain high visibility. The profiles are written in the present tense, with descriptions of present situations referring to conditions at the time of the original interviews and personal recollections fleshed out with material gleaned from research elsewhere.

Nearly four years have passed since that "last night in this location." Eddie Condon's Club never reopened; nor, for that matter, has Jimmy McPartland worked at another New York nightspot since then. Maxine Sullivan and Benny Goodman, both of whom I saw on that last night, have since died.

I still spend a couple nights a week in different clubs, reviewing for the *New York Post* and other publications. And while I've listened to a lot of wonderful music, nothing has meant more to me than hearing jazz history firsthand from the older players I've met. These days jazz seems to be undergoing a resurgence, and it's not unusual to find younger fans with an interest in both the older and the newer styles. Judging from the frequent reissues of vintage recordings, the proliferation of books about older jazz figures, and concerts dedicated to re-creating older recordings, there is considerable interest in our jazz heritage. I think there's no better way to learn about the past than through the words of the people who lived it. Let's listen, one more time, to these voices of the jazz age.

Voices of the Jazz Age

1

SAM WOODING

Bringing Big Band Jazz to Europe

"I wanted to have a great colored band," Sam Wooding tells me, " and I *had* a great colored band." His words do not come easily. He is approaching his ninetieth birthday, a patient at St. Luke's Hospital in New York, now in the final days of his life. No longer able to take food—or even water—by mouth, he is being sustained by tube-fed nutrients. He clears his throat from time to time with an ominous sort of rumble. "In those days," he recalls, "whites stood here . . . and blacks stood there. They were fighting like hell to keep us from being anybody. And we was fighting like hell to be somebody."

Wooding certainly won that fight. One of the pioneering black big band leaders, he made his mark in New York in the early twenties. In 1925 he traveled to Europe with the all-black revue *Chocolate Kiddies,* and his orchestra was the hit of the show. He conquered a continent that had never before seen a jazz big band. His tuxedo-clad musicians, playing his arrangements, continued to tour after the show closed, becoming the most widely traveled black orchestra of the 1920s. They wowed audiences throughout Europe, helping pave the way for the 1930s tours by Duke Ellington, Louis Armstrong, Benny Carter, and others. Wooding recorded in Germany in 1925, the first American jazz orchestra to record in Europe. He introduced American jazz to Constantinople and then to the Soviet Union, where his tour had at least as great an impact as the renowned Benny Goodman tour in 1962. Wooding was also one of the very first—if not *the* first—leaders of a jazz-oriented big band to tour South America.

Back in New York for a breather in 1927, Wooding turned down an offer to open the Cotton Club. His men had no interest in playing in Harlem when they could be touring Europe and living like kings. Wooding headed back to Europe, playing concerts and dances through 1931. In 1932 he returned to a United States that had passed him by. Newer bands had come up in his nearly seven years abroad, and though he played one-nighters for the next few years, bookings were far from steady. He gave up bandleading in 1935 to study music, eventually earning both a bachelor's and a master's degree from the University of Pennsylvania. He taught and led vocal groups in the forties, appearing at Carnegie Hall in 1949. In the fifties, sixties, and early seventies, he toured the world accompanying his protégé, singer Rae Harrison, whom he eventually married. In 1974, at the age of seventy-nine, he re-entered the big band field, playing periodic engagements with his new band into the early 1980s.

Now it is April 1985. Rae Harrison Wooding has agreed to let me interview her husband at the hospital. She cautions me that he is very weak and may not be able to answer my questions. She urges me to be brief. In the hospital room, Wooding seems too far gone to be able to take part in an interview. His eyes appear lifeless, his hearing is poor, his voice is low and hard to understand. The first minutes do not go well. His wife tries to answer for him. Then he interrupts: "Nothing don't mean anything," he says, "if you don't have the beginning. . . ." And now he is off.

Where he is getting the strength from I do not know; yet he pulls the words out of himself. He was playing professionally before the term "jazz" had even come into use, but he's been overlooked, he feels, in the jazz history books. The sentences come haltingly. In three extraordinary interviews, spread over the next two weeks, he manages to get out the story that is clearly so important for him to tell. Behind the failing flesh is a fiercely proud spirit.

I visited Wooding for the last time, at his apartment in Harlem, in July 1985. Two weeks later he was dead. There are no jazz orchestra leaders left who go back as far as he did. This is his story.

Sam Wooding was born in Philadelphia on June 17, 1895, a mere thirty years after the Emancipation Proclamation, he notes. In his boyhood, many blacks, his grandparents among them, still remembered what it had been like living as slaves. He digresses for a moment to recall an old song he learned as a boy, "Trust and Obey," which he says was popular among slaves. In the song, the master is treated reverentially, "like he was God," Wooding says. His parents and grandparents came from Virginia, where, according to him, slaves were known for having yielded more, for having adapted more to white culture.

When Wooding was a boy, his father served as a butler for the Biddles. "The Biddles were Philadelphia stock; they were the great family of Philadelphia," he declares. Wooding's parents had accepted the conventional values of society. They were churchgoing people, Methodists who sent him to a Roman Catholic school to get the best education available in their area. They had high, bourgeois expectations for their children.

"I was given a title by my parents, my brother was given a title, and the oldest boy was given a title," Wooding recalls, explaining that his parents wanted their sons to grow up to be "respected" members of society, such as doctors or ministers. One of his brothers realized that dream, becoming the first black coroner in Philadelphia. He, on the other hand, was given the title of "dentist"; that was the goal his parents had decided he should strive for in life. But music was always in him; and maybe he rebelled against his parents' notions of what was respectable.

As a boy, just learning how to play the piano, he was obsessed with the *new* music: ragtime. "Yeah—well I was aiming at it, 'cause I couldn't play nothin' then," he says. Did his parents approve? "The hell no! I couldn't play it at home. And I *did* want to play it."

Ragtime was no more respectable in his parents' eyes than it was in the eyes of most white people, but Wooding was stubborn in expressing his interest in it. If he truly wanted music, his parents finally allowed, he could dedicate his life to music. "But not this music! They wanted church music. Maybe someday I could be the head of a choir, they said," Wooding remembers. He adds: "I *did* finally head a choir, but that was sixty years later, and it was a jazz choir."

Summers were always spent in Atlantic City, New Jersey. The Biddles would close up their Philadelphia mansion and relax at the premiere seaside resort for both the wealthy and the nonwealthy. Atlantic City was filled with music, and Wooding's exposure to it affected him greatly. One show in particular, which he saw when he was about nine, convinced him that he wanted to spend his life in music: "During one of the seasons in Atlantic City—it must have been about 1904—my father had a little time off, and he had a little money in his pocket. So he decided to take us to see the great Williams and Walker, doing a show. It was on the pier. And seeing these guys, Bert Williams and George Walker. . . . And they wore nice clothes and they all made a great show. They had traveled all over the world with it."

The nine-year-old boy was being exposed to a major cultural event.

Bert Williams and George Walker—black singers-dancers-comedians—were Broadway headliners at the turn of the century; in fact, no other blacks would star in their own Broadway show until the 1920s. They proved to be a smash in England as well, where Williams, at a Buckingham Palace lawn party, taught Edward VII how to do the American cakewalk. Young Sam Wooding was inspired by this great all-black musical, by the widely traveled, widely praised Williams and Walker. He realized there was a whole glamorous world out there, far removed from the life his parents had planned for him. And he wanted to be part of it.

The love of music, Wooding says, was no doubt already in him. But seeing that show really brought it out. "And of course none of us like to do the hard work," he adds in a self-deprecating way. As soon as he was old enough, whether or not his father was working there, he got into the habit of going to Atlantic City. "I was going all the time. . . . And all of the Negroes used to go in the summer to Atlantic City. Because in their own cities, there wasn't much doing, but Atlantic City was sort of a summer resort." It was where the action was, where he saw men who didn't play piano much better than he did, living what appeared to be the good life. Some wrote their own songs. Wooding fancied himself a songwriter as well. His first song, written when he was eleven, he says, was called "Won't You Be My Sweet Little Household Queen?"

At perhaps age fifteen, the boy whose parents had wanted him to become a dentist—or, failing that, a church choir director—dropped out of school. His father was having difficulty supporting the family anyway. Wooding would get by with his piano playing and songwriting, and by whatever other means he could in Atlantic City. At that time, the music business centered on live performances and sales of sheet music. Record sales were but a small fraction of sheet music sales, which reached an all-time high of two billion copies in 1910.

When Wooding turned professional in the summer of 1911, the summer he turned sixteen, musicians in Atlantic City were not yet using the term "jazz" or playing what would later be called jazz. Ragtime was the big thing, Wooding says, as it had been for the past dozen years. Hit songs of 1911 included "Alexander's Ragtime Band," "Ragtime Violin," "Careless Love," "I Want a Girl Just Like the Girl That Married Dear Old Dad," "That Mysterious Rag," "Oh You Beautiful Doll," and "Everybody's Doing It" (which celebrated the popular new ragtime dance step, the turkey trot). It was the year in which Scott Joplin presented his ragtime opera *Treemonisha,* which flopped, and the year in which Al Jolson made his Broadway debut. The term "the blues" was just beginning to come into general use in music. The first published blues song, W. C. Handy's "Memphis Blues," appeared in 1912. Later in the decade, Wooding witnessed the rise of the new hot music that would become known as jazz.

Although the term "swing" would not come into general public use until the 1930s, Wooding states that among musicians he heard the term "swing" used before he heard the term "jazz" for hot music. There was ragtime and then there was swing, he says; the term "jazz" came along later for the new music. That's the way he recollects it.

Who were some of the first good hot musicians Wooding saw in his youth?

> There was a fellow called Jack the Bear. He played in two keys, but he played ragtime. That was in Atlantic City. And I heard Eubie Blake play at Atlantic City, 'cause he used to go there every summer. Eubie was playing at the boathouse, about 1911. 'Cause I wasn't allowed to go in the cabarets in those days. I got in a window that was very near and listened to him.
>
> Eubie played with a drummer. Madison Reid and Mary Stafford were the singers. Eubie Blake was very good. Later I found out that he wasn't the best, but he was a better piano player than Jack the Bear was.

The best pianists Wooding ever heard in his life, a point of importance to him, were James P. Johnson and Willie "The Lion" Smith—"they were the New York boys." New York was the show business capital, and the best in New York were believed to be the best anywhere.

Neither Jack the Bear nor Eubie Blake was yet playing what we would consider jazz. They were playing current rags and Tin Pan Alley tunes, as best they knew how. As a boy, Wooding's understanding was that a *good* pianist was one who could play well what the composer had written—whether that meant "serious" music or ragtime music. You played what was printed on the sheet music. But in his mid-teens in Atlantic City, Wooding learned that a good pianist could—and should—improvise, adapt, change things around. Sometimes the point was to find the most effective way of setting off a singer or dancer; sometimes it was pure showmanship. The best pianists, he realized, weren't merely executing what the composers had written.

Wooding was glad to finally get a job, accompanying a singer and dancer named Josephine Berkeley. She was the one, he remembers, "that give me the *inside stuff*—which threw me back, because until then,

I thought you just played a piece . . . but that was not so." He adds that he became good enough as a pianist to substitute for the great Eubie Blake one night when Blake was sick. That evening he accompanied Mary Stafford, now forgotten but a headliner in her era, who recorded for Columbia in 1921 and became one of the pioneering black female recording artists. Her brother, George Stafford, was a drummer who worked later for Wooding, Charlie Johnson, Red Allen, Eddie Condon, and others. Wooding was now getting to know all of, and be known by, the Atlantic City piano players.

Charlie Johnson proved to be a great help and inspiration. According to Wooding, Johnson was about the first pianist he heard who was playing what would today be considered jazz rather than ragtime—although Wooding says at the time they were calling it swing.

> Charlie Johnson was a piano player from Boston. I met him in 1917. Charlie used to tell me a lot of things, even when I was with Josephine Berkeley. And he's the first one that I heard play like the people, like they's playing now. Well, Percy Adams from Philadelphia, he used to play swing, but he would play mostly dance music. Charlie was three or four years older than me, and he took me, and I took him as a big brother. I used to go and sit in on his job. Charlie Johnson became the greatest in Atlantic City as a cabaret piano player. James P. Johnson didn't come to Atlantic City, and neither did Willie "The Lion" Smith.

Wooding continues: "Charlie didn't have a band then. He didn't begin leading a band until after I left out of New York for Europe in '25, when he started at Smalls's Paradise in Harlem." (Johnson actually had begun his bandleading career a few years earlier in Atlantic City, starting with smaller outfits.)

"Charlie was a *lot* of help," Wooding stresses, not just musically, but personally. He became a kind of surrogate parent, "because my parents wasn't any help to me in the world. . . . they were church members. See, they only knew one thing—do 'the right thing.' And in those days, *everything* was for me. I was trying to be a pimp and everything. See, I was trying to be a great sport, and they wouldn't know nothing about that. But Charlie used to say, 'Sam (or Kid), don't do that. Because that leads you in wrong.'"

There were many bawdy houses in the city that stayed open for the summer, Wooding recalls, and they employed hot young ragtime pianists like him to help draw in customers. " 'Professor'—that's what they used to use [as the term for the pianist] in the bawdy houses, when I was coming up." And the prostitutes made sure that the johns tipped them. "They'd say: 'Give the professor some money,' and the man would give it. And sometimes they'd go to reach in the man's pocket. This was in the white district. . . . From Arctic Avenue up to Atlantic Avenue, it was the white district. And from Arctic down to Mediterranean Avenue was the Negro district. But the Negroes, we didn't go just for the Negroes. We went for the ofay—for the whites."

Wooding tried to get a couple of prostitutes to work for him, but it just didn't work out. Meanwhile, Charlie Johnson helped keep him focused on music. Rapid changes were occurring in music and Johnson was up on the new sounds, like the jazzy stride piano style that was evolving from ragtime.

If any one year can be pegged as the birth year for jazz, historians usually choose 1917, while acknowledging that the music had been developing in New Orleans and elsewhere before that. In 1917 the five-piece Original Dixieland Jazz Band (or "Jass Band," as it was sometimes spelled in the early days) scored a tremendous success at Reisenweber's Restaurant in New York and made the first jazz record—and possibly the first million-selling record of popular music ever: "Livery Stable Blues," backed by "Dixie Jass Band One-Step." Small jazz bands soon began finding audiences in New York, Chicago, and other cities—especially after the authorities closed down the Storyville area (a red-light district) in New Orleans. That had the unintended effect of reducing employment opportunities for musicians, motivating many to head north for better prospects and helping to spur the dissemination of jazz from New Orleans to Chicago and elsewhere. New Orleans lost its greatest jazz musicians, and its importance as a jazz site, within the next few years.

The United States entered World War I in 1917, and Wooding was soon inducted into the army (which, of course, was still segregated). "I lost [touch with] Charlie Johnson after the army started," he says. "I spent a year and a half in World War One, and I never got to hang out with those guys. I sort of missed Charlie."

While in the service, Wooding became a member of an organized band for the first time in his life, playing tenor horn, not piano. The 807th Pioneer Infantry Band, which was a very good band, was led by the distinguished composer-arranger-conductor William Vodery, Wooding recalls: "My own band had its beginning, in a sense, with Bill Vodery's Band in Europe, the 807th. Bill Vodery, you know, he was colored, but he was the arranger for Ziegfeld; he did all of Ziegfeld's theater work. And he inspired me to have a band." Did Vodery's band play any jazz? "No, military music. Marches. But I know enough to know what I wanted. And I had heard Eubie Blake. That's what I wanted to do, because military music was so strict."

Vodery was one of the most prominent black men in music in his day. He was from the generation just before jazz, and his contributions helped lay the groundwork for the jazz big bands that would develop in the 1920s. He was a role model for aspiring black musicians, as were such other noted prejazz black musicians as Ford Dabney, a leader and composer who had also worked with Ziegfeld; James Reese Europe, whose prewar orchestra had been the favorite of dancers Vernon and Irene Castle and whose military band, the Hellfighters, attracted a great deal of attention in Europe during the war; and Will Marion Cook, an orchestra leader and composer who had worked with Williams and Walker and whose Southern Syncopated Orchestra, numbering nearly forty musicians, attracted a following in Europe just after the war.

When the war ended for him in 1918, Wooding says, "I was thinking about my own band. And I thought, if I could get a good drummer, it was a possibility of having my own band. So I thought of, not of trumpet players and trombone players, but I thought of drummers. . . ." He recalls how audiences had really taken notice of drummer Buddy Gilmore, from Will Marion Cook's huge concert orchestra. "And I can tell you, we got George Howe, who was a good drummer."

Sam Wooding returned to Atlantic City in 1919. No longer just a piano player, he led a jazz band, the Society Syncopaters, which played at Scott's Hotel. It was a five-piece group—trumpet, trombone, clarinet, piano, and drums—pretty much the standard instrumentation of a jazz band then. A band might also have a banjo and perhaps a tuba, or maybe a violin, but generally there was no more than one of any particular instrument. There were no sections, as you would later have in big bands, and the music was generally not arranged. Wooding's band wound up playing for a show featuring Ethel Waters and Ethel Williams ("the Two Ethels," he says). He often played music for shows during his career.

In 1920 Barron Wilkins, the black political boss of Harlem, heard Wooding in Atlantic City and hired the band to play at his club, Barron's, on Seventh Avenue and 134th Street. Wooding recalls: "You couldn't do nothing here [in Harlem] if Barron Wilkins didn't give his approval. There was two brothers, Barron Wilkins and Leroy Wilkins. Barron took care of white audiences; his club was for whites. And Leroy Wilkins took care of the Negro. See, they didn't mix in those days." Leroy Wilkins's club, which did not admit whites—the only exception, according to Wooding, was Al Jolson, by then the reigning king of show business—featured the piano players Wooding admired so much: Willie "The Lion" Smith, James P. Johnson, Luckey Roberts, Willie Gant. It was known as a much rougher joint than Barron's, with fights and slayings occurring within its confines. Barron's, one of Harlem's first large clubs, was a more prestigious venue for a musician to play and a fashionable nightspot for white society during the Harlem Renaissance of the 1920s.

Wooding remembers that his band sounded far from polished in its first appearances in New York.

> That first show, we played with Dancing Dotson. And when we opened up, we sounded like a bunch of crazy people. Because we were nervous; we hadn't been out of Atlantic City, where we had started. So [Dotson] walks out there—he was very smart, the way he did it—and he said: "I hear you. Boys, I want you all to cut out that first bit, and play something for the people. I didn't bring you down here for them to hear a clown band." And the people were enjoying it. Because they thought we were really kidding! And we were doing the best we could. Then we got down to business. And we had a success. And what we knew, we really knew, was jazz; we played jazz all the time.

It wasn't the same jazz, by any means, that you could have heard in New Orleans. The New Orleans jazzmen had an affinity for the blues that musicians of the Northeast did not. Wooding's men wanted to play hot, getting some of the spirit of New Orleans jazz but with an urban sophistication and refinement. Their music was commercially slicker, more show-biz oriented than the music being played down in New Orleans (or on the South Side of Chicago by New Orleans–born musicians who had recently moved to that city). At Barron's, they would play for featured singers and dancers and then for patrons who wanted to dance or sit, drink, and listen.

Wooding's band from the Barron's period included trumpet, trombone, clarinet, piano, drums, banjo, and violin. Sidney Bechet sat in with the band one night, Wooding recalls, and did such an awesome job on "Dear Old Southland" that Wooding retired that number from the band's repertoire. There was no way they could duplicate the performance without Bechet.

In the next few years, Wooding became an arranger as well as a pianist and bandleader. The development did not come by choice, however. He wanted his band to have a distinctive sound and initially attempted to hire the services of an experienced white arranger. But the man made it plain that he didn't want to work for a black, so Wooding began working up beginnings and endings for numbers and modifying stock arrangements himself. Before long he progressed to creating his own arrangements.

To set things in historical context, we should note that 1920—the year in which Wooding arrived in New York—was the same year in which Paul Whiteman and Fletcher Henderson arrived in the city.[1] Whiteman was five years older than Wooding; Henderson was two and a half years younger. Whiteman had organized his first dance band in San Francisco in 1918, then he had moved to Los Angeles and Atlantic City before making New York his permanent base in 1920. He was the best-known bandleader in America throughout the twenties; and his million-selling recordings of "Whispering" and "Japanese Sandman" (1920) were pioneering examples of special arrangements.

It was customary for dance bands to play unimaginative stock arrangements supplied by publishers, in which the melody was played by the ensemble for chorus after chorus. But Whiteman's arranger, Ferde Grofe—whose importance in establishing the foundation upon which big band jazz would be built has often been overlooked—kept the music changing. He was most likely the first arranger to treat each chorus differently. He'd harmonize various instruments for a stretch; let the smooth saxes lead as a section for a while, with other instruments playing a countermelody beneath them (foreshadowing, in a faint way, the vigorous call-and-response that Don Redman, Fletcher Henderson, and others would develop in the late 1920s and early 1930s); have various soloists take the lead—all to keep the music interesting. As Whiteman enlarged the band, Grofe enjoyed greater freedom to arrange the music, borrowing—as he viewed it—elements from the worlds of both jazz and symphonic music.

Whiteman's so-called symphonic jazz was presented (and accepted by many) as an improvement upon—a refinement of—earlier, cruder jazz. He used eleven or twelve musicians on his records in the early 1920s; later in the decade, his orchestra would swell to twenty-five or more members. The extraordinary popularity of the music Whiteman made did not go unnoticed by other musicians of the twenties—both black and white. Any bandleader hoping for commercial success had to pay attention to what Whiteman was doing, for the symphonic jazz he was creating in New York had far more commercial appeal than the rougher sounds of authentic New Orleans jazz. Whiteman eventually controlled eleven New York–based bands and seventeen touring bands, and he supplied arrangements to an additional forty bands, all of which extended his sway.

Meanwhile, in 1920 Fletcher Henderson graduated from Atlanta University, where he had studied chemistry and math. He headed to New York planning to do postgraduate research there with the hope—despite barriers of racial prejudice—of becoming a chemist. Instead, low on funds, he wound up taking a job as a song demonstrator. In 1921 he became a house pianist for Black Swan (the first black-owned record company), accompanying not just blues and jazz artists but pop and classical artists as well. He got plenty of exposure via records, as an accompanist and under his own name, and also organized a band to tour with Ethel Waters (autumn 1921 to summer 1922). Tradition has it that a 1922 broadcast by Waters, backed by Henderson's group, was the first performance by blacks on radio. Henderson later worked as a sideman in a band at Broadway Jones' Club and became the leader of his own big band for the first time in January 1924.

Wooding apparently made his recording debut in 1922. The *Chicago Defender,* a black newspaper, reported on May 13 that Sam Wooding's orchestra had recently recorded for Columbia. Although the company did not release any records credited to Wooding, discographer Brian Rust has speculated that "Put and Take" and "Moanful Blues," which Columbia released in 1922 and credited to Johnny Dunn's Original Jazz Hounds (Dunn's name was then bigger than Wooding's), may actually have been by Wooding's orchestra; the cornet playing, he notes, does not sound like Dunn's.[2] The first documented recording by Wooding was made on July 16, 1922, when Wooding's Society Entertainers backed Lucille Hegamin, a black vaudeville performer who sang torch and blues songs in a refined style, on two numbers for Paramount Records: "I've Got to Cool My Puppies Now" and "Send Back My Honey Man." The band consisted of Wooding, piano; Elmer Chambers, trumpet; Herb Fleming, trombone; Garvin Bushell, clarinet and also sax; Rollen Smith, tenor sax; Charlie Dixon, banjo; Joe Young, drums.

Blacks were now making some important breakthroughs in the world of show business. The all-black Broadway show *Shuffle Along* was such a hit in 1921 that it spawned a raft of imitators. Wooding served as musical director for the pit band in one touring black show, *Plantation Days.* When the tour ended, in Indianapolis, he headed back to New York.

In 1923 Wooding's band opened the stylish new Nest Club on 133rd Street and Seventh Avenue in Harlem, which drew a racially mixed crowd. He now had eight players in the band and felt he had hit upon a sound, a musical identity of his own, using augmented chords. Perhaps his star sideman was Garvin Bushell, who demonstrated his prowess on all of the reed instruments. (Bushell had started out as a clarinetist and saxist, but Wooding soon had him doubling on bassoon and oboe, to add color to the symphonic jazz that, taking a cue from Whiteman, he was striving for.) Big-voiced, magnetic Lizzie Miles sang in the revue, and there was Wooding himself, who, if not among the greatest piano players in the city, was certainly one of the better ones. Bushell recalled in 1977 that the Nest became world famous, drawing elite patrons including royalty. Bandleaders such as Roger Wolfe Kahn and Paul Whiteman and Whiteman's star trumpet soloist, Henry Busse, all found their way uptown to check out the show.[3]

If whites were flocking to see black entertainment in the Harlem clubs, some producers speculated, maybe they'd do the same for shows in midtown clubs. Thus, in 1922 Florence Mills played the Plantation Room on Broadway; and in January 1924 *The Creole Follies,* starring Edith Wilson and Fletcher Henderson and His Famous Club Alabam Orchestra—that was the billing, even though the orchestra and club were brand new—opened at the Club Alabam on West Forty-fourth Street, in the heart of the theater district. Henderson's ten-man big band featured Coleman Hawkins on tenor sax and Elmer Chambers (who had come over from Wooding's band) on cornet, with special arrangements by Don Redman (who was just beginning to work out how to play sections off against one another). They became a great hit, the first real jazz-influenced big band to make it in New York.

Hawkins played far hotter and more creatively than any of the musicians in Whiteman's band. An authoritative, big-toned player, he really improvised in his solo spots. Standard dance bands around town stressed musicians reading written parts, mostly ensemble; if a solo instrument got a few bars, it was generally to carry the melody, not to improvise. Henderson was breaking new ground by successfully combining arranged passages with hot, improvised jazz solos. He was offering rudimentary big band jazz and clicking with both the public and other musicians.

A pioneering New York radio station, WHN, put a wire into the Club Alabam and began live broadcasting of the band—making the club one of the first regular radio outlets for a black band. There weren't nearly as many radio listeners in 1925 as there would be just a few years later; still, the broadcasts helped spread the fame of the band regionally. (And in those early years of radio, when there weren't that many stations, signals could often be picked up by quite distant listeners.)

In July 1924, the band was booked into the huge Roseland Ballroom—the city's best-known ballroom; it would have a lock on the room for the next decade. Henderson soon added Louis Armstrong to his band as featured cornet soloist, which made the band hotter and exposed the players to Armstrong's ideas on phrasing. Wooding's band, which had been making such a hit at the Nest, was selected to succeed Henderson's at the Club Alabam.

The Alabam management wanted Wooding to give the public more of what Henderson had been offering—arranged hot dance music with room for soloists to blow, as well as some sweet numbers, in addition to backing singers and dancers in the show. Wooding's band had to grow. He recalls: "There were only eight of us at the Nest. When we went to the Club Alabam, we added three more pieces. That made eleven. That's not counting me." Like Henderson, he was now leading a big band (defined as ten or more musicians), a jazz-influenced big band, at a prestigious New York venue, a band with brass and reed sections that could play separately or provide an ensemble backing for the improvisations of soloists.

In 1924 the big bands of Charlie Johnson, Duke Ellington, and Chick Webb had yet to arrive on the scene. In fact, if you were talking about black, jazz-influenced orchestras in New York, Wooding says, he and Henderson just about had the field to themselves. Small jazz combos were plentiful, but jazz-influenced big bands were new. Wooding adds that the now-forgotten Leroy Smith—the violin-playing orchestra leader at Connie's Inn in Harlem from 1923 to 1926—"had a great band, but he had too many of the old guys in there. One fellow in there played the cello." Henderson, he says, had the best *modern* band—not counting his own, of course.

Wooding takes pride in the fact that he had hit the big time: "People like Gloria Swanson, Firpo, Jack Dempsey, Al Jolson used to come there to the Club Alabam. The Club Alabam had the leading people." He remembers how the scions of some of the wealthiest families would sit on the steps leading up to the bandstand; and he adds, in a clear allusion to the reputation the Cotton Club would later have, "We didn't have no mob guys in there." He knew he had really arrived, however, when in 1924 he was booked to double (from the Club Alabam) at the famed Winter Garden Theater, the flagship of the Shubert empire. "Every Sunday night we played at the Winter Garden Theater—a midnight show. They didn't have Broadway shows on Sundays; they had concerts there. And we also played the Loew's

Theater five times that year." Still, the biggest break for Sam Wooding was yet to come: *Chocolate Kiddies* and the European tour.

Chocolate Kiddies was a 1925 revue designed to give European audiences a sampling of black entertainment from New York. By the early 1920s, black entertainment was selling big. The first sign, perhaps, had come in 1920, when Mamie Smith's "Crazy Blues" (the first vocal blues recording) sold 75,000 copies within a month of its release, spurring record companies to produce many more "race records," as records by black performers were then called. Then, in May 1921 *Shuffle Along,* an all-black show with music by Eubie Blake and lyrics by Noble Sissle, opened on Broadway, the first all-black Broadway production since the pioneering shows of Williams and Walker more than a decade before. *Shuffle Along* had proved to be a smash hit, running for 504 performances, and in the next four years another ten black Broadway shows opened.

The producers of *Chocolate Kiddies* hired top black acts from various productions throughout New York City to take part in their show. The company included more than thirty singers and dancers. They were all listed in the program, along with where they had been appearing: Rufus Greenlee and Thaddeus Drayton, from the Sixty-third Street Theater; Adelaide Hall, from the Club Alabam; the Three Eddies, from the Plantation Theater; Bobby and Babe Goins, from the Club Alabam; Charles Davis, from the Colonial Theater, and so on. Sam Wooding and His Orchestra, from the Club Alabam, initially were just one of many attractions; no one could have foreseen that they would draw more attention than the singers and dancers. Lottie Gee, replaced during the run by Evelyn Dove, was initially expected to be the star attraction. A bon voyage party, thrown by the owner of the Club Alabam for Wooding and the entire *Chocolate Kiddies* company at a "sister" club, the Bamville, featured entertainment by most of Harlem's leading show people, including Florence Mills.

Chocolate Kiddies brings back good memories for Sam Wooding. "Before opening night, I just had the band, I was just playing for the show. But by the second half of the [first] show, it *was* Sam Wooding," he recalls. "After opening night, we *took over*—everything was different." Critics and audiences paid more attention to his orchestra—the first black jazz-influenced orchestra to reach the continent—than they did to the singer and dancers. European dance bands stressed ensemble work, so when Wooding's sax players rose to take hot solos, they were offering something new. His orchestra became the prime attraction of *Chocolate Kiddies* and continued touring, as Sam Wooding's Chocolate Kiddies Orchestra, long after the show closed.

In his autobiography, Duke Ellington says he wrote all of the music for *Chocolate Kiddies* (with Jo Trent penning the lyrics), supposedly in one night. His claim has become part of jazz lore, cropping up in other writers' books about him, as well as in some general jazz retrospectives. Wooding strongly disputes the notion that the complete score was written by Ellington. The evidence suggests that Ellington contributed songs to the show, but that the show, as presented in Europe, did not have a full score by him. "It wasn't a legitimate show; it was a revue," Wooding notes. "And the people all used their own music. Bobby and Babe Goins, Johnny Hudgins, Greenlee and Drayton, they all had their own music. All I had to do was play that music."

Wooding's band also had its own featured concert spot in the program. "Oh yeah, we had our own arrangements. I arranged the music we played. That's what made it a novelty. Yeah. Because it was the same music, but the people were hearing it through a different ear. . . . One strain would be maybe an augmented chord, another strain would be, would be the octave, and I treated each one different." (Ferde Grofe had established the precedent of treating each strain differently, although Wooding strove for a hotter overall feel than Grofe did.) According to Wooding, the band played only one instrumental that he did not arrange, the sedate "By the Waters of Minnetonka."

Chocolate Kiddies opened in Germany in May 1925; by late June ads were claiming the program was "entirely new." Because it was a revue, the singers and dancers were easily able to interpolate into the show different routines from their repertoires, and Wooding was able to present different numbers. A copy of the program from a late-summer engagement in Sweden was reproduced in an article by Bjorn Englund that ran in England's *Storyville* magazine.[4] Although it gives general composer credits to Ellington and Trent, only five songs listed in the program are known to be by them; in some cases authorship is unknown; the rest are known to be by others.

The program lists three acts. The first was set in a Harlem café, purportedly showing black nightlife in New York, and included such things as Bobby and Babe Goins doing an Apache dance and headliners Greenlee and Drayton doing a specialty. The entire second act was given over to a "Symphonic Jazzconcert at the Club Alabam in New York: Sam Wooding and Orchestra." The selections were: "1. Medley American hits. 2. 'Indian Love Call' [written by Rudolf Friml]. 3. 'Shanghai Shuffle' [written by Gene Rodemich and Larry Conley]. 4.

'Some Other Day, Some Other Girl' [authorship unknown]. 5. 'St. Louis Blues' [written by W. C. Handy]." Act three began in a plantation and ended in Harlem. It opened with numbers such as "Old Black Joe" (Stephen Foster), "Joshua Fit de Battle of Jericho" (traditional), "Swing Low, Sweet Chariot" (traditional), and "Swanee River" (Stephen Foster) and also brought in some contemporary hits, such as "Old Fashioned Love" (1923) by James P. Johnson and Cecil Mack.

The only certain Ellington-Trent numbers mentioned in the program are "Deacon Jazz," "Jim Dandy," "Love Is Just a Wish," "With You," and "Jig Walk," to which the ensemble danced the current craze, the Charleston. Ellington's songs thus would appear to have been only a small part of the show as it was presented in Europe; certainly, he was not responsible for the show's success and in fact never saw it, since *Chocolate Kiddies* was only presented overseas. Of course, he may honestly have thought the producers had used his songs throughout.

Wooding's main concern is that his status at the time, compared to Ellington's, be properly understood. After all, he had already been leading a band at Barron's when Ellington, who was four years his junior, first arrived in New York as a pianist in Elmer Snowden's five-man band, the Washingtonians. Ellington took over that small group while it was playing at the Kentucky Club, a speakeasy on Forty-ninth Street, in late 1924. He gradually added players, but it did not become a big band until late 1927, according to Ellington's recollections.[5] Wooding was leading a prominent big band in New York well before then, and he emphasizes that he wants *Chocolate Kiddies* to be remembered as his success—not, somehow, his and Ellington's.

I make the mistake, at one point, of asking Wooding when he first met Duke Ellington. With dignity—and a touch of annoyance that the question has even been asked—Wooding eventually responds: "*He* met *me*. *I* didn't meet him at all. It was through Sonny Greer that I was acquainted with Duke. 'Cause Duke didn't mean nothing. Duke wasn't considered in those days." When I suggested that Ellington may have been a great piano player, Wooding becomes aroused, answering quickly and with real feeling in his voice: "Oh, no! No. Ellington wasn't a great pianist. He wasn't a piano player at all!" The *real* piano players, Wooding says, were the Harlem stride geniuses, men like James P. Johnson and Willie "The Lion" Smith.

While Ellington and the Washingtonians were in New York, Wooding and his eleven-piece orchestra were becoming the toast of Europe, achieving the kind of success that Fletcher Henderson had in New York. "Half a century has passed since the *Chocolate Kiddies* tour of Europe," Bjorn Englund wrote in 1975, "and it is still the best-remembered and most talked about Negro show to have visited our shores. . . .[6] Wooding recalls:

> When we opened in Berlin [on May 25, 1925, at the Admiralspalast], our first show, it was a wonderful experience. But the people in the audience started stomping their feet, and calling out "*Bis!*" Well, we didn't understand what "*Bis*" was—we had just come out of Harlem. We thought they were calling us "beasts"—B-E-A-S-T—but they wasn't. They were calling out "*Bis*"—and some of the boys in the saxophone section had their horns and were going out the door, because they were afraid, and I was with them. . . .

He and his men had no idea that the fervored stomping and shouts of *Bis!* were the German equivalent of clamoring for "more, more."

When Wooding realized that the audience was thrilled, he knew he had them, for the number that had caused such a commotion was far from the best in his repertoire. Europe simply had not had much exposure to American big bands. "We played there for seventy-six performances," he recalls, until July 20. A contract offer from Vox, just ten days after the Berlin opening led to four recordings (in both 10-inch and 12-inch 78 r.p.m. versions): "Shanghai Shuffle," "O Katharina," "By the Waters of Minnetonka," and "Alabamy Bound."[7] "And then we went to Hamburg," Wooding continues, "and from Hamburg we went to Stockholm, where I played a benefit show for the Swedish Red Cross, for the brother of the king. From there we went to Copenhagen, and then back to Germany, played a couple of smaller spots. We went to Switzerland. And from Switzerland we went on to Spain. Then we went back to Paris . . . [and] that's where I met such people as Maurice Chevalier and Mistinguette. We played at Nice, in the Negresco Hotel. . . . We had a big success. And the Lord was with us." The show sold out, despite ticket prices far higher than for other shows.

Reviews generally praised the *Chocolate Kiddies* dancers more than the singers, and the orchestra most of all. The serious critics who covered this new music from America were, for the most part, favorable; they found the music vital, if barbaric. One reviewer was awed at the ruckus the men were making—and at the dignified way in which Wooding conducted, as if he were leading a symphony orchestra. Some disapproved of the inclusion of a bit of Wagner's music in the show, as if black musicians had no right to play classical music. But Wooding was proud that his men could handle anything, whether jazz or so-called serious music. Ads claimed that the reed section was capable of doubling on twenty-five instruments; and the trumpeters could double on French horns. His men could go from sweet commercial numbers to hot dance music and jazz with ease. Wooding wanted them to be as versatile as the members of Paul Whiteman's orchestra.

In Wooding's estimation, the two best musicians in the band were reedmen Garvin Bushell, who played "all of the family of saxophone," and Gene Sedric, who was featured on tenor and, according to Wooding, owned the best instrument. "I think the first time Europe had heard a tenor played solo was when they heard Gene," he says. (Wooding's band, like Henderson's, was featuring jazz tenor solos; Whiteman's was not.) Sedric, who became best known as a member of Fats Waller's band, was, in effect, Wooding's answer to Coleman Hawkins, who was then being featured with Henderson in New York. Wooding says proudly of Sedric: "He was compared with . . . I think he was better than Coleman Hawkins, because he also was a vocal soloist, and Coleman Hawkins never bothered with vocal solos. But Gene was very good." And he was a team player, not just a soloist. Wooding feels the same could not be said of Hawkins. "Why, Coleman Hawkins was like Louis Armstrong," Wooding declares with a touch of disapproval. "He didn't feature nobody but himself. And that was bad."

Initially, Wooding tried to hire Louis Armstrong out of Henderson's band for his own *Chocolate Kiddies* orchestra, but Armstrong declined the offer. He then tried to hire Bob Shoffner, the trumpeter who had succeeded Armstrong in King Oliver's band in Chicago in 1924. Finally, he hired cornetist Tommy Ladnier, who also had worked for a while with Oliver as his featured soloist. Wooding wanted the best possible jazz improviser on cornet, and he went to the same source—King Oliver's Creole Jazz Band—that Henderson had. Ladnier, who died at the age of thirty-nine, is known to many jazz buffs for his later recordings with Henderson, such as "I'm Comin' Virginia," "Rocky Mountain Blues," and "Snag It," and for the group he subsequently co-led with Sidney Bechet.[8]

Some authorities will dispute Wooding's claim that his was the first jazz-oriented American *orchestra* to reach Europe.[9] Music historian Mark Tucker has suggested that a case could be made for Will Marion Cook's thirty-six-man Southern Syncopated Orchestra, which was a great hit in Europe in 1919; however, it was not really jazz-oriented, in spite of the presence of young Sidney Bechet among the reeds.[10] A more plausible claim might be made for Paul Whiteman's band, which toured the continent in 1923 and was promoted as a jazz ensemble—the term "jazz" being used comparatively freely then. Beginning in 1927, Whiteman could boast of truly exceptional jazz soloists, among them Bix Beiderbecke, Frank Trumbauer, and Jimmy Dorsey, but in 1923 he was still offering well-played dance music—often warm rather than hot, and sometimes a bit pretentious. He had outstanding technicians, but he didn't have jazz soloists who could offer anything comparable to the hot chorus that Ladnier, for example, took on Wooding's 1925 recording of "Shanghai Shuffle."

Tucker has also suggested that the orchestra conducted by Will Vodery, which accompanied the American revue *Dover to Dixie* in England in 1923, could possibly have been "the first black jazz orchestra to reach Europe."[11] In the absence of recorded evidence, however, it is impossible to judge at this date just how jazzy that particular orchestra (which included Johnny Dunn on cornet) might have been in 1923. Vodery, who earned considerable success in his career arranging for Broadway and, later, Hollywood productions, is not generally thought of as being part of the jazz tradition; although he was an important inspiration to Wooding and others, he was not out to make a name for himself as a jazz orchestra leader. His *Dover to Dixie* orchestra, which never recorded, had a rather limited impact in Europe, playing in only one British theater; by contrast, Wooding's orchestra—with *Chocolate Kiddies* and on its own—enjoyed great success in country after country. Thus, Wooding seems entitled to claim that his was the first jazz orchestra to reach Europe—or at least the first to reach continental Europe.

Wooding views himself as the Christopher Columbus of jazz, having brought big band jazz to a new world. He helped pave the way for Claude Hopkins, whose band went into Europe with a revue later in 1925; Noble Sissle, whose band became a hit in Paris in 1928; Louis Armstrong, who first reached Europe in 1932; and Duke Ellington, who followed in 1933. But some who define jazz more narrowly than it was defined in the 1920s argue that Wooding's band should not be called a jazz orchestra but a show orchestra. They will note, correctly, that much of what Wooding's men played was not jazz, that in *Chocolate Kiddies* the band played scored music for various acts, besides doing its jazz concert spot. On its own, the band mixed sweet and hot music; it even offered some comedy numbers. Yet all bands had to offer variety back then, if they wanted to make it financially. The important thing here is that on the hotter numbers Wooding would let soloists improvise, and the band would dig into jazz material such as "Tiger Rag" with plenty of gusto. Wooding wanted a jazz feeling in the music he played, and his band was accepted by all of its contemporaries as a jazz ensemble. In fact, its jazz side was what made it so exciting and so newsworthy.

"After a year in Europe, we went to Russia," Wooding remembers. The band played in Moscow from March 16 to May 5, 1926, and in Leningrad from May 8 to May 23. He enjoyed the classical music he heard in concert in Moscow—particularly one concert in which an entire symphony orchestra played without a conductor—and many of the men in the company found the Russian women beautiful. At some point in the tour—Wooding claims it was in Russia[12]—Tommy Ladnier quit the band and Wooding had to give concerts with no one taking the cornetist's place. Europe simply did not have the stock of musicians familiar with American jazz that it would have later, making qualified substitutes impossible to find, except, perhaps, in Paris. "Tommy Ladnier was rather weak, because he left me. . . . He went with Fletcher Henderson. But he later came back to me. He didn't find the same feeling in Henderson's band he had found in my band, and I took him back in my band."

Chocolate Kiddies ended its European tour in Danzig, a little more than a year after it had opened, and Wooding's band continued touring on its own. He recalls Josephine Baker—who was soon to become one of the most celebrated black entertainers—coming to meet him when he was playing at a theater in Germany. "She wasn't nobody then. And she would still have been nobody, if she didn't switch to strip-teasing. . . . She became the greatest artist in Europe."In September 1926 the band recorded another ten sides in Germany, including "Black Bottom," "Milenberg Joys," and "Lonesome and Sorry." The records were of incidental importance to Wooding, however; live performances were the main thing.

Did the people treat Wooding well in Europe? "Oh, I should say so. They were crazy about jazz. And the Europeans liked the Negro's style of jazz better than they did Paul Whiteman's." Wooding's men projected dignity; they wore striped trousers, oxford gray coats, and ties. Of course, they encountered a few snobs who seemed to resent blacks dressing so well, not "knowing their place"—people who might have accepted black performers in raggedy clothes and blackface makeup but were uncomfortable with blacks who looked and acted as if they were world-class artists.

Wooding's band played in Turkey, Egypt, Rumania, Hungary, and other countries before finally sailing from France in the spring of 1927. The musicians returned to New York via South America, where they made a brief tour of Argentina. Wooding recalls: "We toured a lot of cities, I can't remember some of them, in Argentina. . . . Because nobody wanted the old music in Europe or South America. I opened those places up. That's why I want that to be understood, that Europe,

Sam Wooding (at piano) and his band in Atlantic City, circa 1920. (Author's collection. Courtesy of Mrs. Sam Wooding.)

Sam Wooding (at piano) and his orchestra in Copenhagen, 1925. It was a mark of honor for Wooding's sidemen that they could double on bassoons, oboes, French horns, and so on. (Author's collection. Courtesy of Mrs. Sam Wooding.)

Sam Wooding stands proudly in front of posters for the new sensation, *Chocolate Kiddies,* in Berlin, Germany, 1925. (Author's collection. Courtesy of Mrs. Sam Wooding.)

Sam Wooding (far right) and his orchestra in Frankfurt, Germany, June 1929. Singer Edith Wilson stands at the far left. (Author's collection. Courtesy of Mrs. Sam Wooding.)

The Sam Wooding Orchestra of the 1970s, with Wooding's wife, Rae, on vocals. (Author's collection. Courtesy of the Institute of Jazz Studies.)

Sam Wooding, enjoying his eighty-ninth birthday party in his memento-filled Harlem apartment, June 1984. Standing alongside Rae Wooding is U. S. "Slow Kid" Thompson, aged ninety-seven, who was married to Florence Mills and was a highly praised dancer in the 1920s. (Author's collection. Courtesy of Mrs. Sam Wooding.)

Argentine—." He begins to hum. "And the waltz, *da, da, da, dum . . .*" That stately type of music had been in vogue in so many countries, but the vigorous strains of hot American dance music and jazz replaced it.

Back in the United States in the summer of 1927, Sam Wooding proudly told reporters of having played for European royalty. His success appeared phenomenal, and he had no trouble getting musicians to work for him. His players, some of whom had adopted continental manners and airs, having hobnobbed with the elite of Europe, were the envy of jazzmen who had been stuck in New York, scrounging around for jobs to pay their bills. After playing dates in New York, Buffalo, Boston, and other cities, Wooding says he soon had two offers to weigh: to go into the Cotton Club, where Andy Preer had been leading the house band; or to do another tour of Europe. He invited his musicians to make the decision, knowing full well which offer they'd choose. To him, there was no choice.

"It was a joke," Wooding says. "Which you would rather do—go into the Cotton Club or go to Europe?!" He had no way of knowing how popular the Cotton Club was about to become—he knew that Jack Johnson had tried running a club in that spot but had failed—and felt he had already done the New York club scene. Having played Barron's, the Nest, and the Club Alabam, why should he base himself in another New York club when he could instead return to Europe, where people clearly appreciated jazz—and jazz musicians—more and where there was far less racial oppression. New York was still Jim Crow in many ways. Black bands, for example, were not yet being hired for the big hotel jobs, and only white musicians got to back white singers on records or in most clubs. Black musicians could play for white audiences at certain clubs and dance halls in New York, but they were not supposed to fraternize with the public; they had to remember their "place." By contrast, Wooding says, blacks could revel in the freedom they felt in Europe.

Wooding volunteers a key reason why he feels Europe seemed so attractive to black musicians back then, one you don't see in most jazz histories: "There were white women in Europe, and the boys were crazy about white women. Yeah. You see, because we hadn't too long been freed. Abraham Lincoln freed us. The novelty's worn off now. In Europe, you'd take a white woman and have fun all around—." His wife, uncomfortable with such statements, tries to cut him off—"I don't want you to say that . . . "—but he continues. That *was* an important factor in his musicians' wanting to return to Europe, he says, at least for some of them—himself included. "Of course there was no future in no white woman," he adds. "You didn't get nothing but a bum. You didn't have a *good* white woman." But black musicians did walk freely about Paris, arms around white women—something you simply didn't see in the United States.[13]

Wooding's wife interjects: "Why would they want to go back to Harlem, where they've been all their lives? So they say, 'What the hell, let's go on back to Europe.' " She adds, maybe a bit defensively: "White women *were* an attraction for some of the men in the band. But we must remember that most of the men in the band carried their wives with them. Most of the men carried their wives—including him. He didn't go there and just . . . he just did, what the thing is like anybody else'd do: 'Well, we have some fun, but I'll come on home. I got my wife at home,' things like that."

Another motivation, Wooding says, is that his musicians were paid handsomely everywhere they worked in Europe. And he was paid three times as much as the sidemen. Certainly, the band would have received more than the $1,100 a week the Cotton Club was offering, which struck them as insulting—after all, they were world famous. Garvin Bushell comments in his 1977 oral history that Duke Ellington, who ultimately accepted the offer to go into the Cotton Club, had no place better to go. However, he adds that if the members of Wooding's band had known what radio could do, they would have *paid* $1,100 a week to be based in, and broadcasting from, the Cotton Club. But radio had not been a big factor in the music business when the band sailed for Europe in 1925—the first network, NBC, was formed in 1926—and radio executives seemed to give the best airtime to the most insipid, commercial, white orchestras, like the Cliquot Club Eskimos. In 1927 no one could have foreseen the impact that Ellington's broadcasts from the Cotton Club would have.

The booking Sam Wooding rejected became the break of a lifetime for Duke Ellington, who enlarged his group to ten pieces for his opening on December 4,1927, at the Cotton Club. Ellington had been gradually building up a reputation over the last couple of years via a steady stream of recordings and postmidnight regional broadcasts on WHN. But it was his live, early evening broadcasts from the Cotton Club over the fledgling CBS network in 1929 and 1930—the first ongoing nationwide radio exposure ever given to any black band—that really made him. The club became his vehicle to national fame.

Would it have been the same for Wooding, if he had opened at the Cotton Club in December 1927? "No. I would never have stayed [there] as long as Duke did," he says. "No, I was like Paul Whiteman. Paul Whiteman never stayed nowhere. Even his own club—they set him up in a club and . . . Paul Whiteman worked a while, and then he burnt the club down rather than stay there any longer. And I was the same way." Of course, and more important, Wooding's arrangements lacked the creative brilliance of Ellington's, whose often-astonishing writing made his band unique and immediately recognizable on the air.

In 1927 annual record sales in the United States reached nearly 100 million; a successful record could spread a band's fame nationwide. The records Wooding had made in Europe had not been released in the United States, which meant he was largely unknown in his own country. But in 1927, people in cities far from New York were beginning to buy Ellington's records of "Black and Tan Fantasy" and "East St. Louis Toodle-Oo." Wooding wasn't worried about making records because he wanted a band that could put on a great live show. So he stayed busy playing theaters—that's where the money was—until European bookings were lined up. The band did not cut any records during its 1927–28 stay in the United States, and by the time Wooding returned in 1932, record sales had dwindled to just 6 million annually, with most companies extremely cautious about signing "new" artists.

Wooding and his orchestra, with some changes in personnel, sailed for Europe in June 1928, where they experienced more triumphs: command performances for royalty and seasons at exclusive hotels, from Constantinople to Tunis, from Vienna to Bucharest. The 1929 version included: Bobby Martin, Doc Cheatham, and Tommy Ladnier, trumpets; Albert Wynn and Billy Burns, trombones; Willie Lewis, Jerry Blake, and Gene Sedric, reeds; Freddy Johnson, piano; John Mitchell, banjo; King Edwards, tuba; Ted Fields, drums; and Willie Lewis and Ted Fields, among others, doubled as vocalists. They covered everything, from hot jazz to sweet pop ballads, although they didn't offer much in the way of blues.

In Barcelona in 1929, the band recorded ten sides, including "Tiger Rag," "Krazy Kat," "Carrie," and "I Can't Give You Anything But Love." Later that year, in Paris, Wooding and company recorded another seventeen sides, including "Hallelujah!" "Button Up Your Overcoat," "Singin' in the Rain" and "Can't We Be Friends?" These recordings show a tremendous advance over the 1925 sides. The saxes swing with a loose, relaxed, Harlem feel that is still attractive. Scat vocals—reflecting the rapid rise of Louis Armstrong and the popularity of his scatting since the band's earlier recordings—are commonplace, as are cheerful "wa-ta-da-da" vocal interjections by two or three members of the band, in emulation of Paul Whiteman's Rhythm Boys.

On "I Can't Give You Anything But Love," the vocal is first offered in a straight—almost overly dignified—fashion, before giving way to a joyously free-wheeling scat chorus. On "Bull Foot Stomp," a growl cornet answers playful "wa-ta-da-da" vocal comments. The band is hotter than Whiteman's—it has a chewier, more elastic feel—but the Whiteman influence is obvious. When the vocalists and the cornet converse, one thinks a little of Whiteman's famed 1928 recording of "That's My Weakness Now" with Bix Beiderbecke and the Rhythm Boys. Bobby Martin's growling trumpet is juxtaposed with Willie Lewis's wild, laughing-like-a-hyena clarinet on a couple of numbers. While the effect is striking, it's more show-biz than heartfelt, as is the comic falsetto Lewis sometimes uses to impersonate a woman, with Bobby Martin, in a baritone, answering him as a man. A fun, campy recording, "I Lift Up My Finger and I Say Tweet, Tweet (Shush Shush, Now Now, Come Come)" appears to be mocking the high-falutin' ways of some people the band members were encountering.

Wooding's band had to entertain in its concerts, and that meant offering humor, film tunes that had nothing to do with jazz (like "The Wedding of the Painted Doll"), current pops, as well as some straight-out hot music (like the exciting "Breakaway"). It had to put on a good show, just as Jimmie Lunceford's band, for example, would in the 1930s. Wooding's soloists got to play hot jazz much more frequently than those in Whiteman's band, but certainly not on every number. No band in the late 1920s could make it commercially by playing just hot jazz. Wooding's was a jazz-influenced big band that tried to cover as many bases as possible.

The band remained a great favorite with European audiences, playing what were billed as "jazz concerts," even though Doc Cheatham, who played lead trumpet in the band, told me he felt the band was beginning to sound a little corny. He thought Wooding had spent so much time overseas that he had not kept up with the latest developments in American music. Cheatham remembered a shortwave radio broadcast of McKinney's Cotton Pickers from Detroit, circa 1930, that knocked him out. McKinney's men were certainly outswinging Wooding's. Cheatham left the band to return to the United States; within a year, he was trumpeting with McKinney.

The Great Depression, beginning in late 1929, had combined with increased competition from radio to put a serious damper on the record business. Yet in 1931, in Paris, Wooding's band recorded another four sides, including "Love for Sale" and "I Surrender, Dear." Wooding might have been content to play in Europe almost indefinitely, but his tour fell apart when the band lost nine months of booking commitments due to the Depression—three months in Germany and six in England, all planned for 1932. In addition, he feels, attitudes were changing in Germany. Hitler was not yet in power, but there was a rising surge of Germany-first feelings, and booking an American black jazz orchestra was no longer in vogue. (Within a few years, Hitler would flatly ban records by American jazz musicians.)

Wooding's European tours came to an end in Belgium in November 1931. "The boys in the band had a lot of money," he recalls, "and I had three times what they had. When we come home, they seemed to have too much money." His musicians went their separate ways, rather than wait to see what future they could make if they stayed together as an orchestra in the United States. A few of them decided their future lay in Europe. Clarinetist Willie Lewis became the leader of the best-known black orchestra in Europe in the remainder of the 1930s; his band included such former Wooding sidemen as Bobby Martin, Ted Fields, and Billy Burns.

Because Wooding had been overseas almost continuously since 1925, in 1932 his name meant little in the United States. The big bands of Duke Ellington, Chick Webb, Cab Calloway, Bennie Moten, and Claude Hopkins, among others, had become nationally famous in the interim. Wooding put together bands for one-nighters, using some first-rate players (including Sid Catlett on drums, Frankie Newton on trumpet, and his longtime star Gene Sedric on tenor), but it was an uphill battle. Even many well-established bands were going through rough times. Fletcher Henderson's superb band was not working steadily; in fact, Henderson, who had become one of the greatest of all big band arrangers, was unable to meet his payroll commitments and was forced to disband for a while in 1934.

Wooding played the Arcadia Ballroom, the Pelham Heath Inn, and the Liberty Theater. In 1932 he was reunited with erstwhile Club Alabam and *Chocolate Kiddies* star Edith Wilson, in a revue at Harlem's Lafayette Theater. In 1934 his was the second big band ever to play the Apollo Theater (Benny Carter's was the first). But he was unable to secure a record contract, which was essential if he was to build a national reputation. His band, including Frankie Newton on trumpet and Gene Sedric on reeds, made a test recording for Columbia, in 1934, of "My Gal Sal" and "Weary Blues," but it was never released.

Newer bands now had the public's eye. After finishing a run at Pleasure Beach Park in Connecticut in 1935, Sam Wooding gave up trying to make it as a bandleader.

Looking back, he had much to take pride in. He had played top spots in Europe and in the United States. He had enjoyed two seasons at the Bellevue Casino in Biarritz, three seasons at the Hotel Negresco in Nice. He had given command performances for King Carol of Rumania, for the Prince of Wales, for King Alfonso and Queen Victoria of Spain, for Prince Carl of Sweden, and for high officials of the Soviet Union. He had gone over as big in theaters in England as in Harlem.

Wooding opened a music studio for a while. From 1937 to 1941 he directed a choir, the Southland Singers, which appeared at the 1939 New York World's Fair. He took courses at Temple University and went on to earn both a bachelor's degree (1942) and a master's degree (1945) from the University of Pennsylvania. For the first time, Wooding says, he truly understood harmony, having learned the mechanics of arranging. He no longer needed to work out the notes by trial and error, looking for things that simply "sounded good." His parents would have been proud of his educational achievements.

When anyone addressed him now as "professor," Wooding winced; he didn't want to hear that term. Although he knew they meant it as a sign of respect, he was reminded of the days when prostitutes in Atlantic City bawdy houses would refer to piano players as professors, and he didn't want those memories "mixed up with the education." He had, after all, absorbed some of his parents' attitudes about the importance of "respectability."

With his degrees in hand, Wooding supervised music instruction in the Wilmington, Delaware, public schools. His most successful pupil was trumpeter Clifford Brown, whom he taught as a high school junior and senior and who went on to become one of the greats of the bebop period. Wooding didn't really like teaching, though, and he didn't teach for long. The pay seemed insignificant, he adds, after what he had made back in the old days in Europe. He led a vocal quartet for a while, which played Carnegie Hall in 1949, but he was still restless, unsure of how best to use his talents. Finally, he concentrated on promoting the career of a young protégé, singer Rae Harrison, who eventually became his second wife (he had been previously married during his bandleading days). She had been interested in classical singing; he coached her in jazz and pop.

The two lived abroad throughout most of the fifties, sixties, and early seventies. They believed that Europe was a more hospitable environment for black artists, and it's not surprising that Wooding would want to return to scenes of his greatest successes. They performed together as the International Duo in such varied countries as Germany, Turkey, Greece, Israel, and Japan. He would play piano; she would sing. Rae Harrison is particularly proud of her appearances at the swank Nouvelle Eve in Paris, various European Hilton hotels, and at the Palace Theater in New York, where Wooding played piano with the orchestra in the pit. She sang songs he wrote for her. He hoped to help make her a star.

The Woodings resettled in New York in the early 1970s. Sam formed his final big band after Duke Ellington died in 1974. Eager to prove he still had new sounds to offer, he imagined that Ellington's passing might leave an opening for him. But it was too late to relive the triumphs of the twenties. Wooding made sporadic appearances with the band—with Rae on vocals—until about two years before his death. The band didn't sound like anybody else's, and it surely wasn't peddling nostalgia. It might play an oldie like "Royal Garden Blues," but it did so in a hard-driving way that was not suggestive of the jazz age. Wooding was keen—perhaps too keen—on proving he was very much part of the present. He preferred hiring young musicians to veterans. A promotional brochure, prepared when he was eighty-two, stressed that he was "hot, funky, and right now!"

Wooding cut an album with his new band, appeared at the Zurich Jazz Festival, the Kool Jazz Festival at Waterloo Village, New Jersey, and on television. Although the band was not impressive, he got a flurry of media attention because of the history he represented. He continued writing and arranging numbers almost until he died. In fact, the last time I visited the Woodings at their photo- and memento-filled Harlem apartment, two weeks before Sam's death, his wife was still hoping he'd be able to make one final recording session. He had charts that deserved to be recorded, she said.

I attended Sam Wooding's wake on August 3, 1985. A handful of family members and friends gathered in Rodney Dade's Funeral Parlor in Harlem as tapes of Wooding's big band of recent years played softly over the p.a. system. Rae Harrison Wooding said she still hoped to reassemble his band for one last recording session, to preserve for posterity some arrangements of his from the old days as well as some from modern times, to remind a world that needs reminding what a pioneer Sam Wooding was.

2

BENNY WATERS

Hot Jazz Uptown

> In the '20s, I was real well established, because I was working in Charlie Johnson's band, see? And we were recording for Victor, and that was the biggest thing in that period. For a Negro band to record for Victor Records then was quite an asset, because Victor was prestigious. They were so cranky about Negroes working back then. They said, "They can't play so and so . . ." —you know what I mean? So they chose us. We went to Camden, New Jersey, the main office, and recorded. And you should hear those records! You'd be surprised how well they came out. Right now you can buy them. All the instruments—you can hear the violin, blended, you know?

Benny Waters is remembering with pride records he made between 1927 and 1929. Victor had a technological lead over every other company, so the records *were* exceptionally well produced for their day. But the pleasure with which he recalls his career in the 1920s seems tied to the fact that he reached heights back then, as a soloist in one of the greatest bands of its time, that he never surpassed in the many years that followed.

Waters never achieved the degree of renown he would have liked; but, ironically, it is his lack of national prestige that allows him to be more candid in his recollections than many better-known jazzmen. Because he has not had to maintain a public image the way an Ellington or Basie did—a concern that greatly limited the value of their memoirs—Waters can speak more freely about his experiences in the jazz life.

His voice is deep, resonant, self-assured—I am reminded a bit of James Earl Jones—and his speech, appearance, and general demeanor suggest a much younger man. It comes as a bit of a surprise when he mentions that his first influence on sax was Johnny Hodges: "Because I had the privilege of working with him back in Boston. He was thirteen years old. I was eighteen." That makes Waters eighty-five. Based in France since 1952, he still works actively as a musician and at the time of our interview in 1987 was visiting the United States to play at the West End Cafe in New York and at various festivals.

Music came naturally to Waters. Born in rural Brighton, Massachusetts, on January 23, 1902, he was no more than five or six, perhaps younger, when he first sat down at the organ in his home. He had received no instruction, he says, but he had seen others in his family play. His recollection is that he managed to play tunes he had heard—mixed together, but clearly music, not just noise—from his very first attempt. His three older brothers all played instruments, and eventually he joined them in bands. He also gave piano concerts in local churches and halls, billed as a child prodigy. He hadn't heard anything like jazz yet—in fact, the term "jazz" was not then in use—just hymns and folk music.

"My mother was a seamstress and my father a carpenter," Waters says. "Just middle-living people, country people, you know. I guess by her being a professional seamstress and my father being a professional carpenter, I may have had an advantage over some of the other kids, because we made more money" (although there wasn't much to spare). His mother was a strict Methodist for whom "sinful" activities like card playing and dancing were taboo. She inculcated in Waters the habit of regular churchgoing; if he missed, he got spanked. While she worshiped at church, his father drank with buddies at the local bar. Waters had no interest in boyhood athletics, nor was he much good when he tried to help his father with manual work. But none of that mattered, his mother told him, because *he* was going to be a musician.

Waters's mother died when he was perhaps seven years old. In her will, she expressed a wish that someday he would study music at a conservatory—she wanted him to become a proper musician—but she had no money to leave to ensure that it might become a reality. Waters went to live with his maternal Aunt Mamie and her husband, Fred Garner, in Haverford, Pennsylvania, just outside Philadelphia. The Garners were, in what Waters indicates was the parlance of the era, "Negro rich": they had achieved some financial success and were respected within black society. His uncle, a landscape gardener with five or six people working for him, owned a ten-room house and—extraordinary for that day—three automobiles. The Garners socialized with blacks who had achieved success in business, government, and the arts. Waters remembers, for example, the distinguished black singer Roland Hayes being a guest at their home.

Living with the Garners for the next several years, Waters experienced luxury that was new to him. He indulged himself. At age sixteen or so, for example, he was going out, in one of his uncle's cars, with a driver, picking up women and taking them to hotels. Not many youths, white or black, were enjoying chauffeur-driven rendezvous in that era. His sexual life started quite young, Waters recalls, and he was never shy about fulfilling his desires. The Garners might have envisioned him eventually marrying a respectable member of the black upperclass—for a while, he did try dating the daughter of the president of a black insurance company—but he was more interested in having a good time than in bourgeois respectability.

Schoolwork did not much interest him, but music did. Waters had switched from piano and organ to clarinet and then saxophone, which he settled on as his preferred instrument. "I was self-taught on the saxophone. My brother was a saxophonist and a trumpeter, and he just passed his instrument over to me. The first band I worked with was my brother's little group. We'd work for the rich people in their parlors—little parties that they had. It wasn't so much jazz; you'd play the melody of songs that they knew, like songs from shows." Caught up in the musicians' world, he didn't complete high school. The Garners realized he was going to follow his own desires, and they figured they had done about as much as they could for him.

Waters says he was perhaps fifteen or sixteen (which would have been around 1917–18) when he first began working with Philadelphia-based professional bands, led by Charlie Miller and Lonnie Polk. He was associating with adult musicians all of the time now, drinking and smoking with the best of them. Because Waters was underage, Polk had to get permission from the police to have him travel to engagements in New Jersey. A trombonist in the band acted as his guardian.

At perhaps age sixteen (he isn't certain about the exact dates of many events), Waters began irregular studies at the Boston Conservatory, taking courses there part-time over the next five years or so. The Garners, he stresses, were not supporting him.

> I went to the conservatory on my own. My aunt only gave me $50 when I went there. That's all I had anyplace—$50. I worked my way through. I got a job in a restaurant. I got

fallen arches by walking on the hard floor, doing that to make a living before I got established in Boston.

I think it's good to do things on your own. It makes it better when you work your way through things. Even the drinking and smoking, the things that I used to do, I never did let that interfere with music, because *I* wanted it myself. But if you're sent with a whole lot of money by your parents, you know, it makes you a little blasé. You don't study as much. But I wanted it myself, so I didn't let nothing interfere. I really got quite a lot of knowledge out of that. I didn't study the saxophone in conservatory; I studied harmony, theory, and solfeggio. Solfeggio—that's the study that pertains to sound. You know, you strike one note; like the teacher gave you a C, then you'd make E, G, and so forth.

I'm not the greatest saxophone player, nothing like that. But harmony and theory—I kind of boast with that. I know what I'm doing, and I know what the other player's doing. And that's important, because if you know what the other fellow's doing, then you can copy. If you hear a saxophone player that's playing wonderful chords—if you know what they're doing, you can do it. But if you don't know what they're doing, you can't do nothing except admire it. So it was an advantage for me to study, and it *was* rare, at that age, to study.

Waters initially stayed with a brother who lived in Boston. He worked as a busboy until his feet became swollen from walking all day on a tile floor; later he got a job cleaning rooms at a hotel. For a time he even lived as a pimp, staying with a Panamanian woman named Anita. She'd go out every night to turn tricks with white customers; then she'd return, awaken him, put perhaps fifty dollars in earnings on his chest, and they'd make love. In that period Waters was taking classes three days a week at the conservatory and picking up jobs as a musician when he could. When Anita told him he would have to choose between her and the music—she wanted him to herself—he told her the music came first. That ended their relationship.

Waters got a job working with banjo player Bobby Johnson, who would later be musical director of Charlie Johnson's band. He also gave lessons to young musicians. (One of his pupils, Harry Carney, who was eight years younger than he was, grew up to become a key member of Duke Ellington's band.) Basically, though, he took whatever jobs in music came his way, not necessarily playing "hot." A Boston radio orchestra for which he played, for example, mixed

Schubert serenades with occasional pop tunes. He also worked in a couple of different settings with Johnny Hodges, who would be a star in Ellington's band throughout most of 1928–70.

Hodges was only thirteen, according to Waters, when the two first worked together; in fact, Hodges (who may actually have been fourteen or fifteen) was so young that initially he was only allowed to play afternoon gigs, like Sunday tea dances. Hodges, who had not yet learned to read music—Waters says they had no trouble doing popular tunes without music—looked perennially bored, but he already had a superior tone on sax and played jazz and blues as well as anyone Waters knew in Boston. Both played soprano sax as well as piano and alto. According to Waters, Hodges was already so impressive a soloist that bandleader Ted Lewis used to go to hear him. Waters acknowledges: "When I was very young, I listened to Ted Lewis playing C-melody saxophone. He wasn't playing that much jazz, but I liked his approach." (Later, Coleman Hawkins would be Waters's ideal, but in 1923 Waters had not yet heard Hawkins and Lewis's records were big sellers.)

In 1923 or 1924, Waters headed to Philadelphia; by 1925 he had moved on to New York. He says: "I made records in Philadelphia that I never heard. Perry Bradford, he was a record promoter. It was during the Mamie Smith days. But I never heard those records, never heard them in my life." (Bradford, who was singer Mamie Smith's musical director, sang and led recording bands of his own.) Brian Rust's discography, *Jazz Records, 1897–1942,* does not list any records by Waters in this period; either his work is uncredited on some obscure 78s or the records were never released. But none of that seems important to Waters because in 1925 he joined Charlie Johnson's band.

"Charlie Johnson's was the first big band, name band, *known,* that I went to. And that consisted [at one time or another] of some of the greats, such as Benny Carter, Jimmy Harrison, Dickie Wells. And we had Edgar Sampson, the composer of 'Stompin' at the Savoy.' We had a great band there." In the summer, the band often played at an Atlantic City cabaret, the Paradise. Most of the year, however, was spent at Smalls's Paradise, at 2294½ Seventh Avenue in Manhattan. Smalls's had a capacity of 1,500 and caught on with the public immediately upon its opening in the fall of 1925. People knew they'd have a good time there. It was more than just the music—the whole atmosphere was hot and festive: waiters doing the Charleston; Monday morning breakfast dances. A fantasy world in the midst of Harlem.

"Smalls's Paradise was one of the biggest cabarets in America. The crowds were 80 percent white at least, maybe more, maybe 90 percent,"

Waters recalls. "We had about thirty-five or forty people in the shows. It was a big thing. The show would last about two hours. It went on twice a night, sometimes three times. We'd have requests. Many times some movie actors like Wallace Beery used to come up there, George Raft used to come up there, many movie actors. Sometimes they would be late, come in at the end, and they'd request the show. We'd do it again for them. They'd give us a tip, you know. That has happened many times." The show changed every few months with Johnson overseeing the hiring and firing of all the talent, not just the musicians in his band. The most popular show, according to Waters, was *Kitchen Mechanics,* with music by James P. Johnson. The performers portrayed cooks and maids.

Variety reported on February 17, 1926, that Smalls's Paradise "has a floor show of colored people, fast dancers who work too hard for the number of performances they give nightly." Since Harlem had become an "in" spot, parts of it were, in effect, being staged for the benefit of visiting whites, just as parts of Paris were being staged for the benefit of visiting Americans. The dance floor at Smalls's, *Variety* noted, was filled with whites from downtown—"all in evening clothes. . . . Johnson's Band is hot and it makes them dance. Any price charged to go on the floor for the whites would not be too much for that band."[1] Waters remembers Johnson often getting drunk, standing out in the audience and asserting what a great, great band he had. Banjo player Bobby Johnson served as the band's musical director.

Johnson's band did not have a strong stylistic identity of its own, although Waters notes that it sometimes did the "doo-wah, doo-wah" with muted brass that later became identified with Glenn Miller (and he wonders if Miller might have gotten it from Johnson). The band played music for the shows as well as music for dancing; and, as was common in the mid-1920s, it played a goodly number of stock charts, or arrangements—often undistinguished—furnished by the music publishers.[2] Members of Johnson's band also contributed some arrangements. Benny Carter, for example, wrote many during his tenure (1926–28); it was the start of his career as an arranger, which continues to this day. Waters and trumpeter Jabbo Smith sometimes improvised arrangements on an informal basis. After Carter left the band, Johnson commissioned Waters to write two arrangements per week, which he did for the next couple of years, in addition to arranging music for the shows.

Waters was hired by Johnson because he was a good all-around musician, not just a jazz soloist. More than capable of handling whatever section work on sax or clarinet was required, he was also the band's tenor sax soloist. But as a jazz soloist, Waters was overshadowed by such greats as alto saxist Benny Carter, trombonist Jimmy Harrison, and trumpeters Sidney de Paris and Jabbo Smith. Then, as now, he was most comfortable playing ballads and swinging tunes. While he didn't have a natural affinity for the blues—he had come from too bourgeois a background—to protect his job he learned to play some gutbucket blues when required.

The music world in the 1920s was publicly segregated, with white and black musicians belonging to separate unions and playing in separate bands. But Johnson's band lured the best of them—white as well as black—who would come and sit in. Many great players found their way, late at night, to Smalls's. Waters says:

> Yeah, our place was more famous than any place in Harlem for that. Such big stars as Jimmy Dorsey and not so much Tommy but Miff Mole. Miff Mole was a great trombone player, you know. Jack Teagarden was there every chance he got, to jam with Jimmy Harrison. Charlie Teagarden. Benny Goodman's brother, the bass player [Harry Goodman]. Another guy that used to come there often, Gene Krupa. Man, I've jammed many times with those guys. They came up there to jam with our band.
>
> Frankie Trumbauer came to Harlem, but he didn't play. Frankie was a little bit timid. I don't know why, because he played beautiful. That song that he made, "Singin' the Blues," will always be, as long as there is music—because he had such a beautiful *tone* on the saxophone. That will never die.

Waters doesn't recall Bix Beiderbecke ever coming up to Harlem, but he remembers hearing Beiderbecke and Trumbauer in Jean Goldkette's band, when both Goldkette and Johnson were working in Atlantic City. He notes, "Jean Goldkette had a great band."

White musicians headed to Harlem for various reasons, Waters believes. Some went to learn from or borrow ideas from jazzmen they recognized as superior. Others were simply doing it for the love of it. Still others wanted to test themselves by taking on musicians they had heard were great but with whom they couldn't work because of racial prejudice.

Waters vividly remembers an after-hours cutting contest that occurred one night in the late 1920s at the Melody Club , upstairs at 131st Street and Seventh Avenue. On that night, Jimmy Dorsey—who Waters feels was egotistical, inclined to brag about the musicians he triumphed over—came up to Harlem to jam with the best black alto saxmen. At the Melody Club, Dorsey cut Johnny Hodges but was in turn cut by Benny Carter, whom others had gotten out of bed just so he could take on Dorsey. Why didn't Waters participate? "I didn't have my saxophone. I couldn't play that much sax anyway. At least, I didn't think I could. And it was for alto saxes. Jimmy Dorsey, Johnny Hodges, and Benny Carter—three altos, no tenors." As Waters tells it:

> . . . Jimmy made—knew a little bit more harmony than Johnny. Johnny, in his harmony, wasn't too advanced, you know what I mean?
>
> So Jimmy was like that, you know. He used to say "I cut this guy. I blow him out." So somebody said, "Call up Benny Carter." So Benny came up around there with his own piano player—I forget his name, Freddy somebody. Benny started playing "Georgia Brown," which at that period was very popular. But Jesus! When Benny Carter got through playing "Georgia Brown," Jimmy got all red in the face and practically hauled up and walked out—looked like a drowned rat. And here's what Benny was doing: Benny played along with Jimmy, and every four bars he'd move into a different key—and Jimmy too, that's the way they used to do—all the way back to the first key [where] he started again.

By the session's end, Hodges had stopped, Dorsey had gone home, and only Carter remained, playing by himself, triumphant.

Waters's crowd didn't put Jimmy Dorsey in the same category as Carter. Dorsey was a superb technician—looked up to by countless sax players—but he didn't have the feeling for jazz that Carter did. According to Waters:

> . . . Benny was so far advanced, you see. He's still far advanced. If you don't think he's far advanced—you see, I know Benny; people don't. Benny's not a showman. He plays like this. He knows so much saxophone, he'll do like this [Waters scats effortlessly, easily], and it sounds so beautiful. But you say, "He ain't doing nothing, just fooling around." Then you start pushing it, then all these things come out, all kinds of things come out. And he still can do it! He's rich now, he don't have to do certain things. I know his character. When you work beside somebody for two years, you learn the character.

In his view, Carter is still the number one sax player today.

Waters, who played tenor back then but now mixes tenor and alto sax, says his inspiration on tenor was Coleman Hawkins. "Anyone who hear me play tenor saxophone would know I'm from the Coleman Hawkins school. I don't sound like Coleman, but I'm from the school. I'm not from Lester Young's school." One night, back in the early days, he and Hawkins got to jam together. "It was only Coleman and me," he remembers happily. "That's the way it started. It used to be fantastic in that era." But he is too much of a realist about his own abilities to imagine he could have ever cut Hawkins. He didn't even try, he says: "I knew that I couldn't play as much as he could . . . so I played my three or four choruses—I did my little thing—and stopped. And left it all—Hah! hah! hah! hah! You know, instead of getting a good bucket of milk and kicking it over, I kept my milk in the pail."

Many Americans in the late 1920s would probably have viewed Benny Waters's life as one of incredible self-indulgence. Asleep during many of the hours the average citizen was working, he'd play hot music at night, then head off to other clubs to hang out. (This was particularly easy to do in Atlantic City, where clubs would take turns offering free drinks to entertainers and musicians from other clubs.) Because in those days a lot of places had no cover charge, Waters might take in as many as five clubs before heading home. He also indulged in cigarettes (regular and marijuana), illegal liquor, and sex with a gusto that would have stunned the general public, most of whom suspected in some undefined way that jazz was connected with immorality.

Nowadays, there are those who are shocked by the attitudes toward sex and drugs expressed by some rock musicians. Their grandparents would have been no less shocked by the attitudes of many jazz musicians. But the people who have created uninhibited music, then and now, have often led comparatively uninhibited lives. Waters gratified his desires more freely than the average citizen did—it was all part of the scene—and doing so may have yielded more relaxed and creative playing. Alcohol and pot lowered his inhibitions, while a rich and varied sex life kept his energy level high, gave life and freedom to his playing.

There was always someone you could buy reefer or bootleg liquor from; and sometimes you didn't even have to buy it. Waters remembers a bus tour with the Charlie Johnson band through the South, from Georgia to Texas. He and Jabbo Smith would pick marijuana, growing wild in the fields, whenever the bus stopped and then let it dry out in the back of the bus. Just about everyone in the band also drank—perhaps none more than Waters. But he didn't see that as a problem. He had to be in control to execute all of the show music—the scores called for a good deal of disciplined ensemble playing, not wild improvisations—and he felt fully in control of his drinking.

Although alcohol is a depressant, Waters thought of it as a stimulant that helped to keep him going, and soloing freely, through long, long nights—for example, when the band would double at a theater besides playing at Smalls's Paradise. He recalls one time when the band drove down to Camden, New Jersey (a couple of hours away), to record during the day, then put in a full night at Smalls's (until about four o'clock), and then played a breakfast dance until nine. He drank gin, beer, and bourbon that night, and everyone, in his recollection, told him he sounded good. Apparently he hadn't reached the point yet where too much drinking would slow down reflexes and harm one's playing.

Sex was something Waters accepted as a natural source of pleasure. He didn't have any Puritan hangups about it; in fact, he inhabited a moral universe different from that of the average American. He still attended church regularly—he always had an interest in religion, he says—but he had his own opinions about sexual matters. (Waters was not shy about recounting details of his sexual history in his memoir, *The Key to a Jazzy Life,* a copy of which he gave to me.[3]) From the time he arrived in New York, he and a couple of buddies would go to sex "circuses" together, where they could watch all varieties of sexual acts and then bed down with prostitutes. One trumpeter he knew had a house in Harlem where musicians could go after hours to smoke dope, drink whiskey, gamble, and enjoy homemade soul food. Waters met one woman there he never forgot: when he got into bed with her, he discovered she was a hermaphrodite. He says he tried his best to satisfy her.

At one time, Waters recalls, he was seeing two women. One of them was regularly giving him money from her gambling winnings; the other one was regularly getting money from him. That arrangement screeched to a halt when the first woman—justifiably outraged—discovered where her money was going. Waters also liked having a different woman for each night of the week. Although he was living at reedman Ben Whitted's home, he had some privacy, so this wasn't a problem.

Of course, Waters's life wasn't all play. He was putting in lots of long nights in his profession, and he was picking up occasional outside free-lance assignments as well. But his approach to life was far different from the Protestantism to which many Americans subscribed. He figured he was overdoing things when he came down with appendicitis and was hospitalized for almost two months (in that pre-antibiotics era, appendicitis was sometimes fatal). Seriously ill, he had to recuperate a few more months at home after his release. He blamed his ailment on too much drinking and too many women!

Waters got married for the first time, to a woman named Margaret, when he was twenty-seven; it lasted about five years. The two met at Smalls's Paradise one Sunday afternoon. (Although Smalls's drew a mostly white crowd at night, on Sunday afternoons, when prices were lower and the band would play but there was no show, it drew a mostly black crowd.) Husband and wife both drank to excess. And they fought a lot. One night he cut their mattress in half with a razor; another time she locked him out and he broke in through a window.

Although Waters denied that alcohol was part of the problem, he recalls a night-long binge of whiskey, wine, gin, and pot that left him too dazed to climb the stairs to his apartment. After sitting on the bottom step, in a stupor, for about an hour, he swore off marijuana and, because smoking was reducing his wind for playing, later gave up cigarettes as well. But the drinking was something he would not, or could not, stop—and, in the end, may have limited his growth as a musician.

In the late 1920s, Waters gave every appearance of being an up-and-coming arranger. He arranged such Charlie Johnson recordings as "Walk That Thing," "Harlem Drag," and the classic "Boy in the Boat," with its slightly sinister, late-night feel, as well as music for the shows at Smalls's. He also arranged some King Oliver recordings of 1927–28, including "Tin Roof Blues," "Sobbin' Blues," and "Aunt Hagar's Blues." Waters used to enjoy talking with Chick Webb about arranging, taking notes as they talked, but he never fulfilled the promise that he showed back then. His arranging slowed to a trickle after leaving Johnson's band.

Waters was doing some free-lance recording at the time: instrumental sides for Clarence Williams in 1927–28 and for such vocalists as Esther Bigeou, Katherine Henderson, and Sara Martin (all backed by Williams's group). Waters says he never heard those records until he went to Paris in 1952, when collectors played them for him. According to Waters: "I also was recording with King Oliver's band during the same period I was working with Charlie Johnson. These were Oliver's songs. For him to declare those songs that he made, he had to get them on record. Then they were obviously his songs. So that made him make many sessions. Fast. He got me on some. He got any bunch of musicians that could read and fake. He would hire them for the record date, that's all." Oliver, whose playing had passed its peak, was not leading an organized band in that period but continued to lead bands on record.

Playing live each night in Charlie Johnson's band was Waters's main activity, of course. Because Johnson felt that working live was the main thing, he didn't push much to get his band on record or on radio, which was a miscalculation. Apparently, he didn't realize how important those media were to building and maintaining a group's reputation. His band, which was riding high in 1926, through 1929, gradually fell behind, in terms of fame and popularity, as other bands courted—and reaped the benefits of—record and radio exposure. Waters nonetheless wants the status of Johnson's band in its peak years to be clearly understood. It was, he asserts, "a great band from the beginning."

Charlie Johnson did not have the first black jazz orchestra on the scene, of course. Fletcher Henderson had already gained renown at the Club Alabam and at the Roseland Ballroom, in 1924, before Johnson opened at Smalls's Paradise in 1925. Waters notes: "Fletcher was like the first big band to gain recognition. Particularly, the first Negro group to gain recognition. That's why Benny Goodman picked him out to arrange, to get a sound, as Benny said himself, like Fletcher. Which he did." Was Sam Wooding's band well known at the time? "No, not as I know. I think Sam was in Europe in the period. Sam Wooding was the first Negro band to tour—maybe first any kind of a band, I guess. Sam Wooding was one of the first any type of jazz band to tour Europe as a big name. They've been all over Russia and all that stuff."

Even as he notes that the most well known band of that period was Henderson's, Walters mentions several others: "Fess Williams at the Savoy [starting in 1926]. He was the one who actually put the Savoy on the map, see. Chick Webb followed him [in 1927]. They had Earl Hines's band [in Chicago]. They had many bands from the West. Like the Sunset Royalers was a group that was from the West that was very, very good. And they had McKinney's Cotton Pickers from Detroit. And another group that was going at the same period, very famous—Andy Kirk's."

Waters is quick to stress that Charlie Johnson's name was big before Ellington's. "Many prizes we won over Duke Ellington," he says. "We used to have battles of the bands. I remember one particular—I forget the name of the place here in Harlem—we had a battle for a cup. We won. But at that time, I think [Ellington] was just getting together with his big band." Walters continues:

> [Ellington] came to New York at the Kentucky Club [1924–27] with just a six-piece—or maybe he had seven—a six-piece band. Good, too. Then his big band was formed right

at the Cotton Club. He was a little rusty at that period. And our band had been well established at Smalls's Paradise. So we had the lead on him, see. Of course, it didn't take him long to get straight. Ha-hah!

But at the Cotton Club he had the big band. I think he had maybe more than ten musicians. But ten musicians was a big band at that period. . . . It wasn't eighteen and twenty at that period. One of the first ones that had more than ten was Paul Whiteman. He was trying to make a symphony of jazz. We didn't accept Whiteman's as a great *jazz* band. We just called it great music. He had some terrific musicians in that band. Miff Mole and Frankie Trumbauer and Bix Beiderbecke—oh, he had the cream of the white musicians in that band. He could afford to pay. He got a lot of them from Jean Goldkette.

New York's nightlife began to subside after the stock market crashed in the fall of 1929. People didn't have as much money to spend at places like Smalls's, and things only got worse in 1930–32. By then, Charlie Johnson's band no longer enjoyed the prominence it once had; nor did Smalls's Paradise, which had lost some of its cachet. Duke Ellington and the Cotton Club had exploited radio wisely, making themselves nationally famous. (And Ellington's band, unlike Johnson's, had developed its own unmistakable style.) Chick Webb's band also was winning widespread acclaim, via broadcasts from the Savoy Ballroom. And new bands were cropping up left and right. "During that period I worked with other little groups," Waters recalls. No longer part of Johnson's band, which had left Smalls's Paradise, he did whatever he had to, to make a living in music.

It is significant that after 1932 Waters did not find a job in another name big band. He toured briefly in a vaudeville package with Bill Robinson and Ethel Waters, but mostly wound up working in dancing schools for the next few years. Musical excellence and originality were hardly expected from the combos that played in such schools, which he feels were high-class houses of prostitution: men paid to slow-dance with the hostesses or dancing teachers, whom they'd sometimes arrange to meet after work for more intimate activities. He remembers playing short choruses of one tune after another, all at slow tempos, and working long hours at relatively little pay. He also remembers meeting another dancing-school musician who told him about Christian Science. A regular churchgoer—and back in the twenties and thirties, he indicates, that was not the norm among jazzmen he knew—

in the 1930s, Waters adopted Christian Science as his faith. He has been a follower of it ever since.

In 1935 Waters got into Fletcher Henderson's band. Though the band did not have the prestige it enjoyed in the mid- and late twenties, when it was on top of the heap, joining it was an enormous step up from working in dancing schools. Waters got his chance thanks to a bassist who had worked with him in Johnson's band and was now playing in Henderson's band. One day the guy showed up at Waters's apartment to tell him that Henderson needed a tenor player. Though Waters was hung over when he auditioned—he had been drunk and fighting with his wife—he got the job.

Waters's drinking, however, soon soured things for him. Drunk one night, he took offense at a remark made by trumpeter Frankie Newton and tried to punch him. Newton blocked the punch, breaking Waters's arm. Waters wound up being hospitalized for a long stretch—his well-to-do uncle Fred Garner covered the bills—and it took months of physical therapy before he could regain full use of the arm. In the meantime, Henderson had hired a replacement. Having squandered a good opportunity, Waters went back to working in a dancing school.

Waters has some vivid recollections of his brief (perhaps six months') stay in Fletcher Henderson's band:

> That was in the same time that Benny Goodman started his band. All those arrangements Benny Goodman played, I played before. Because Fletcher had to see if the score was correct so he could sell it to Benny.
>
> One time we were *supposed* to be playing at the Savoy for the benefit of the union. Benny Goodman was there; he played first. And after Benny played all of Fletcher's arrangements, Fletcher didn't have no numbers to play, so he told us, "OK, boys, pack up," because he had sold Benny Goodman the arrangements—and some of the best numbers. I guess Fletcher was afraid to play, after Benny.

"Benny and John Hammond used to come up to Fletcher's house, on 138th Street, many times when I was there. Fletcher was arranging for Benny then," Waters notes. He adds that Henderson's wife helped out a great deal but did not get any recognition.

> Fletcher did the arranging. He made the score, and then his wife did the extracting. To take it and make it for all of the instruments is work. And that's what his wife did. If you have

> ten pieces, you have to make it for ten parts—extract—from what Fletcher writes. The arranging is the knowledge of how to arrange. But the real *work* is the extracting—taking it from the score and giving it to the trumpets and the saxophones. His wife was a musician, so she did that.
>
> That's why he could turn out so many arrangements a week. And his brother, too, Horace. He used to do a lot of arranging, too, for Benny Goodman. But not directly for Benny—for Fletcher, his brother. Horace was working for his brother. Fletcher would pay him and pass it on to Benny Goodman. A lot of people don't know that. They think that Fletcher made all the arrangements. But not all.

Waters believes that some arrangements credited to Fletcher Henderson were actually by Horace. "Not too many, though. I can only remember one that I *know* that Horace made, 'I'll Be Loving You Always.' Some others, too, but I can't pinpoint them." Waters adds that he, too, arranged "a couple of songs" for Henderson.

Charlie Johnson took Waters back into his big band, which was playing once again at Smalls's Paradise, in 1936–37. Waters was happy to be back, although the peak years for the club and the band had clearly passed. Still, it was great, after the scruffy dancing schools, to be working in a place where a young Buddy Rich was likely to drop by and sit in on drums, or where Phil Harris and Alice Faye would often come to dance.

Since the opening was for an alto, not a tenor player, Waters joined Johnson on alto sax and wound up playing quite a bit of it in various bands over the next half dozen years.

> As far as the alto saxophone was concerned, I was influenced by three guys—first, Johnny Hodges. Because I had the privilege of working with him when he was in Boston, when he was thirteen years old. I was eighteen. But he could play. I think he was playing more jazz then than he did with Duke.
>
> And I worked right beside, for two years, Benny Carter, in Charlie Johnson's band. Benny Carter was *young* and great! He's great now. And I had the privilege of working and arranging for the great Earl Bostic. But I listened to other people. New York is a mecca for jazz, so there's a lot to listen to. I liked Don Byas, as one of my favorites. I like Art Pepper's playing on alto. But so many—I listen to everybody. I always used to go around. I still do that.

Benny Waters's exuberance comes across in this publicity shot by Leon Bosc, probably taken in the late 1940s. (Author's collection. Courtesy of Benny Waters.)

Benny Waters, in the 1980s, plays in an immensely appealing style—careening with reckless abandon on uptempo numbers, making the most of very few notes on slow ones—clearly rooted in the 1920s. (Author's collection. Courtesy of Edith M. Rothman.)

* * *

From the mid-1930s until 1952, when he went to Europe, Waters worked for a odd mix of name and no-name bandleaders, alternating between jazz and commercial bands. He even passed as a Cuban musician for a spell, when he worked briefly for Alberto Socarras, the superb Cuban flute player.

> We were in Columbus, Ohio, working this exclusive joint up there. No Negro band had ever worked there. Now Alberto's my color; Alberto's not light at all. We all had on these shirts way wide and this big bandanna around here, all that kind of stuff. And he says, "Now Benny, you're not no Negro, you're Cuban. We're all Cuban."
>
> Finally, because I was drinking in that period, I thought, How the hell can I get a drink if I can't say nothing? So I go to the bar, and go like this [Waters pantomimes that he wants to drink]. And the guy says, "What'd you say?" I was ready to talk. Oh! I couldn't talk, because if I talked, he'd know that I'm a Negro. And I didn't talk. Because Alberto had told me in the front, "You're not no Negro, you're Cuban."
>
> That club was exclusive, had never hired a Negro band. A lot of Cuban bands work where Negroes don't work. Sure. Cuban music swings like mad. Cuban music is something else.

Waters worked for a while in Coleman Hawkins's band. He was also in Hot Lips Page's big band, on tenor sax, in 1938 at Smalls's Paradise (and played on Page's record of "Small Fry"); then in 1941, he was with Page's smaller band on Fifty-second Street. "Hot Lips was a buddy of mine," he notes. "I made an arrangement of 'Gee Baby, Ain't I Good to You' for him." He played in various commercial bands, too, such as violinist Norwood Penner's society music–type quintet and Dave Martin's orchestra, which played at hotels. In 1940–41, Waters was in Claude Hopkins's big band, on tenor. "That was an underrated band," he says, "—much better than people thought. I did a few arrangements. And I did some recording" (for example, such 1940 sides as "Yacht Club Swing" and "Out to Lunch").

From about June 1942 through December of that year, Waters was in Jimmie Lunceford's band, on alto (longtime Lunceford star Joe Thomas got all the tenor solos). He had a featured alto sax solo on "Margie," which he inherited from Ted Buckner, but he had to play it note for note the way Buckner had on the hit record. Not being able to express himself was frustrating, he says. Still, Lunceford's band had something for everyone. While Henderson's and Johnson's bands were both excellent musically, Lunceford offered greater showmanship, with musicians standing and waving their instruments in unison, and more variety in vocals, including the effective use of a vocal trio. The band's most-requested numbers were those arranged by Sy Oliver, who had left in 1939. Waters recalls: "I made arrangements for Jimmie Lunceford, too. I made an arrangement of 'Out of Nowhere' for the band. That was most likely the greatest band I ever worked with, for all types of music, and entertaining also."

Waters didn't become buddies with Lunceford, because that wasn't Lunceford's style. "Jimmie was pretty close-mouthed. He kept by himself; he didn't hang out with the boys." Lunceford was also more refined than most musicians he had associated with. From Waters's point of view, "Jimmie was an intellectual. You know, he graduated from a school down there, a Negro university. He was a professor." (Lunceford graduated from Fisk University in 1926 and taught music at Manassa High School in Memphis.) He was also very strict.

> Discipline—he demanded that. The guys drank, like they do in any other band, but they didn't get drunk. Like I was the one that was drinking more, most likely. No drunks. Because they respected him. He didn't drink. Strict. He'd tell you what he wanted. And he demanded it. Calm. Like if somebody'd get out of line, he'd say, "Now, you know I don't do that. . . ."
>
> I got in trouble with Jimmie Lunceford. I got my little whiskey in me, and I wanted to go out and meet those chicks at a little jazz club. A guy told me, "Come on up, man, and jam. There's all these chicks out here." I get my horn and go out there and jam. Jimmie heard about it. He give me hell! I mean, I should know that—because there's a bylaw in the union that's against that.

Sober, Waters knew that if a band was hired to play an exclusive engagement, its members could not jam at competing clubs. But once again liquor had clouded his judgment—and may well have limited his career more than he realized. He heard, for example, that saxophonist Ted McRae wanted him to take his place in Cab Calloway's band but that the straw boss of the band had vetoed the idea because Waters was known to be a "juice head." One wonders what other jobs he might have been considered for but lost out on because of his reputation as a drinker.

Waters got married again for a while, this time to a pianist named Lorraine. He formed his own small group, with his wife on piano,

Kaiser Marshall (who had been with Fletcher Henderson from 1924 to 1930) on drums, Herman Autrey (an alumnus of Fats Waller's, Henderson's, and Johnson's bands) on trumpet, and Eddy Gibbs on guitar. They worked in a minor New York club, the Red Mill, on 174th Street and Jerome Avenue. "It was a good, more commercial band. Because we didn't have time to play no jazz. We had these shows and things to play. All we did was play a couple of numbers, the spectacular for the show. And dancing." Waters says he went the small-group route by choice, but it was clearly a comedown for him. If he had been offered a spot in a top-flight big band like Basie's or Ellington's, he would have taken it. He just wasn't getting the offers.

His wife got work playing in USO shows, and so they headed out to California together, where Waters had a little combo just outside of San Diego. "I had a band in California that played everything. I had a bass saxophone; I sounded like Adrian Rollini at times. I was playing mambas, congas, Viennese waltzes in California. On a Saturday night the place would be half full of Mexicans, because San Diego, where I was, is only fourteen miles from Mexico. They wanted their music. I played all kinds of stuff. I was singing in the group. I used to put on hats, like a cowboy, and sing those songs, that 'Water.' " Whatever the locals wanted to hear.

Waters says he preferred working in small groups. "The big bands, I found, was much more work. You don't have a chance to play a lot of solos in a big band because you have too many other people." And just playing section parts got tiresome. "In a small group, you kill yourself blowing till you knock yourself out. That's why I prefer it." He was, however, really on the periphery of the music world now. Playing commercial music in a little café near San Diego, hoping for an occasional good tip from a patron, he was far from the glory days of the twenties at Smalls's Paradise. The jazz world of the mid- to late 1940s was in ferment. Bebop was emerging. But Waters could only follow the new developments from a distance.

What did he think of Charlie Parker? Was he impressed with him?

> Yeah, Charlie was great; he changed the whole scene. I had my own opinion; I always liked Benny Carter, see. But Charlie, he changed the scene. He changed the scene of the alto players. He changed the scene, the same as Lester Young. Because when I came up, there was nobody but Coleman Hawkins; that's all you could hear, Coleman Hawkins. But Lester came and he changed the scene. I never thought Lester played as much as Coleman, not for me. And I still don't think

that Charlie played as much as Benny Carter. I may run into a little argument about that statement. But that's my own opinion. I listened to them both.

That don't keep Charlie Parker from being a stylist and changing the scene. So you can't take that away from him. He changed the scene of the alto playing. And for the young boys, that's all they know, is Charlie Parker. That's all you hear till Coltrane came up and changed it around.

Waters once again got to tour when he joined Roy Milton's jumping small band, and he also played on such 1946 Milton recordings as "Groovy Blues" and "R. M. Blues." But here, too, he felt frustrated because Milton insisted he play just what was on the records. Waters would have liked to have made a name for himself as a featured soloist in a big band and then gone off on his own, as had, say, Illinois Jacquet. But he could see that that simply wasn't going to happen. So one night in Oklahoma, loaded on moonshine, he said to hell with everything and, when Milton was away from the stand, did his own thing on "Roy Milton's Blues."

Shortly thereafter, Waters returned to Philadelphia and moved in with a woman he'd known since he was young. In his words he was semi-pimping, living in her ten-room house and taking a breather while he tried to figure out, as 1950 arrived, where he was going to fit in the current music scene.

By now, the big band era had passed. Many bands had broken up in 1948, and those that had survived were struggling. Bebop had come to dominate the small-group jazz scene, but it was not Waters's kind of music. Rhythm and blues was coming up strong, too, but like bebop it was mostly being played by musicians much younger than Waters (he was now forty-eight)—and he had never been big on blues anyway. So, like a number of older, swing-oriented black musicians, many of whom were not happy about the latest developments, he found a new niche for himself playing Dixieland. He had to learn the melodies and the routines of oldies such as "That's A Plenty" and "Jazz Me Blues" because he hadn't played them back in the twenties. But they were related enough to the swing music he had favored for him to make the adjustment. There was a certain segment of the public supporting Dixieland now, and if playing it would ensure his survival, he'd play it.

From 1950 to 1952, Waters played clarinet and soprano sax, not tenor or alto, at Jimmy Ryan's, on Fifty-second Street in New York.

Trombonist Jimmy Archey led this Dixieland group, with Dick Wellstood on piano, Henry Goodwin on trumpet, Tommy Benford on drums, and Pops Foster on bass. How did Waters feel about playing Dixieland? "I liked it," he maintains. "Sure, I had never played it before. It took me several weeks before I could get into it, on clarinet. And by not being an exclusive clarinetist, it took me a little while to get into some of that stuff. But finally I got straight. And we had a good band over there."

To some of the younger black musicians who were 100 percent into bebop, going into Dixieland seemed akin to selling out, giving white audiences what they wanted just to make a buck. In their view, playing Dixieland seemed like Uncle Tom–ing. But Waters was fairly comfortable playing this music, and he was working in the company of some excellent and dedicated musicians. It was never his first preference, he admits; he'd still rather play ballads and swing than Dixieland (or blues or bebop or anything else). But he was *able* to do it. It gave him visibility in New York, which he hadn't had in recent years.

Playing Dixieland also led, unexpectedly, to Waters becoming an expatriate. "In 1952, I went to Europe with Jimmy Archey's Dixieland group. I had no idea, when I went, that I was going over to stay. I was going over there for one month, that's all. But Archey disbanded. So Bill Coleman, who's very famous over there, asked me to join his group. I said, 'Well, here's a chance to see Europe.' And I've been there ever since! Now I'm quite established in Europe." Unlike some other expatriates, he wasn't trying to escape racism. In fact, he believes that "there's just as much racial prejudice in France as there is in New York. No difference. That's international." He adds: "I never did think of that racial prejudice. Racial prejudice was always stupid to me. I wasn't raised that way. I used to walk to school with a little white girl, hand in hand. I was only about eight or nine, something like that."

Waters feels that it's possible for a jazz musician to do better in Europe because of less competition—"See, because the States is blasé. America's pretty tough." He says that European audiences accepted him, whether he was playing Dixieland, which he played when he first reached Europe, or in more of a swinging mainstream vein, which he preferred and which he concentrated on as soon as he could. Also, in Europe he was treated as a more important figure—Benny Waters, a jazzman *from America*—than he had been in the States. He has since performed on more than twenty albums and cassettes, released on labels in France, Germany, Belgium, Switzerland, Italy, Sweden, England, and Czechoslovakia. Initially, he recorded as a sideman (*Bill*

Coleman and His Swing Stars), then later as a leader or top-billed guest artist (*Benny Waters in Paris, Benny Waters with the Swiss Dixie Stompers, Ben Waters with the Harlem Blues Band,* etc.).

From 1952 to 1968, Waters generally played under the leadership of others, mostly in France but also on tours to other countries, including Switzerland, Germany, Belgium, and Italy. For years he worked at La Cigale in Paris, in a band led by a fellow expatriate, trumpeter Jack Butler. After Butler returned to the United States in 1968, Waters became the bandleader at La Cigale for a few years. Around that time, he also permanently gave up drinking—or, as he puts it, his drinking problem was cured through Christian Science. And in the past two decades, he has established himself under his own name, rather than as a sideman. He tours as a soloist, working with local rhythm sections, "in about fifteen different countries for the last fifteen years, or maybe more than that. When I go back, I already have lined up about eight countries."

Waters is a flexible musician. His conservatory training in music theory, he feels, has served him well, enabling him to play compatibly with modern, younger musicians. While he's happy playing old standards such as "Body and Soul" and "Laura," he doesn't mind taking challenges from bebop-oriented younger musicians. He notes:

> I played with this little kid. He was concentrating on bebop, the choruses note for note. [Waters scats, as an example, Thelonious Monk's "Well, You Needn't."] OK, he'd play that. So I'd say, "OK, let's play a song like 'Laura,' something like that, that already has chords in it. Then he lost. A lot of them—because they concentrating on Charlie Parker too much.
>
> I had that experience in Paris with a guy from Guadaloupe who played just like Charlie Parker. He copied the records, he had the sound and everything. He played three choruses of Charlie Parker—note for note what he heard on the record. I would play three choruses of *my own* interpretation of the number. And I would get more hands than he did. Because a copy is a copy. You can't beat a guy that's originating things.

The 1986 release of the film *Round Midnight* prompts Waters to comment that he's jammed with its star, Dexter Gordon, many times in Paris.

> . . . He used to come down to the place where I used to play on Sunday afternoons to jam with us. *Round Midnight* was a wonderful movie. I thought his acting was great, although he

was just acting himself. The playing—OK. I mean—thousands of saxophone players, you know.

In France, now, they flock in to play the Free Jazz. But they don't know what they're playing. They go by what somebody else said. So if a bunch of people like Free Jazz, then they get in like a clique—"I only like Free Jazz." And the Free Jazz stuff sometimes is kind of crazy. It's so weird that even the musicians don't even like it.

But I've heard Free Jazz that I like. Anthony Braxton—I've stayed there all night—all night—and I enjoyed every note. He was real free. But I mean he was doing it. And then he turned around and played "Lester Leaps In" just like I would, or anybody would, or like Lester [Young] would. That shows you he was a musician. Sometimes the guys are playing Free Jazz that don't have that much ability. They copy from the records or from other big stars.

Today, Waters gets enthusiastic receptions wherever he plays. He tells of sharing a stage with Scott Hamilton and getting the bigger hand, which he figures is because he plays naturally in an idiom Hamilton is trying to reach back toward. Of course, part of the audience's enthusiasm for Waters may be due simply to his having survived for so long. If he gets greater ovations now than he did years ago, it's not because he's playing better; it's partly a gesture of respect for his age. The applause acknowledges that he is one of the last survivors from a so-called golden age of jazz. People are surprised to see someone well into his eighties playing with such vigor. He boasts: "I call myself 'The World's Most Modern Saxophonist over Eighty.' Everywhere I go, they're always talking about how modern I play. I might as well use it—wag your own tail. I do play quite modern. That's on account of me studying harmony and theory and solfeggio."[4]

On this particular visit to the United States, Waters notes, he played first for the Cape Cod Jazz Society, in Boston, then headed down to New Orleans for almost a week, playing at the Hotel Meridien and at the New Orleans Jazz and Heritage Festival. He went on to Denver, Maryland, and Washington, D.C., before hitting New York. After his upcoming five-day gig at the West End, he is booked to play George Wein's festival in Saratoga Springs. For the West End he'll be playing tenor sax, alto sax, and clarinet, and he'll also sing a bit on the bandstand. "I don't say nothing about that singing," he murmurs. "I sing, but I mean—it goes over."

His biggest success of this trip, Waters suggests, was on May 2 at the New Orleans Jazz and Heritage Festival. "I had a stand-up ovation of about 3,000 people. I'd never seen that before. I was working with a white band [the Creole Rice Jazz Band], but I wasn't playing Dixieland, I just played the way I play. Here's where I criticize. Those people, the musicians and some of the promoters, they think that Dixieland's the only music. If Dixieland is the only music, how can I have a standing ovation? I sure wasn't playing no Dixieland. I was swinging, playing saxophone with a rhythm section. It isn't what you play, it's how you play it."

He confides that he is a bit disturbed to note that traditional New Orleans jazz seems to be kept alive only by younger white musicians. Where, he wonders, are the young blacks who can preserve the heritage of men like King Oliver, Louis Armstrong, and Jimmie Noone? "I didn't see no Negro band playing Dixieland. All the bands were white. You look at the *Mississippi Rag,* you'll find hundreds of those groups that play like Louis Armstrong or Bix Beiderbecke, things like that. You don't hear no Negroes. Negroes don't like to play that. Since Wilbur de Paris broke up, I don't know of any Negro band that's following Louis Armstrong in New Orleans. May be, but I don't know of any." He adds that he knows of plenty of great young white Dixieland bands, particularly Jim Cullum's, which features Allan Vache on clarinet: "Allan's a hell of a clarinet player. I've worked with Warren Vache many times. He's a hell of a little trumpet player—and his brother is just as good on clarinet."

Now in his mid-eighties, Waters is thinking about moving back to the States. After living abroad for some thirty-five years, he would like to spend his final years here. He also hopes to rework and find a U.S. publisher for his colorful memoir, *The Key to a Jazzy Life.* His health is good, he says, and he doesn't want to wait until it declines before moving. Still, he wonders what he'll have to do to establish himself in New York, if he'll have to play Dixieland again, as he did before he left for Europe in 1952.

> I know it's hard in New York, because I was raised in New York; I know the conditions. But if I feel like it, I'll do it. Or I could just go out and jam with some of these little young kids that think they can play everything. That's all you got to do.
>
> I know the conditions here. I know that bebop is coming back in line. I know that Dixieland, in certain parts of the country, is still here. I know that Dixieland is divided among the young white musicians. In fact, the only way that a Negro

> musician can get in is to form a Dixieland group. Well, I can do that. If I came here, if I wanted to, I could get some *good* musicians and start a Dixieland band.
>
> There's nothing wrong with that. If I came back and started a Dixieland band—in connection with other things—I'd work all over the damn place. It's a fault of the Negro, that the Negroes say, "I don't like that crap." I'm not talking *all,* I'm talking about the average Negro. You can tell by what they're playing, what they like. If you say something about Dixieland, they're liable to insult you.

Waters recently played Dixieland for the first time in years, sitting in with a Dixieland band in Germany, and he says it was quite successful. So he feels confident that he could get into it again, if he had to, to earn a living in the States—although, he adds, he doesn't think of himself as a Dixieland player at heart. Rather, "I call myself mainstream." He'll do whatever is needed to get by, however. He may not have much money, but he's always been able to support himself by playing. And he can't imagine *not* playing.

"I'm working Wednesday night at the West End with some boys young enough to be my sons. I've worked with them for three or four years. Don Coates—very good piano, nice guy, too—I like Don because he knows all of these songs that I play. I work with young guys," he reiterates. "It's kind of hard to find anybody older than me."

3

BIX BEIDERBECKE

An Appreciation

Bix Beiderbecke's life lasted but twenty-eight years (1903–31). His recording career spanned but six years (1924–30). And he produced most of his greatest recordings—the ones that really secured his reputation—within just two years (1927–28). The impact he made in so brief a period is little short of astonishing.

Nearly six decades have passed since Beiderbecke's death, and most of the people who heard him play live have by now died. But Beiderbecke's music continues to attract new listeners. His solos—sometimes jaunty, full of life; other times poignant, shaded by a sense of loss—spring forth from the grooves to touch us, to move us.

As a jazz critic, I'm exposed to an awful lot of jazz in all genres, week after week. It's always a pleasure for me to get back to the Beiderbecke sides, though. Listening to some of them is like stepping into a bracing mountain stream. The best of his solos seem absolutely perfect: one cannot conceive of them being improved upon. The beauty in form and in tone is both striking and immediately apparent. But beyond that there is an emotional content that gives the playing its full impact. You listen to, say, "I'm Comin' Virginia," and the melancholia pervades you. From sixty years in the past, a human spirit is making contact with you. I've heard a number of other cornetists play Beiderbecke's solo, note for note, on "I'm Comin' Virginia," yet invariably they fail to re-create the *effect* of the original recording. For there is something subtle and elusive and powerful in Beiderbecke's work. It is easy to imitate but seemingly impossible to duplicate.

Beiderbecke had a rounded, ringing tone—Max Kaminsky said,

"Bix's tone was so pure, so devoid of any tinge of sentimentality or personal ego, that it was the nearest thing to heaven I have ever heard"[1]—and a percussive way of tumbling through certain passages of notes, so that the listener hears each note being struck in succession. Modern players tend to smooth out such passages a bit, to blend the notes into more of a seamless, connected whole. But the wondrous effect of the original gets lost. And, of course, Beiderbecke's emotional undertones cannot really be copied. His imitators—even the very best ones—tend to sound somewhat superficial after awhile. Hearing excellent cornetists try, yet not quite manage, to duplicate what Beiderbecke did reminds us anew of the value of his contributions.[2] Rex Stewart commented in 1967: "In my book, Bix was a once-in-a-million artist. I doubt if what he played will ever be surpassed on trumpet. He was one of the all-time giants, and I feel that his gifts remain today as unsullied and strikingly refreshing as when he lived."[3]

Beiderbecke's legacy is one of lyricism, of restraint. He showed how a ballad could be interpreted in a genuine jazz fashion, with grace and subtlety, and without excessive sweetness. Generally acknowledged to be one of the two most important trumpeters—technically, he always played the cornet—to emerge during the 1920s, he also enjoyed playing piano, which he had taught himself long before he first picked up a horn. He left a handful of piano compositions, the greatest of which is "In a Mist," that suggest an unfulfilled potential as a composer.

The questions jazz buffs always seem to ask about their musical favorites are, Who were their influences? How did they come to play the way they did? What made them what they were? I'm convinced, having profiled many outstanding musicians, that some things ultimately remain a mystery. You can track down early influences and identify musicians your subject studied under; yet, ultimately, the talent of the truly great artist seems almost a given. It was *there.* It blossomed. It had a life of its own.

Jazz singer Red McKenzie said that when he heard Beiderbecke for the first time, "I got so excited that I couldn't eat anything for two weeks."[4] Hoagy Carmichael said that Beiderbecke's playing literally knocked him off his feet. If such responses seem exaggerated, you should bear in mind the state of jazz at the time Beiderbecke came onto the scene. Listen to the primitive recorded jazz that preceded him, and then listen to his playing. Try to imagine how his music must have hit audiences when it was fresh. People can talk about this musician or that musician influencing Beiderbecke, but when you get right down to it, he was an original. No jazzman recording before him sounded anything like him.

Beiderbecke received very few newspaper write-ups during his lifetime, although the first one came early. The *Davenport Daily Democrat* announced, "SEVEN-YEAR-OLD BOY MUSICAL WONDER, Little Bickie Beiderbecke plays any selection he hears!" The reporter was quite clearly impressed:

> Leon Bix Beiderbecke, aged seven years, is the most unusual and the most remarkably talented child in music that there is in this city. He has never taken a music lesson and does not know one key from another, but he can play in completeness any selection, the air or tune of which he knows.
>
> "Little Bickie," as his parents call him, has always had an ear for music. When he was two years old, Mrs. Beiderbecke says that the child was able with one of his chubby fingers to play the tune of "Yankee Doodle." . . . In fact, so acute is his ear for music that if his mother plays a piece in another key than that in which "Bickie" has always played it, the child will sit down and play the piece in exactly the same key with proper bass accompaniment. . . .
>
> When "Bickie" is playing the piano, he never looks at the keys; he never watches his hands. To one watching and listening to the child playing the piano, it might seem that the child's mind was not on what he is playing, because his eyes are centered upon objects about the room or he is looking into space with apparently no thought of the piece he is playing. But a careful observation of that gaze and of the child indicates that his mind is absorbed in the music, in the melody that he is playing.[5]

Where did that flair for music come from? It seems to have simply been there.

If the young Bix was in a world of his own when he was making music—so consistent with countless descriptions of the adult Bix—it was no doubt a far more interesting world than the one inhabited by his father, Bismark "Bix" Beiderbecke, a businessman with the East Davenport Lumber and Coal Company.[6] The elder Beiderbecke was a solid, conservative, financially comfortable citizen. His younger son's facility for playing music on the piano was hardly of great importance to him and conceivably might have been somewhat unsatisfying: most fathers—especially Germanic ones—seem to have conventional hopes that their sons will excel in stereotypically masculine pursuits, which piano playing is not. The youngster no doubt felt closer to his mother, who had played organ in church before her marriage and who encouraged her son. A childhood friend, Leon Werentin, remembered that Bix was often at his grandmother's house, playing piano. According to Werentin, the two were "great buddies."[7]

Beiderbecke attended President John Tyler Elementary School No. 9, which was directly across the street from his home on Grand Avenue in Davenport. In 1911, a few weeks after starting the third grade, he had to withdraw due to a severe, long-lasting case of diarrhea, followed by scarlet fever. It must have been hard for him to stay home, a sickly child, while his peers attended classes and played together during recess, all within earshot.

Missing out on a formal education as well as the normal socialization that goes on in any school, Beiderbecke found himself with time for introspection, time to rely on his imagination to keep himself occupied. He was also spending a greater part of the day with his mother than most boys. By the time he recovered, the school year was too far along for him to be re-enrolled. So to help him make better use of his time, his mother hired a music teacher, who came to the house once a week. The lessons proved unsuccessful, the teacher concluding that his young pupil, while clearly precocious, lacked the discipline needed to properly benefit from the instruction offered. The boy played the assigned pieces, not as written, but with inventions of his own, the teacher noted with dismay.

Beiderbecke returned to school in September 1912. He was now a grade behind his old friends, which no doubt reinforced his sense of being set apart. And after a year on his own, he was not in the habit of applying himself to daily schoolwork. Classroom studies weren't of much interest to him anyway. He was more intrigued by music. Leon Werentin recalled: "When we'd go to the silent nickel movies, Bix didn't care about the plot. He just wanted to hear the guy who played piano accompaniment. As soon as the show was over, he'd hurry back to his grandma's to play on her piano what he'd just heard." George Von Maur, who was a few years older, remembered: "His parents would take Bix along when they went to parties in various houses. I can remember them bringing him to our house on many evenings. He'd make a beeline for the piano. Bix loved to play it. And he'd do it to everyone's confusion. He knew what he was doing, but that sure didn't help the card games. But even if his music tended to spoil them, Bix would keep playing—even if no one wanted to hear it."[8]

Davenport was basically a quiet, respectable middle-American community, many of whose residents were, like the Beiderbeckes, of German stock. But its location along the Mississippi River introduced an element not found in most other midwestern communities of similar socioeconomic status: hot music. The infectious sounds from calliopes and bands as the riverboats made their way north from New Orleans wafted easily to the Beiderbecke home: syncopated dance music, ragtime, and the beginnings of what would become known as jazz.

Although respectable parents like the Beiderbeckes did not want their children hanging around the waterfront, where they might come into contact with lowlifes and riffraff and get into who knows what kind of trouble, it proved a tempting area for many youths, and especially tempting for one with an interest in music. We can imagine how Beiderbecke's parents felt when they got a call one night from a riverboat captain in Muscatine who had found their son on his boat after it had pulled out from Davenport earlier in the day. The boy had slipped aboard and offered his services as a calliope player.

When Bix's older brother, Charles Burnette Beiderbecke, who had served in the army in World War I, was discharged in late 1918, he bought a wind-up Columbia Graphophone and a few records for the family—some "serious" music and a recording of the Original Dixieland Jazz Band playing "Tiger Rag" and "Skeleton Jangle." His parents were hardly thrilled by the raucous, frenetic sound of the ODJB, but his brother—then fifteen and a freshman at Davenport High School—definitely was. It must have startled the Beiderbeckes to see their younger son, who had never been too disciplined about learning how to play music "properly," devote himself to learning this strange new music. Bix played the record repeatedly, at a slow speed, so that he could learn cornetist Nick LaRocca's every note, which he then duplicated on the piano.[9]

By mid-January, Beiderbecke had borrowed a cornet from a friend down the street, and eventually he taught himself how to play it. The fingerings he stumbled upon by trial and error were not the so-called correct ones; yet it was his lifelong use of alternate fingerings that contributed to the individuality of his sound and the style he developed.[10] By March, he was doing his first gigs as a musician, playing piano—he was still just experimenting with cornet—in a group made up of fellow Davenport High students, for Friday afternoon tea dances at the school. His friends were just learning how to play Dixieland jazz themselves.

The ODJB made a lasting impact upon Beiderbecke. Tunes it popularized, such as "At the Jazz Band Ball," "Sensation Rag," "Original Dixieland One-Step," and "Fidgety Feet," with LaRocca credited as composer or co-composer, became staples in Beiderbecke's repertoire. For as long as he lived, if he had to play a hot jazz tune, he was apt to fall back upon something that had first been recorded by the ODJB. Even his masterpiece, "Singin' the Blues," had actually been introduced by the ODJB. Because he possessed an imagination, a sense of lyricism, and an understanding of advanced harmony that no members of the ODJB had, Beiderbecke's later recordings of the ODJB's early numbers were considerable improvements upon the originals and are the versions generally remembered today. Even in his novice years as a cornetist, according to contemporaries, he didn't just punch out the lead with short, separate statements the way LaRocca did; he connected his phrases to produce more flowing lines. Beiderbecke nonetheless retained a respect for LaRocca, who was probably his first musical hero, for as long as he lived—long after most jazz players had written off LaRocca as crude, primitive, old hat.

Although several of his high school musician friends worked that summer of 1919 in a band on a Mississippi River excursion boat, Beiderbecke, then sixteen, was deemed too young. Still, he spent plenty of time hanging around the riverfront. In August, the sternwheeler *Capitol,* sailing out of St. Louis, reached Davenport carrying piano/calliope player Fate Marable's band, which included Johnny St. Cyr on banjo, Warren "Baby" Dodds on drums, and Louis Armstrong on cornet. Beiderbecke and Armstrong met for the first time during the boat's stay in Davenport. Beiderbecke did not yet own a cornet; Armstrong, nineteen, was an unknown sideman in a riverboat band. Armstrong later recalled: "He'd come down to hear the bands, and then go home and practice what he heard. [Bix] and I became friends the first time we met—he was the type of youngster I admired all the way. No matter how good the solo was that he played, he wasn't very much satisfied with it. He never seemed satisfied with his efforts; this was true in later years, too, even while he was driving all the cats wild."[11]

Beiderbecke bought his first cornet, from a schoolmate, at the start of his sophomore year. While he had his share of innocent dates in high school (his girlfriend, for a while, was Vera Cox), it seems clear that making music held the greatest interest for him. Leon Werentin recalled: "At any Davenport High School dance where there was an orchestra, Bix was there, always borrowing an instrument so he could sit in. It didn't matter what it was, he could play it. A lot of times Bix would take a date and just forget about her if someone else let him play the trumpet or piano. It didn't really bother him to leave the girl alone all night. He wasn't really that gung-ho about going out with girls anyway."[12]

Chet Salter, who joined the same Davenport High School fraternity as Beiderbecke did, in their freshman year, recalled: "Three or four times a year we'd have a fraternity dance at the Davenport Orchestra Club, with a hired orchestra. And every time, there'd be Bix talking them into letting him sit in on the piano. The minute he got there, the music got terrible. It was absolutely no good, as far as we were concerned. We told Bix several times to quit sitting in, and when he wouldn't we just blacklisted him from the fraternity." The high school kids couldn't understand his music; he was probably ahead of them. Salter adds: "I can't say I was too friendly with him. His butting-in on the music was one reason. Another was that he was bumming around with some fast company."[13] "Fast company" is, of course, a relative term. Some of the older professional musicians Beiderbecke knew and worked with when he could—those who smoked and drank and hung around with show people—must have seemed pretty fast, but Beiderbecke's teen years were no doubt quite innocent by today's standards.

Beiderbecke wrapped up his sophomore year by taking part in the Davenport High School Concert and Vaudeville Night at the Grand Opera House. He played cornet in a group, composed of four other students plus the school's adult piano accompanist, billed as the Black Jazz Babies. (Jazz was then thought of, basically, as black music.) His parents hoped that eventually he would go on to college and a respectable career in business. But his scholastic performance was weak, and his music, always pleasurable, was now beginning to put a little money in his pocket.

With several school friends, Beiderbecke worked that summer of 1920 in a local "novelty orchestra." And he continued playing gigs, as opportunities arose, when school resumed in the fall. He failed an audition to join the musicians' union (presumably because of his inability to read music), but was able to get work in the orchestra at the Columbia Theater. A contemporary, Rolla Chalupa, recalled vaudeville star Sophie Tucker, as she took her bow after a performance, pointing out Beiderbecke and introducing him as " 'the greatest trumpet player in the world.' And he was just a high school kid." Chalupa, who also remembered his friend playing hooky, to sit by himself at the theater to watch Tucker perform, added that he personally witnessed principal George Edward Marshall "take Bix by the ear" out of the theater and back to school.[14]

Beiderbecke was failing courses in school—enough so that at the end of his junior year he was told he would not be promoted. His parents decided to enroll him in Lake Forest Academy, a prep school thirty-five miles northwest of Chicago. Officials there decided that, due to his poor record, he would have to start in the fall as a sophomore.

In the summer of 1921, Beiderbecke briefly played his first riverboat jobs and also got his first booking as a group leader. While a student at Lake Forest, he played for campus dances and elsewhere, occasionally visiting Chicago and sitting in with a hotel orchestra. In Chicago he heard the second major white jazz band to emerge: the New Orleans Rhythm Kings. There are those who say that Paul Mares, cornetist of the New Orleans Rhythm Kings, had more of an influence on Beiderbecke's playing than Nick LaRocca. But the influence of either player should not be exaggerated. Ultimately, Beiderbecke did not sound like anyone but himself, and he wound up making the work of both LaRocca and Mares seem primitive by comparison.

In May 1922, Beiderbecke was expelled from Lake Forest Academy. The nineteen-year-old had been caught outside the dormitory too often after lights-out. Drinking may have been a factor. He spent the summer gigging as he could. In Chicago he saw Louis Armstrong, who had just joined King Oliver's band. Armstrong had not yet recorded, much less achieved national fame, but his playing was already astonishing musicians who went to hear him. Hoagy Carmichael later wrote that when he and Bix listened to Armstrong slash into a magnificent, high-speed version of "Bugle Call Rag" one night in Chicago, he wondered why everybody in the world wasn't there to hear it. According to Carmichael, Beiderbecke "was on his feet, his eyes popping."[15]

Armstrong recognized that Beiderbecke was for real: talented, not trying to copy anyone, playing from the heart. He later wrote: "The first time I heard Bix, I said these words to myself: there's a man as serious about his music as I am."[16] Plenty of white musicians purportedly playing jazz in 1922 were not at all serious about their music. They were commercial players without any real feel for jazz, just trying to keep up with the latest trends. They would copy superficial aspects of black jazz playing, hoping to sound hot and novel. Still, many of them made good money as "jazz artists"—much better than the black originators. In the mid-1920s, the average white record buyer probably would have named Ted Lewis—who in retrospect clearly had little jazz talent—as a prominent jazz clarinet player but would have had no idea who gifted black jazz clarinetists Johnny Dodds and Jimmie Noone were.

While in Chicago, Beiderbecke met Eddie Condon and other young jazz players. Then, in late October 1922, he made his first trip to New York, where he met Nick LaRocca and other members of the Original Dixieland Jazz Band. By December he was back in Davenport, working—rather unhappily—in the office of the East Davenport Coal and Lumber Company, where he weighed coal and helped collect bills. He had no desire whatsoever to follow his father in the coal business, or to settle down in Davenport, but what options did he have? He hadn't been able to cut it in public or private school, and his father didn't want him just lounging around the house. He couldn't earn enough money playing cornet to support himself, probably because most bands didn't want a cornetist who couldn't read music.

Under his jaunty exterior, Beiderbecke probably didn't have the highest opinion of himself. He was also something of an embarrassment to his parents. Being thrown out of prep school after failing in high school was bad enough, but playing *jazz* was worse. Jazz was the music of uneducated lowlifes, clearly beneath the Beiderbeckes of Davenport, Iowa.

Beiderbecke lived with his parents through June 1923, gigging on cornet in and around Davenport. Thelma Griffin, an assistant buyer in a Davenport department store, remembered him playing in the orchestra when the store put on a fashion show; she never dreamed he would attain the status he did within the next couple of years. She said that he used to come in regularly just to see her, that he was friendly but seemed shy. Once, he left a Valentine on her desk rather than give it to her in person. She played piano then and still plays "Somebody Stole My Gal," which was popular that year, the way he showed her.[17]

The Chicago-based Benson Orchestra played two dates in Davenport in April 1923, and Beiderbecke got to meet briefly a young saxophonist who would later play an important role in his life: Frank Trumbauer. That summer he found work on a riverboat, and for most of August he played in the same band as a fourteen-year-old clarinetist from Chicago—who also couldn't read music too well—by the name of Benny Goodman. By now Beiderbecke's playing was getting stronger; he was being recognized locally as a hot cornetist. In October he finally got his union card, which enabled him to find jobs more easily. But he was not always appreciated. His forward-thinking ideas often sounded "wrong" to other musicians, who'd tell him to stick to the melody.

What Beiderbecke really needed was a steady job in a band of young jazz players, where he would have the freedom to express himself and to develop. He found exactly what he needed in Chicago in November 1923: an octet that, one month later, adopted the name the Wolverine Orchestra.

When the Wolverines entered the Gennett studio in Richmond, Indiana, on February 18, 1924, to cut their first sides, only one of the eight musicians—banjo player Bob Gillette, who had recorded a few sides with the New Orleans Rhythm Kings the previous July—had ever made a jazz record. More significantly, six of the eight would *never again* make a jazz record after leaving the Wolverines. Bassist Min Leibrook eventually wound up, along with Beiderbecke, in Paul Whiteman's orchestra, but none of the others achieved a fraction of the success in jazz that Beiderbecke did. The Wolverines were hardly jazz heavyweights, and the critical listener can spot shortcomings in the playing of the individual members of the band. But oftentimes in music, the whole can be greater that the sum of the parts. And collectively, the Wolverines came up with a sure rhythmic thrust that set them apart from most groups of the day. Their vigorous, emphasized rhythm won them a strong regional following.

The Wolverines started their recording career with numbers such as "Fidgety Feet," "Lazy Daddy," "Sensation Rag," and "Jazz Me Blues"—all of which had been introduced three to six years earlier by the ODJB. The new recordings were not mere imitations, however. The Wolverines produced a smoother sound, one that seemed to gain in momentum over the course of a performance. With the ODJB, you heard players going off in all different directions; with the Wolverines, the energy seemed more focused.

At the heart of the band was Beiderbecke. (Just how important his contributions were became apparent after he left: the band never again sounded anywhere near as good, and its importance rapidly diminished.) He stayed in the Wolverines for almost a year, during which the band recorded fourteen sides deemed acceptable for release. Among those sides were "Tiger Rag," "Royal Garden Blues," "Copenhagen"—which proved so popular that Melrose Music published a stock arrangement based on the Wolverines' version—and an original, "Riverboat Shuffle," written for them by Hoagy Carmichael.

Carmichael had been awed by Beiderbecke's talent from the beginning. He later recalled how moved he had been when he first heard the young cornetist, who took out his horn and played just four notes, but "hit 'em like a mallet hits a chime." The pure richness of sound made Carmichael rise from the piano bench and stagger over and fall onto the davenport. Of the man who would always remain his personal favorite, Carmichael observed: "Bix's breaks were not as wild as Armstrong's but they were hot and he selected each note with musical care. He showed me that jazz could be musical and beautiful as well as hot. He showed me that tempo doesn't mean fast. His music affected me in a different way. Can't tell you how—like licorice, you have to eat some."[18] He also found himself drawn to Beiderbecke as a person, touched by Beiderbecke's unusual gentleness.

Carmichael got the Wolverines plenty of work that May at Indiana University, where he was studying law. And the band's records were beginning to win them admirers nationwide. The Wolverines were the first important jazz group made up of white midwesterners.

Beiderbecke's talent matured noticeably during his tenure with the Wolverines. In his free time, he explored the music of modern "serious" composers. His parents still hoped that he would straighten out, go to college, find the kind of work they deemed worthy of a gentleman, and settle down. But the band was developing a strong following now, and Beiderbecke was beginning to receive acclaim from other players. With each passing month, he was getting more caught up in the life of a jazz musician, making it increasingly difficult for him to fit into the conventional world of his parents. Playing cornet nightly was certainly more appealing than going to an office somewhere from nine to five. The very freedom of the life he led was seductive.

Bootleg gin was part and parcel of the jazz world. Marijuana was around, too. Some of Beiderbecke's friends smoked regularly. He may have done no more than experiment with it, though; liquor was clearly his preferred vice. And sexual mores were more relaxed among jazz musicians than in the world at large. The rules were different here than in Davenport. Beiderbecke's parents would have expected him to be looking forward to marrying and raising a family, presumably near them. But in his world, he was more likely to meet women—who found jazzmen glamorous, exciting, perhaps vaguely dangerous—amenable to spending nights with men without any strings attached. Bix reportedly did spend some nights that summer with one woman who followed the band around. He also noted there were women who thrust themselves at the Wolverines' handsome leader, pianist Dick Voynow—who'd tell them bluntly that he wasn't interested in women. Voynow, as the band members knew, was homosexual, and comfortably so. Beiderbecke was now in a far more live-and-let-live world than the straitlaced, bourgeois one in which he had been raised.

During the summer of 1924, the band was taken over, temporarily, by drummer Vic Berton, who had played in everything from Sousa's band to jazz groups and would later gain prominence for his work with Red Nichols. Berton, twenty-eight at the time, had a bigger name and more contacts than any member of the Wolverines. He could get the band jobs that it wouldn't be able to get otherwise.

Beiderbecke came to know Berton's brother Gene, aged twenty, a renowned concert artist/singer of modern Russian and French songs, and his kid brother Ralph, aged thirteen, who grew up to become a jazz writer (his book *Remembering Bix,* published in 1974, will be of interest to all Beiderbecke fans). A frequent visitor at the family's Chicago home, Beiderbecke was intrigued by Gene Berton's commitment to serious music. Here was a man who had no interest at all in jazz, who had toured Europe and had personally met masters of modern music that Beiderbecke revered.

Gene Berton was homosexual. He introduced Beiderbecke to his friends, who were homosexual, and once took him, along with precocious younger brother Ralph, to a party at which many of the guests were in drag. Beiderbecke reportedly witnessed it all with a kind of I-never-saw-anything-like-this-back-in-Davenport attitude. One thing led to another, and Berton and Beiderbecke would up having a homosexual fling. Berton later acknowledged that Beiderbecke was basically heterosexual but seemed amenable to trying new things (unless he could think of a pretty compelling reason not to). He doubted that women or sex were all that important to Beiderbecke, however; music clearly came first.

Berton believed that Beiderbecke's overall attitude was expressed by a phrase he so frequently tossed out: What the hell? He also observed that Beiderbecke seemed to look up to him because of his high-level involvement in the world of serious music. Berton was doing with his life what Beiderbecke thought he should have been doing with his own. Despite all of his success playing jazz, Beiderbecke still felt, according to Berton, that playing serious music was a higher calling.[19]

Neither the Wolverines nor Beiderbecke were household words, but their style was certainly being noticed by other musicians. In New York, bandleader George Olsen's pianist/arranger, Eddie Kilfeather, was so impressed with the cornet solo on the Wolverines' recording of "Jazz Me Blues" that he transcribed it and wrote it into an arrangement of "You'll Never Get to Heaven with Those Eyes" (which Olsen's band recorded, with Red Nichols on trumpet, on June 26, 1924). When Kilfeather told Nichols that the solo had first been played by the Wolverines young cornetist, Nichols knew he wanted to meet Beiderbecke—which he did in July, when he crossed paths with the Wolverines in Indiana. Nichols was happy to sit in with the band, and he and Beiderbecke became friends.

Years later Wolverines tenor saxist George Johnson commented that Nichols clearly fell "under the influence of Bix's genius."

> Red probably will not like this statement, but it is my personal opinion that much of Red's playing today is the direct result of the absorption of ideas gained from listening and playing next to Bix, together with the learning, note for note, of Bix's recordings. Even before we landed in New York, we had heard a recording of Red's called "You'll Never Get to Heaven with Those Eyes," in which he used Bix's chorus in "Jazz Me Blues" note for note.
>
> Bix was a fountain of ideas that were spontaneous, as unexpected to himself as they were to us, while Red's playing has ever been methodical and carefully thought out, with each note planned ahead. Each was an artist, but Bix had the natural flow of ideas which, once played, were discarded and never used again. There were too many yet unplayed to bother with repeating.[20]

Nichols was ever sensitive to charges that he had borrowed too heavily from Beiderbecke's style. At one point, he commented: "Bix made a tremendous impression on me, and I'd be the last one to deny that his playing influenced mine. But I did not consciously imitate him. I had already evolved the 'style' identified with me in later years, and the same was true of Bix. We both derived inspiration from many of the same sources. Only a person who is musically ignorant finds any marked similarity between my work and that of Bix."[21] Nichols liked to recall after-hours sessions when the two men were working in New York, during which they would exchange ideas on playing and alternate fingerings. They were contemporaries who learned from each other, he suggested.

Pianist Jess Stacy, who was playing piano and calliope on Mississippi riverboats, also met Beiderbecke for the first time during the summer of 1924. He was struck by the originality of Beiderbecke's playing—on piano as well as cornet, even if his piano playing was of only secondary importance. Stacy found Beiderbecke to be a shy fellow, unaware of how great he was. He also noted that Beiderbecke took much longer solos in jam sessions than he ever did on records.

Like Stacy, clarinetist Mezz Mezzrow met Beiderbecke in 1924 and was impressed by his style of playing. Mezzrow wrote in his autobiography, *Really the Blues,* that he considered Beiderbecke's "more a polished riverboat style than anything else. That style was second nature to Bix because he'd grown up in Davenport, Iowa, and always hung around the waterfront."

> I have never heard a tone like he got before or since. He played mostly open horn, every note full, big, rich and round, standing out like a pearl . . . with a powerful drive that few white musicians had in those days. Bix was too young for the soulful tone, full of oppression and misery, that the great Negro trumpeters get—too young and, maybe, too disciplined. His attack was more on the militaristic side, powerful and energetic, every note packing a solid punch, with his head always in full control of his heart.[22]

At summer's end, the Wolverines left for New York, opening on September 12, 1924, at the Cinderella Ballroom at Forty-eighth Street and Broadway. They impressed musicians (even Paul Whiteman came to the band's opening night) and critics (*Variety*'s Abel Green wrote that, "as a torrid unit, [the Wolverines] need doff the mythical chapeau to no one"[23]), but their uncompromising jazz failed to click with the general public. The average New Yorker seemed more receptive to conventional dance bands, which mostly played the melody as written and only sparingly let a soloist take a hot half-chorus.

Beiderbecke accepted an offer from orchestra leader Jean Goldkette and left the Wolverines on October 12. He was replaced by Jimmy McPartland, who still speaks enthusiastically of the time he was invited to join the band. He knew all of the Wolverines' records, and when he got to New York, Beiderbecke took the time to teach him routines on numbers the band had not recorded. He even picked out a cornet for McPartland to use. McPartland savors the memory of Beiderbecke telling him: "I like ya, kid. Ya sound like me, but you don't copy me." To McPartland, Beiderbecke was important because of the polish he brought to jazz. He was, in simple terms, "the master."[24]

Before Beiderbecke left town, he participated in his first free-lance recording date with a sextet bearing the contrived name of the Sioux City Six, led by C-melody sax player Frank Trumbauer. The two sides cut that day were not memorable. "Flock of Blues" mainly proves Beiderbecke was out of his idiom when he tried to play blues the way black players did. However, the session marked the beginning of one of the decade's most important musical partnerships: Beiderbecke and Trumbauer.

Beiderbecke was in Detroit on October 15 to play at the Graystone

Ballroom, Jean Goldkette's base. Goldkette was not a jazzman. He was an astute businessman who often ran several different orchestras, fronted by others, at the same time. If he didn't really have a feel for popular music or jazz—he was personally more comfortable with classical music—he did have an understanding of what the public liked. He noted the success of the Wolverines' records, recognized the importance of Beiderbecke's contributions, and figured Beiderbecke could prove to be an asset to his own orchestra.

Unable to read music well enough to cut the charts that the Goldkette orchestra played, Beiderbecke simply wasn't a viable section player. He was great when it came time to improvise a solo, and jazzmen in the band, such as Tommy Dorsey and Don Murray, were all for his presence. But the orchestra played a lot of music, including some semisymphonic things, that just didn't require the services of a jazz improviser. A sample radio program from this period included: "By the Waters of Minnetonka," "Romance," "After You've Gone," "Fox Trot Classique," "No, No Nanette," "Poplar Street Blues," and "Mandy Make Up Your Mind."

Goldkette's book was written for two trumpets, so he had to keep two trumpeters on the payroll to handle the section work. Beiderbecke thus was a costly proposition for the relatively little use Goldkette made of him as a soloist. In addition, A&R man Eddie King, who didn't like jazz, initially had control over the band's Victor recordings, and he preferred letting people hear the melody "properly," rather than as reconfigured by a player like Beiderbecke.

After less than two months in the Goldkette band, Beiderbecke was fired. He didn't get to play on any of the Goldkette records made and released during his tenure in the band, though he did take part in the recording of two numbers that were only released decades after his passing. He soloed, not too impressively, on a take of "I Didn't Know," but King, who failed to appreciate his hot jazz style, insisted after the second take that he was making too many mistakes. On the three subsequent takes, trumpeter Fred Farrar played the melody straight while Beiderbecke sat out. ("I Didn't Know" was not released until 1960, when the second take was used on an LP.) A brief, third trumpet part was created for Beiderbecke so that he could participate in the recording of "Adoration," arranged by George Crozier. Although test pressings were made, "Adoration" was not released commercially until Sunbeam Records included it in a boxed set of Beiderbecke's complete works.

Obviously, Beiderbecke really wasn't ready for the Goldkette band in 1924. He knew he would have to develop his reading skills if he ever wanted to work in a big-time outfit again.

Back in Davenport by December 20, living at his parents' home and seeking whatever gigs he could find, Beiderbecke played briefly with a local band, Merton "Bromo" Sulser's Iowa Collegians. He also organized a Gennett record date under his own name, using some friends from the Goldkette band, including Tommy Dorsey and Don Murray. (Dorsey even provided the name for an original Beiderbecke created: "The Davenport Blues.") The players drank heavily during the session, so much so that the last two sides recorded were unusable. Drinking was very much a part of the scene; at the time, it seemed like harmless good fun.

On February 2, 1925, Beiderbecke enrolled at the University of Iowa. His parents sent him money from home, no doubt delighted that he was getting back on the "proper" track. Because he had never graduated from high school, he was told to take courses as an "unclassified" student, until his work was deemed to be up to freshman level. Enrolled heavily in music courses, he lasted exactly eighteen days. Whether he withdrew voluntarily or was asked to leave is uncertain. He may have been expelled after getting into a drunken brawl at a café.

The idea of Beiderbecke going to college was probably doomed from the start. He was nearly twenty-two, older than most of the seniors and much too old to be sitting contentedly in classes with gangly freshmen. He had *lived* more than the other students on campus had. The courses in religion, physical education, and military training that the college wanted him to take all seemed irrelevant, a waste of time.

Beiderbecke headed to New York City in March and moved in with Red Nichols for a week at the Pasadena Hotel, on Sixtieth and Broadway. Nichols was enjoying great success in the California Ramblers, a ten-piece band whose members then included Adrian Rollini and Tommy and Jimmy Dorsey. The Ramblers were immensely popular with the collegiate set, and Beiderbecke was happy to sit in with them. Nichols always insisted that, during this time period, he and Beiderbecke recorded together, but he could not recall on which records. The mystery has never been solved.

Next, Beiderbecke headed to Chicago, where he worked for three and a half months at the Rendezvous Cafe for a bandleader named Charlie Straight. Not all Chicago musicians were impressed by Beiderbecke. He wasn't the greatest technician, and he couldn't read music.

Harmonically, his thinking was ahead of his time, but some of his contemporaries only perceived that he sometimes went for effects that seemed "strange." He was drinking a lot after hours—to the point that, when under the influence of liquor, he would go from a generous, sweet-natured guy to an insulting one—but felt he was still in control.

That summer of 1925, Beiderbecke worked for a month in one of Goldkette's bands, billed as the Breeze Blowers. The group, including such notables as Don Murray, Jimmy Dorsey, Bill Rank, and Steve Brown, played at a Michigan resort area, Island Lake. Frank Trumbauer came into the band when Dorsey left, but he didn't stay long. He had aspirations of leading his own band, and when an opportunity arose, he took it—and took Beiderbecke with him.

Beiderbecke worked in Trumbauer's band (nine musicians plus a singer) at the Arcadia Ballroom in St. Louis for eight months—from September 8, 1925, until the ballroom closed for the summer on May 3, 1926. It was one of the few times in his career that he stayed in one spot for such an extended stretch.

Because he was not much of a reader, Beiderbecke initially had to learn the melodies by heart. Before starting a number, he would turn to another musician to ask what his first tone should be; then, once the band started playing, he could take it from there. By the end of the season, he had learned how to read fairly well and was no longer asking others what note to come in on. He was also getting regular parts to play.

Working together night after night gave Beiderbecke and Trumbauer a chance to develop a tight musical rapport. They'd revel in chase choruses—trading phrases, one after another, seemingly answering each other on their instruments. They, and the band as a whole, worked out routines on certain numbers, giving them a foundation they could build upon in subsequent years. The two were the drawing cards of the band and Beiderbecke's salary was second only to Trumbauer's. Both were gaining fine reputations among fellow musicians, Trumbauer having already won respect for his work with Ray Miller's orchestra and the Benson orchestra. Beiderbecke, meanwhile, awed other players with his uncannily accurate ear. (If someone struck any notes simultaneously on the keyboard, he could call out exactly which notes had been struck.)

A then-unknown Pee Wee Russell worked with Beiderbecke in this and other bands. He later noted: "The thing about Bix's music is that he drove a band. He more or less made you play whether you wanted to or not. If you had any talent at all, he made you play better.

It had to do for one thing with the way he played a lead. It had to do with his whole feeling for ensemble playing. He got a very large tone with a cornet. Records never quite reproduced his sound. Some come fairly close, but the majority don't."[25]

After hours there was time for getting high on moonshine and listening to music by modern composers such as Stravinsky and Ravel. (Beiderbecke didn't care for such old masters as Mozart and Brahms.) And he could always find a band someplace to listen to or sit in with. He went to concerts by the St. Louis Symphony and even tried to take lessons from Joe Gustat, first trumpet in the symphony. Fortunately, for posterity, Gustat turned him down. Had Beiderbecke learned to play like a symphony musician, he would have sacrificed his individuality. His idiosyncratic fingerings (which were responsible for the percussive quality in some of his passages that imitators can never quite seem to duplicate), his use of vibrato, his phrasing—all of these were wrong by symphonic standards. Gustat believed Beiderbecke was better off following his own path than trying to become a more conventional player.

During the season in St. Louis, Beiderbecke entered into a sexual relationship with a young woman, Ruth Schaffner, who lived down the street from the Arcadia Ballroom, in an apartment with her two sisters. Schaffner must have believed that the affair would culminate in marriage—no self-respecting nineteen-year-old midwesterner in 1925 would have thought otherwise. In later years, she suggested to interviewers that her involvement with Beiderbecke had been the most important part of her life, that he had always been thoughtful and considerate—no doubt a romanticized, idealized recollection. She also recalled that their regular correspondence stopped within a few months after he left St. Louis and that, although they got together on subsequent occasions, he did not necessarily bother to let her know in advance when or if he would be in town. By Beiderbecke's final year, 1931, she had lost contact with him entirely.[26]

Beiderbecke no doubt was attracted to Schaffner and did care for her in his fashion, but she was not his top priority. While Schaffner may have remembered him speaking of marriage, it is revealing that others who knew him did not seem to recall him talking about her, or saying he expected to marry her, or even admitting he had a fiancée someplace. Some did recall Beiderbecke saying at a later date that he had not found the right girl yet. Others say he showed comparatively little interest in women in general. Eddie Condon thought Beiderbecke was simply "obsessed" with jazz music. "With the aid of prohibition and its artifacts," Condon wrote, "he drove away all other things—food, sleep, women, ambition, vanity, desire. He played the piano and the cornet, that was all."[27]

On May 13, 1926, Beiderbecke and Trumbauer returned to work for Jean Goldkette, who split his large main orchestra into two units for the summer, hiring extra players to bring both up to full strength. He made Trumbauer the leader of the unit booked into the Blue Lantern Casino in Hudson Lake, Indiana, ninety miles east of Chicago. Besides Beiderbecke, the unit included Pee Wee Russell, Sonny Lee (trombone), Fuzzy Farrar (trumpet), Doc Ryker (alto sax), and Irving "Itzy" Riskin (piano). Key Goldkette players Don Murray (clarinet), Ray Lodwig (trumpet), Bill Rank (trombone), and Steve Brown (bass) were in the unit that played at Island Lake.

Goldkette's Island Lake band played traditional fare, just as the public would have heard at the Graystone Ballroom in Detroit. But the Hudson Lake band bore the mark of Trumbauer's leadership and of Beiderbecke's ideas of what sounded modern. Goldkette rarely went out to Hudson Lake to see for himself how the band was doing; he stayed in Detroit and oversaw the booking and promotion of his various bands. The Hudson Lake unit was thus hotter and more forward-looking than Goldkette's past outfits had been. One newspaper account of a performance by the band noted that Beiderbecke added variety by playing Eastwood Lane's "The Legend of Lonesome Lake" on the piano.

Beiderbecke was one of six musicians in a shared cottage that summer. In later years, the others would recall his dreamy temperament and his lack of concern for mundane matters such as eating, sleeping, or bathing. He was apt to leave open sardine cans around the place; when he put off bathing too long for his colleagues' liking, they took him out to the lake and threw him in. Pianist Itzy Riskin remembered playing Beiderbecke to sleep with Stravinsky, Debussy, McDowell, and Eastwood Lane—Beiderbecke moaning with pleasure in his bed as Riskin came to intriguing harmonies.[28]

Tenor saxist Bud Freeman and some of the Austin High Gang, who were working in Chicago, drove out to Hudson Lake one night after their own gig had ended. Arriving at four in the morning, they knocked on Beiderbecke's cabin door but received no answer. So they barged right in. They were able to wake up Pee Wee Russell, who invited them to have some bootleg hooch (which was absolutely black in color, according to Freeman). After a few drinks, the musicians went into a loud and lively jam session in the cabin. Beiderbecke, who was out cold, slept through the whole thing.

Freeman came to be awed by Beiderbecke's playing. He already idolized Louis Armstrong and King Oliver. In fact, he felt there was no greater trumpeter than Armstrong, who had such a great beat and such a great sound. Yet for Freeman, in some way, "Bix was the perfect player of our time."[29]

Business was poor for the Goldkette band at Hudson Lake that summer. The locals preferred the more conventional music of a South Bend dance band that split evenings with the Goldkette unit. (The latter appealed to musicians, as so often happens to a band ahead of its time. Chicago jazzmen Benny Goodman, Mezz Mezzrow, Davey Tough, and Jimmy McPartland, among others, often came up on weekends to sit in and crash with their Goldkette friends.)

At summer's end, Goldkette reorganized his main orchestra, utilizing the best players from both units. He put Trumbauer in charge of this reconstituted band, which meant that now the main Goldkette band was to sound more like the bands Trumbauer had led at the Arcadia Ballroom and at Hudson Lake. When that reconstituted band came together, it was probably the greatest white jazz-inflected orchestra in the nation. It could offer dance numbers with finesse, and its hot jazz specialties were a romp, thanks to Beiderbecke and Trumbauer. Steve Brown was also featured, slapping the bass on up-tempo numbers. Goldkette drummer Chauncey Morehouse said that Beiderbecke "was the jazz outlet for the whole band."[30] His fellow band members were inspired by him; they admired his creative gifts, which they realized were beyond their own.

Hot music was but one offering of a band like Goldkette's, which in the course of a night might play waltz medleys, musical comedy medleys, and semisymphonic arrangements. Goldkette occasionally would play something serious at the piano, with his orchestra accompanying him. Like Paul Whiteman, he aspired to lead an all-purpose orchestra. In 1926 the average American would have named Whiteman's as the nation's pre-eminent band; certainly he was paying his musicians far more than Goldkette did. However, Goldkette topped Whiteman when it came to jazz soloists.

Virtually no one had heard this new Goldkette orchestra; it had not yet cut any records. But on a September New England tour, the band dazzled listeners night after night. And with the hiring of Bill Challis as a full-time arranger, all of the pieces came together. Challis's work was downright inspired. His music was graceful, ahead of its time, and he knew how to showcase Beiderbecke and Trumbauer to best advantage. They played Challis's charts with panache.

The band was scheduled to open in New York City at the Roseland

Ballroom, opposite Fletcher Henderson, on October 6, 1926. Henderson's musicians had played at the Graystone Ballroom, where they heard how great the Goldkette band supposedly was, but it was easy to dismiss the claims as loyalty to a local favorite. Past recordings by Goldkette's orchestra, which predated the arrival of Beiderbecke, Trumbauer, and Challis, gave them nothing to worry about. The Henderson band was known to be tops in New York—the best jazz soloists and the best charts. It featured Rex Stewart, who had recently succeeded Louis Armstrong, on cornet, Joe Smith on trumpet, Buster Bailey on clarinet, and the master, Coleman Hawkins, on tenor sax. The arrangers included Don Redman and Henderson himself.

The night of October 6 was a big one, by any definition. Fats Waller sat in with Henderson's band on a few numbers. Bandleader Roger Wolfe Kahn guest-conducted the Goldkette band on a few numbers, and Kahn's star trombonist, Miff Mole, also took some solos. Songwriter Benny Davis sang a few songs. But by night's end, there was no doubt: the Goldkette band had triumphed. It had torn up the place in a battle of the bands. "Most everyone who is anything at all in the music business was present," noted *Orchestra World,* which added: "Whoever is responsible for the Goldkette arrangements should be elected to the hall of fame. They are nothing short of marvelous."[31]

Henderson's star trumpeter, Rex Stewart, wrote many years later in his book *Jazz Masters of the Thirties:*

> We were supposed to be the world's greatest dance orchestra. And up pops this Johnny-come-lately white band from out in the sticks, cutting us. . . . We simply could not compete. . . . Their arrangements were too imaginative and their rhythm too strong. . . . We learned that Jean Goldkette's orchestra was, without any question, the greatest in the world. . . .
>
> You can believe me that the Goldkette band was the original predecessor to any large white dance orchestra that followed, up to Benny Goodman. Even Goodman, swinger that he was, did not come close to the tremendous sound of Goldkette or the inventive arrangements of the Goldkette repertoire, not in quality and certainly not in quantity. . . . [32]

Billboard predicted that the Goldkette band, which was about to record, would produce some scorchingly hot records. But it didn't happen. Although the band might have scored in the dance hall with Challis's spirited arrangements of "Tiger Rag," "The Blue Room," "Baby Face," and so on, those were not the numbers Victor had them record. The record company played things safe and conservative. Eddie King, it turned out, had apparently already decided which tunes *he* wanted the Goldkette orchestra to record. He wasn't interested in what hot numbers had wowed New York City musicians. He was weighing commercial possibilities, based upon his experience in the business.

The first two record dates thus included such trivialities as "Hush-A-Bye" (with Frank Bessinger on vocal), "Cover Me Up with Sunshine" (Bessinger), and "Just One More Kiss" (Al Lynch on vocal). "Sunday" was the only tune with a flavor of hot jazz. Even though it was largely given over to a vocal by the Keller Sisters and Lynch, the zesty brass chorus that followed their vocal caught the attention of those with good ears.

Sixty years later, Challis makes plain the frustration he and the players in the band felt when they realized Victor was not going to capture the greatness of that orchestra:

> Geez, I think they picked out the *stinking-est* tunes for us. We didn't really get any good tunes to do. The best one, I think, was "Sunday." And that, you know, that hit a little bit.
>
> Eddie King picked out the tunes for us. We got a couple of waltzes. And then they gave us singers—we didn't have any singers. So we had guys like Billy Murray. They just brought them in for the record dates. For instance, Don Murray made an exceptional arrangement on "Sunny Disposish." And then to do the vocal, they got a hold of the Revellers, who were very big at that time. But they weren't for our band. We had an exceptionally good dance band. And it was far ahead of its time.[33]

According to Challis, King and the other powers at Victor didn't seem to appreciate Beiderbecke. "They could take Henry Busse and his 'Hot Lips'—that sort of thing—but they never took any of the style of Beiderbecke. They didn't want any improvising. They were trying to make a hit, and in doing that, they made us play the melody. . . . Bix used to steal in on the last eight bars of some of the tunes—even though they were real corny tunes—Bix would stand and improvise right over the band. And some of it sounded pretty good."

For the recording of "Sunday," Challis sneaked Beiderbecke in by having the other trumpeters play along with what would have been Beiderbecke's solo. "If we wanted to get the flavor of Bix on the record," Challis notes, "the only way we could do it would be, he would dictate his chorus, and then I'd harmonize it with the two other trumpets. On 'Sunday,' Bix played the lead, and the other two guys played under him, and it was fairly jazzy. It wasn't the melody anyway. We got away with that. And it was very well liked. The Keller Sisters and Lynch—they weren't with the band, they weren't for us. But the jazz part with the trumpets was. That's what we were trying to get across."

King wouldn't have been in his job if he had not had a pretty good feel for what was and was not commercial. Some jazz buffs may disparage "Idolizing," but it sold 123,770 copies; "Sunday" sold 137,856; and "I'm Looking Over a Four Leaf Clover" (with Billy Murray's stolid vocal) sold 109,810. By contrast, the superb "Clementine"—prized by many collectors—sold only 45,629 copies; "My Pretty Girl" sold 38,869. Musical quality obviously did not necessarily mean big sales.[34]

While King may not have cared for Beiderbecke, he was not dead set against all jazz. He brought in Joe Venuti and Eddie Lang—who were not regular members of the Goldkette band—for recording sessions, and he gave them space to play. He acknowledged that they had made names for themselves and would help sell records.

Some of the tunes aren't as bad as Challis's recollections might suggest. "Idolizing," for example, is a charming, poignant piece, and Beiderbecke's work on it compels attention. But such tunes were frustrating for others in the band, since they knew they didn't capture the band at its best. Vocalists like Frank Bessinger and Billy Murray were considered square and old-fashioned by the young, forward-thinking hot musicians of the band. And, as Stewart noted, when Goldkette's band was at its peak, "recording was in its infancy and reproduction at that time did not project anything like the real performances. So, naturally, the Goldkette recordings did not reflect the verve and consummate artistry of the ensemble."[35]

Rex Stewart shared a locker with Beiderbecke during the first Roseland engagement, in October 1926. They also hung out together in a speakeasy in the building and jammed in the band room after hours. He recalled: "Admiring Bix as I did, it was not difficult for me to copy his memorable solo on 'Singing' the Blues'. . . . As a matter of fact, there was a lot of copying going on. It was a mutual admiration society, with Fletcher and Goldkette exchanging arrangements. . . ."[36]

The band stayed at Roseland for only twelve days on this trip, then returned to the Graystone Ballroom in Detroit. But it had had a tremendous impact on the New York music scene. Throughout the engagement, musicians had come out to Roseland and been wowed by the Goldkette trumpet section. The band permanently changed the sound of all big bands, as bandleaders switched over from two trumpets to three in emulation of Goldkette—though they didn't understand that the change had not resulted from a deliberate stylistic decision. It had arisen because Beiderbecke was not considered reliable enough as a reader for him to serve as a regular member of the section. The book was primarily written for two trumpets, and Fuzzy Farrar and Ray Lodwig—both superb readers—handled those parts. Beiderbecke sometimes improvised a third part and took the hot jazz choruses. The tremendous drive that Steve Brown got on bass likewise motivated some bandleaders to switch from using a tuba to using a string bass.

Cornetist Wild Bill Davison, who worked mostly in Chicago in the late 1920s, played for about a month in a band led by Joe Hooven in Detroit. He frequently got over to hear Beiderbecke at the Graystone. Surprisingly often, he recalled, Beiderbecke would sit in with the much less important band that Davison was playing in. "I always thought that the reason Bix and Trumbauer used to come over and sit in with our band was that he didn't get enough playing in that big band—he didn't get to play enough jazz in that band; although they had jazz arrangements, and good arrangements, I don't think he and Trumbauer got enough playing it. They used to come over and play in our band because we went to six in the morning."[37]

In January 1927, the Goldkette band returned to New York, to play once again opposite Henderson's at Roseland and to record. The recording sessions between January 23 and February 3 were not supervised by Eddie King, so the band had a chance to record sides that more accurately represented what it liked to play, including "My Pretty Girl" and "I'm Gonna Meet My Sweetie Now," which satisfied musicians *and* sold a respectable 179,929 copies. It also recorded "Stampede," a hot Henderson specialty, which Victor never released.

This star-studded orchestra was a prestige item for Jean Goldkette, but it was costly to maintain. One-nighters brought in better money than could be made at the Graystone Ballroom, but lining up reasonable tours was not always easy. When the band was not at the Graystone, Goldkette discovered, he could put in less-expensive bands and the dancers would turn out just the same. Among his other bands were the Orange Blossoms, which later become known as the Casa Loma Orchestra, and McKinney's Cotton Pickers. Goldkette took profits from the ballroom and used them to subsidize his main orchestra, though such an arrangement could not continue indefinitely.

The main band, which became popular with the collegiate set, headed out on the road, up and down the East Coast and as far west as St. Louis. Many musicians changed their style of play upon hearing Beiderbecke and Trumbauer and those gorgeous Challis charts. They discovered that hot jazz could be sensitive; it could be pretty. A young Artie Shaw, whose clarinet work was to become a model of grace, was among those affected. When I asked him in 1985 who his earliest influences were, he replied: "I think probably Trumbauer and Bix, first." He knew them initially from records, he told me. "Then when they came nearby, when I was living in New Haven, I made a pilgrimage to Bridgeport—and in those days, Bridgeport was a long way away. The Goldkette band was playing there, at the Ritz Ballroom, and I stood in front of that band open-mouthed."[38]

The musicians who heard the band realized that Beiderbecke and Trumbauer were doing a lot more than was being captured on the band's Victor records. Singer Red McKenzie was so knocked out that he persuaded Tommy Rockwell of OKeh Records to record the two. Those sides, with anywhere from eight to thirteen musicians on a given date, were released under the billing Frankie Trumbauer and His Orchestra (Trumbauer used virtually all-Goldkette personnel at first). For nearly a decade, there would be a continuous flow of records by Frankie Trumbauer and His Orchestra, although the important ones were all produced during the Beiderbecke years, 1927–29.

It is fortunate, for posterity, that OKeh decided to make the Trumbauer orchestra records, even though they didn't sell very well, for they capture some of Beiderbecke at his best. (If we knew him only from the Goldkette orchestra records in this period, we would probably wonder why his contemporaries had praised him so highly.) In 1927 Victor was wasting him on such trivial records as "Look at the World and Smile" and "Proud of a Baby Like You." But OKeh let Trumbauer and Beiderbecke make the records *they* wanted to make—and the results were sometimes spectacular. "Singin' the Blues," a masterpiece from first note to last, came from their very first session together, on February 4, 1927 (which also produced "Clarinet Marmelade"). "Ostrich Walk" and "Riverboat Shuffle," two great examples of Beiderbecke's hotter side, were recorded at their second session, on May 9, 1927. Four days later, they cut "Way Down Yonder in New Orleans" and the haunting, unforgettable "I'm Comin' Virginia." An incredible outpouring of talent in a very brief period.

The brilliance of "Singin' the Blues" was recognized immediately—one of those rare creations so perfect that, from then on, other musicians playing the number invariably have stayed as close as possible to the Trumbauer-Beiderbecke recording.[39] Initially, saxists copied Trumbauer's solo just as faithfully as trumpeters copied Beiderbecke's, but only Beiderbecke's has stood the test of time. Plenty of bands put "Singin' the Blues" in their books. Fletcher Henderson had Bill Challis write an arrangement based on the Trumbauer-Beiderbecke recording, which his orchestra recorded in 1931 with Rex Stewart on trumpet.

Jazz buffs may argue over which recording was Beiderbecke's greatest—"Singin' the Blues" is usually cited as the favorite, although I'm most affected by "I'm Comin' Virginia"—but all would agree that 1927 marked a period of peak creativity and productivity for Beiderbecke, and that his recordings with Trumbauer captured him in unsurpassed form. Those OKeh recordings are usually freer, jazzier in feeling than the Goldkette Victors, and they gave Beiderbecke chances to play longer solos. The Goldkette band was more of an ensemble orchestra than was Trumbauer's recording band.

The series was not without its duds, of course. Trumbauer's records gradually seemed to grow more commercially oriented, and the talented saxist suffered the delusion that he could sing, which marred some of the sides. He didn't have much of a voice, and his attempts at essaying black dialect (as on "Take Your Tomorrow" or "Bless You Sister") didn't help matters. It was not unusual in those days for white performers to do stereotypical blacks in a bid for humor, but such routines sound offensive today.

Still, the best moments from the Trumbauer OKehs make us gladly overlook the shortcomings. Beiderbecke and Trumbauer could often make much even of shoddy material. No one would ever suggest, for example, that "Borneo" represents great songwriting. But the two used it as a good vehicle for a chase chorus of the sort they had been doing together since their Arcadia days. "Borneo," incidentally, sold but 3,000 copies; by comparison, some of Red Nichols's jazz sides in this period sold in the hundreds of thousands.

By 1927 Beiderbecke's talents were coming into full flower. There were players who tried to copy his phrasing, his sound, whatever they could get from him. But nobody equaled him at what he was doing. "There was an ethereal beauty of Bix's tone, with its heart-melting blend of pure joyousness and wistful haunting sadness," marveled trumpeter Max Kaminsky in his autobiography, *My Life in Jazz.* Like other musicians who came of age in the 1920s, Kaminsky stood in awe of Beiderbecke's playing. "There was his sense of form, his hotness, his shining fresh ideas, his lyricism, his swing, his perfect intonation, and his impeccable matchless taste. His intervals were so orderly, so indescribably right, like a line of poetry."[40]

In this same period, Louis Armstrong was also approaching full realization of his powers. In 1927 he recorded such impressive sides as "Wild Man Blues," "Potato Head Blues," "Gully Low Blues," and "Struttin' with Some Barbecue." He was flexing his muscles, moving toward the perfection of "West End Blues," which he would record in June 1928. Like some unstoppable natural force, his was a searing, passionate, extroverted kind of playing, always on, always up. He had set aside the cornet for the sharper, more aggressive sound of the trumpet, and he was interested in exploring the virtuoso possibilities of that horn.

Beiderbecke, by contrast, preferred the mellower sound of the cornet, whose timbre more closely approximated the human voice. He worked within a limited range, uninterested in showing how high he could play or how long he could hold a note. He was making the cornet *sing*. His sound was clear and ringing. He wasn't out to produce growls or slurs, to sound "dirty" or low-down. His playing was more generally circumspect, more restrained, in keeping with his middle-class background. He was more concerned with form and elegance. And there was, at times, a certain tenseness in his work, an intimation of his own fragility. There are times when Beiderbecke's playing will get hot, and it feels as if he is breaking free of restraints, as if some passion is suddenly bursting to the surface. Armstrong, by contrast, is apt to sound unrestrained from beginning to end; with him you don't sense that struggle to get free from inhibitions.

Armstrong and Beiderbecke were developing along different paths. And Kaminsky, who wholeheartedly appreciated both, was among those who felt they were "the two great originators of jazz."[41] Some jazz writers have implied a parity between Beiderbecke and Armstrong by referring to Beiderbecke as the greatest white trumpeter of his day and to Armstrong as the greatest black trumpeter. Beiderbecke *was* the greatest white trumpeter of his day. Armstrong was, quite simply, the greatest trumpeter.

Jean Goldkette was not interested in running a great *jazz* orchestra per se. Rather, he wanted an outstanding all-around orchestra, one that could satisfy jazz buffs with a lively "Ostrich Walk" (Bill Challis adapted the arrangement he had written for Trumbauer's OKeh recording session so that the whole Goldkette band could play it) and then just as effectively present "Rhapsody in Blue" or a waltz medley.

Perhaps Trumbauer was too jazz-oriented for Goldkette's liking. Or maybe he was getting so prominent that some listeners were starting to think of the band he conducted as *his* band, not Goldkette's. For whatever reason, Goldkette chose to assign violinist/arranger Eddie Sheasby to split conducting duties with Trumbauer. Soon afterward he appointed Sheasby the sole conductor of the orchestra, relegating Trumbauer to the sax section. This had unforeseeable, dire consequences when Sheasby—who was a temperamental fellow and a heavy drinker to boot—simply walked off one night in July and took all of the band's arrangements with him. Goldkette didn't see Sheasby again for a half-dozen years or so. He never got back the arrangements.

Meanwhile, Paul Whiteman had lured Bill Challis away from Goldkette. Challis could hardly have turned down the invitation, for Whiteman was considered the most prestigious bandleader in the country. He paid well, and he carried far more musicians than anyone else. Challis would be able to write more complex charts, get greater variety in tone and color. Whiteman made bids for Goldkette's star players as well, aided by Goldkette's difficulty in lining up enough one-nighters to keep his band going. In September 1927, following a successful stand at Roseland and a recording session that yielded one of the band's best recordings, "Clementine," Goldkette disbanded. He would reorganize other bands in the future, but they would never again approach his stellar 1926–27 outfit.

Just before the Goldkette band came to an end, Beiderbecke recorded his timeless "In a Mist," the first recording of the unusual piano improvisations with which he had been enthralling other musicians after hours. The creation showed his interest in Ravel and Debussy as well as jazz. He didn't have the piece down on paper at the time he recorded it—Challis would help him get it down and into fixed form later, although the published version is not exactly the same as the recorded version—he simply played. He was given a signal when there was only fifteen seconds of recording time left so that he could bring the work to a suitable conclusion. Thus, casually, was a classic performance born. As Louis Armstrong commented years later, "You couldn't find a musician nowheres in the whole world that doesn't still love Bix's 'In a Mist.' "[42]

Beiderbecke, Trumbauer, and several other of Goldkette's best hot players eventually wound up in Paul Whiteman's band—though they might not have gone with Whiteman if they could have found steady work in a more jazz-oriented ensemble. Whiteman had tried to hire Beiderbecke and Trumbauer at the same time that he had hired Challis, but they had both turned him down. Beiderbecke's feelings toward the Whiteman orchestra were ambivalent. He recognized that the musicians were the best available in terms of technical proficiency and that the orchestra was an internationally popular attraction. But it wasn't very committed to jazz, and some of its arrangements sounded pompous, pretentious. One of his Davenport friends, Esten Spurrier, recalled that during the time Beiderbecke was with Goldkette, he put down Whiteman's band in no uncertain terms, saying that he'd never join it, no matter what Whiteman might offer.[43]

Beiderbecke and Trumbauer first went with Adrian Rollini, the brilliant jazz bass sax/vibes player who was putting together an all-star eleven-piece group that would be far more jazz-oriented than anything Paul Whiteman had ever led. The personnel consisted of key Goldkette-associated musicians Bill Rank (trombone), Don Murray (reeds), Chauncey Morehouse (drums), Joe Venuti (violin), and Eddie Lang (guitar), plus Sylvester Ahola (trumpet) and Bobby Davis (sax), who had played with Rollini in the California Ramblers, and Frankie Signorelli (piano) of the Original Memphis Five. It was a hot combination, and Beiderbecke probably would have been content to work in such a band indefinitely. But the band stayed together for little more than a month; it couldn't get work.

Rollini opened at the Club New Yorker. Musicians turned out, for the band seemed to be a continuation of the hot side of the Goldkette band and of the Trumbauer recording band, but the general public did not. Perhaps this reveals something about the general public's enthusiasm for hot jazz, even when played by the best. It was common wisdom among musicians in those days that if a band was too jazz-oriented, it couldn't make it big. And that belief prevailed until Benny Goodman's band finally broke through in the mid-1930s.

Trumbauer used Rollini's band as his recording band for OKeh in late September and October, adding Pee Wee Russell for one session. Beiderbecke used six men from the band for sides he cut under his own name (without Trumbauer) for OKeh sessions in October, recording such numbers as "At the Jazz Band Ball," "Royal Garden Blues," "Jazz Me Blues," and "Since My Best Gal Turned Me Down." On the last-named tune, the men played a routine the Goldkette band had played but had never recorded.

Beiderbecke soloed on a couple of sides in this period: "There Ain't No Land Like Dixieland to Me" and "There's a Cradle in Caroline" (September 29, 1927), which include a second horn that some Beiderbecke aficionados, searching for the elusive sides he and Nichols allegedly made together, believe to be Red Nichols (although the standard Rust discography places trumpeter Hymie Farberman, not

Nichols, on the date).[44] Other have speculated that Nichols and Beiderbecke may have both taken part in an October 20, 1927, Sam Lanin session, but there is no conclusive evidence.

Nichols, who was enjoying considerable success, paid tribute to Beiderbecke in 1927 by recording two of the numbers associated with him: "Davenport Blues" (February 11, 1927) and "Riverboat Shuffle" (August 15, 1927). Nichols may not have had Beiderbecke's great gift for improvisation, but he was an excellent all-around musician and a natural leader. Recordings by Nichols-led groups were notably more cohesive than recordings by Trumbauer- or Beiderbecke-led groups; they had admirable structure.

Beiderbecke mostly worked as a sideman throughout his career; he was not a leader type. Nichols, by contrast, was always hustling to get record dates and to get the very best players and arrangers for those dates. At one point, in fact, Trumbauer tried to enter a recording partnership with Nichols. The idea was that Nichols would use Trumbauer on recording dates *he* lined up and that Trumbauer would use Nichols, instead of Beiderbecke, on *his* dates. However, Tommy Rockwell would have none of it, insisting that Trumbauer use Beiderbecke on all of his OKeh recordings.

When the Club New Yorker folded, Rollini's all-star band was unable to get work elsewhere. At that point, Beiderbecke and Trumbauer accepted Whiteman's invitation and joined his band on October 27, 1927. They found, mixed in among his acres of musicians, such ex-Goldkette musicians as Steve Brown and Tommy and Jimmy Dorsey. Bill Challis was writing arrangements, although Ferde Grofe was still considered Whiteman's number one arranger. Maybe, just maybe, they felt, they could sustain the type of playing they had been developing in the Arcadia band, the Goldkette band, and the Rollini band.

The Paul Whiteman Orchestra reached its peak during the two years that Beiderbecke was a member. Most of the best-remembered Whiteman recordings are from this period and include at least brief solos—absolutely essential to the overall success of the pieces—by Beiderbecke, whose work was set off beautifully by the arrangements of Challis.[45] Yet it would be a mistake to assume that Beiderbecke was considered the band's prime attraction by the general public. The numbers that featured his solos were but one portion of a widely varied bill of fare served up by the Whiteman orchestra. Audiences got samplings of light classics—perhaps the "William Tell Overture" or the "1812 Overture" or "Rhapsody in Blue." They got numbers in which the featured trumpeter was Henry Busse, whose work sounds quite dated today. And even on the numbers in which Beiderbecke was used, he was often used only briefly.

Years after his death, when Beiderbecke became famous among jazz buffs, Whiteman would state that Beiderbecke was the finest musician he had known. But Whiteman never paid him a salary that would indicate he really believed that. A January 1928 Whiteman band payroll sheet indicates that Beiderbecke was being paid $200 a week. Meanwhile, trombonist Wilbur Hall—whose novelty specialty consisted of playing "Stars and Stripes Forever" *on a bicycle pump*—was being paid $350 per week. Others making $350 were Bob Mayhew (trumpet), Jack Mayhew (sax), Chester Hazlett (sax), Henry Busse, and the band's manager, J. F. Gillespie. Getting $300 per week were Harry Perrella (piano) and Mike Pingatore (banjo). Among those earning $200 a week were Bill Rank, Jack Fulton (trombone, vocals), Charles Gaylord (violin), Austin "Skin" Young (vocals, banjo), Charlie Strickfaden (sax), Hal McLean (sax), Jimmy Dorsey, and Frank Trumbauer. Earning $175 were such men as Steve Brown, Kurt Dieterle (violin), Mike Trafficante (bass, tuba), Charlie Margolis (trumpet), and arranger Bill Challis. Vocalists Bing Crosby, Harry Barris, and Al Rinker, along with violinist/arranger Matty Malneck, were paid $150.

When Beiderbecke and Trumbauer joined the Whiteman orchestra, it swelled to twenty-seven musicians, plus the three Rhythm Boys: Crosby, Barris, and Rinker. It was far and away the best-paid band in the nation, with a weekly payroll that reached nearly $10,000, or three times that of the star-studded Goldkette orchestra. Keeping so costly an orchestra afloat was a challenge.

Whiteman offered a hodgepodge of different styles and sounds. He wanted an orchestra that could play anything. Jack Fulton offered falsetto vocals, Bing Crosby a more virile baritone, while the Rhythm Boys performed an act complete with slamming the lid of an upright piano up and down to keep time. The band played dances and concerts, did some theater dates that included unrelated vaudeville entertainers, and provided music for Broadway shows, such as *George White's Scandals*, the *Ziegfeld Follies*, and *Whoopee*. It also recorded Christmas carols. Impressed by Don Redman's arrangements for Fletcher Henderson, Whiteman once hired Redman to write some originals for him—but his men could not swing nearly as well as Henderson's.

Beiderbecke had previously scoffed at the Whiteman orchestra—whose tendency toward ponderousness was easy for jazzmen to deride—but once he joined, he expressed pride in being a member. Underneath that rebellious jazzman's exterior, he still had enough of the "proper" bourgeois Davenport boy in him to take some satisfaction in having been accepted into Paul Whiteman's orchestra. It was a prominent organization, respected by the average American as being the foremost purveyor of tasteful popular music. He knew that Whiteman musicians such as Chester Hazlett and the Mayhews were not jazzmen, but they were excellent technicians who produced beautiful tones.

Still, being in the Whiteman orchestra was also a source of repeated frustrations for Beiderbecke, frustrations that wore heavily on him, whether he verbalized them or not. He had to sit for endless stretches while the band played music far removed from anything resembling jazz; he didn't get a fraction of the opportunities for self-expression that, say, Louis Armstrong was getting. In Whiteman's Carnegie Hall concert on October 7, 1928, for example, Beiderbecke played "In a Mist" on piano. And he got in some hot cornet licks, in a spot tracing the supposed history of jazz and on such numbers as "Sugar" and "Tiger Rag." But the preponderance of the evening was given over to such things as "Gypsy" (vocal by Charles Gaylord), Gershwin's "Concerto in F," "Just Like a Melody Out of the Sky" (vocal by Austin Young), "Valse Inspiration" (an alto sax solo composed and played by Chester Hazlett), "My Melancholy Baby" (vocal by Austin Young), Ferde Grofe's "Metropolis," "Chiquita" (vocal by Jack Fulton), "American Tune" (vocal by Austin Young), and "Band Divertissement: Free Air: Variations Based on Noises from a Garage" (a Wilbur Hall specialty in which he worked a bicycle pump with his right hand and altered sounds by pressing his left palm on the hose).

It's hardly surprising, then, that after hours Beiderbecke was apt to head for other bands where he could really blow. John Hammond recalled being fortunate enough in his youth "to hear Bix sit in with Charlie Johnson's Orchestra at Small's Paradise and a somewhat inferior band at the Renaissance Casino. Harlem's musicians worshipped Bix and provided him with an escape from the shackles of Whiteman and his commercialism." (Benny Waters, who played in Charlie Johnson's orchestra in those years does not recall Beiderbecke ever sitting in with the band.)[46]

There were young musicians and fans who felt—as Artie Shaw put it—that Beiderbecke simply never belonged in the Whiteman orchestra, that his talents were wasted there. They believed it was demeaning for him to be given so little exposure and thought he should have been playing more, with players who shared his sense of swing. Beiderbecke didn't complain—he wasn't the complaining type—but the situation must have been demoralizing. The relentless pressure of the heavy Whiteman schedule—for Whiteman accepted all of the work he could get (theaters, dances, radio)—also took its toll.

It should be noted that Beiderbecke's technical skills had reached maturity by the time he joined the Whiteman orchestra. He could read well and was able to execute challenging legitimate passages if requested to, as his solo work on the recording of "Concerto in F" proves. But there was no creative satisfaction in simply reading parts well.

Some have argued that the frustrations of working in the Whiteman orchestra drove Beiderbecke to drink. That's inaccurate. Although his drinking accelerated during those years, it had started long before he joined Whiteman. Drinking was very much a part of the jazz scene, despite denials by musicians like Whiteman, who told the *Daily Princetonian* in 1928: "People speak of jazz, crime, and booze all in the same breath. How do they get that way? Jazz is music, beauty of sound. It is the greatest rhythm yet discovered. . . . Jazz has nothing more to do with drinking than the soft waltz of the 'little German band' at a Turnverein picnic has to do with the number of kegs of beer which are consumed during the festivities."[47] Whiteman, who was a heavy drinker himself, always wanted jazz to have the best image possible.

Whiteman turned out an incredible number of records, first for Victor and then, from May 12, 1928, on, for Columbia. It's easy for jazz critics to find fault with the worst of them (they're commercial, they don't swing, the symphonic trappings can get pretentious, etc.), and it's true that he tried too hard, at times, to make jazz respectable. But his band could—and did—produce some sheer masterpieces. Who would want to change a note on "Lonely Melody" (recorded on January 4, 1928), "San" (January 12, 1928), or "Dardanella" (February 9, 1928)? The arrangements for all three, by Bill Challis, are elegant, perfectly structured. They have forward movement, and the voicings intrigue us still. For sheer beauty of sound, the Challis-Whiteman specialties are hard to beat.[48]

Challis knew how to utilize all of the elements in the orchestra wisely. Oftentimes he had to incorporate vocals, perhaps by Bing Crosby or the Rhythm Boys, into the charts, and they became a part—but not an overwhelming part—of a satisfying production. Consider his treatments of "Washboard Blues" (November 18, 1927), "Changes" (another masterpiece; November 23, 1927), "'Tain't So Honey, 'Tain't So" (June 10, 1928), "Because My Baby Don't Mean 'Maybe' Now"

(June 18, 1928), "Sweet Sue" (September 18, 1928), and "Oh! Miss Hannah" (October 4, 1929). He knew how to mix the hot with the sweet. But he wasn't the only one turning out memorable, jazz-inflected charts for Whiteman. Matty Malneck was responsible for the great "(What Are You Waiting For) Mary" (November 25, 1927) and "From Monday On" (February 28, 1928), which proved a memorable showcase for Beiderbecke's hot work. Tommy Satterfield produced "There Ain't No Sweet Man That's Worth the Salt of My Tears" (February 8, 1928) and "You Took Advantage of Me" (April 25, 1928). Such arrangements were widely admired.

When the Whiteman orchestra began a three-week stay in Chicago on July 2, 1928, Louis Armstrong hurried to the theater to hear Beiderbecke. As he later commented: "This was the first time I witnessed him in such a large hellfired band as Mr. Whiteman's. . . . I had been diggin' him in small combos and stuff. Now my man's gonna blow some of these big time arrangements, I thought . . . and sure enough he did. . . ." Armstrong recalled the band going into "a beautiful tune called 'From Monday On.' . . . My, my, what an arrangement that was. They swung it all the way . . . and all of a sudden Bix stood up and took a solo . . . and I'm tellin' you, those pretty notes went all through me." He added that when the Whiteman orchestra played the "1812 Overture," through all of the bombast, including the shooting of cannons, "you could still hear Bix. . . . You take a man with a pure tone like Bix's and no matter how loud the other fellows may be blowing, that pure cornet or trumpet tone will cut through it all."[49]

After hours in Chicago, Armstrong and Beiderbecke would jam together. They weren't out to cut each other, Armstrong recalled, but to blend, "to see how good we could make music sound, which was an inspiration within itself."[50] It's a pity that no recordings were made of Armstrong and Beiderbecke together. Armstrong was number one in Beiderbecke's book, the only musician he claimed he'd go out of his way to hear.

Jimmy McPartland recalls that when Beiderbecke arrived in Chicago in 1928, he'd forgotten his tuxedo and borrowed one from him, which he never saw again. But McPartland didn't mind because shortly afterward Beiderbecke picked out a new Bach cornet for him. They went down to the Dixie Music House, Beiderbecke tried out four horns, picked the one that sounded best, and plunked down nearly the full price. (He laid out perhaps $145 toward the $175 price, letting McPartland pay the store the remaining $30 at $5 a week.)

Beiderbecke broke the horn in for a week or so, then turned it over to McPartland for good.[51]

Music was pretty much Beiderbecke's life. If he wasn't playing, he was listening. In Chicago in the summer of 1928, the Three Deuces, at 222 North State Street, was a good spot for late-night jamming, along with perhaps the Dorsey brothers, Hoagy Carmichael, Gene Krupa, George Wettling, Joe Sullivan, Eddie Condon, and Jess Stacy. There were times when Beiderbecke would let Jimmy McPartland take all of the cornet work while he played piano. Sometimes Bing Crosby would join in the sessions as well, playing the drums or the cymbals. And there were always new records to savor. Beiderbecke loved Bessie Smith and Ethel Waters. He'd spin their sides over and over.

Stacy, who adored Beiderbecke's work—he said he bought his first phonograph because he wanted to be able to play Beiderbecke's recorded solo on "Sweet Sue"—remembered him playing a piece called "Clouds" in a jam session once. (Evidently Beiderbecke never got around to writing it down.) Stacy had never heard anyone come up with some of the harmonies Beiderbecke would play on piano.

Beiderbecke was making big money by 1928 standards, although he had nothing to show for it. Besides his $200 per week salary from Whiteman, he was getting $67.50 for every side he recorded for Whiteman. And he was earning additional money for the sides he recorded under Frankie Trumbauer's name and under his own name for OKeh. But the money was of no significance to him. He never held on to his dough for too long.

Jimmy McPartland recalls one time in 1928 when the Whiteman band and the Pollack band both played at a swank New York party. Pollack's band had been laying off for a stretch, and McPartland had run out of money. So he asked Beiderbecke for a loan: $5, $10, anything so he could buy some groceries. Beiderbecke pulled four $50 bills from his pocket and gave them to McPartland. McPartland protested, but Beiderbecke would hear none of it, answering that he had plenty of money and knew McPartland would pay him back when he could (which he did). McPartland never forgot his friend's generous, impulsive gesture.[52]

Beiderbecke played jazz because he wanted to, because he *had* to, not because of the money. The records he made under his own name weren't as good as they should have been, since the sidemen he used were usually far below his abilities. He just wasn't a leader. He didn't have what it took—the force of character, if you will—to get first-rate recording bands and to get the very best out of his colleagues. At one time or another, Beiderbecke played with all of the greatest jazzmen of his era. But he recorded with relatively few of them.

Beiderbecke responded passionately to great talent in the arts and shared his enthusiasm with friends. McPartland recalls being taken to see Ethel Waters in her show *Miss Calico.* One of the Princeton musicians remembered Beiderbecke making sure that he checked out Ben Pollack's band—the best jazz band he could hear in New York—shortly after it arrived the city. And Bud Freeman wrote that Beiderbecke nearly got him fired from Pollack's band. The band was taking a break at the Little Club in New York, according to Freeman, when "Bix very excitedly came running down the stairs of the club and yelled, 'Bud, for God's sake hurry up; John Barrymore is doing Hamlet on radio!'" Freeman immediately left with his friend and was an hour and a half late getting back to the bandstand. But he was grateful to Beiderbecke, for Barrymore was an unbeatable Hamlet.[53]

According to Freeman, it was Beiderbecke who started getting leading white New York musicians into the habit of going uptown to Harlem to jam. He took Freeman and McPartland to hear Willie "The Lion" Smith, for example, and eventually Benny Goodman and other members of the Pollack band wound up going to Harlem to sit in. Beiderbecke was, Freeman says, one of the very few early white jazzmen who really understood the black man's music.[54]

Beiderbecke's family was not impressed by his accomplishments, however, or by the fact that he was revered by other jazz musicians. The world of jazz was foreign to them; they associated it with loose morals and excessive drinking. On the rare occasions when they saw their son, his penchant for liquor was all too obvious. Although he dutifully wrapped and mailed home new records as he made them, his parents never bothered to play them. Beiderbecke was startled, when he finally did get home, to discover that all of the records he had sent were in a closet, unopened. On November 23, 1928, when the Paul Whiteman Orchestra played in Clinton, Iowa, just thirty miles from Davenport, no one from the family, except for his brother, went to see him.

Beiderbecke never took good care of himself. He didn't eat right, and he didn't get enough sleep. Countless people proudly proclaimed themselves his friends, glad to be able to say that they were close to the prominent jazz cornetist. He'd smile and drink with them, and he always had money to buy them liquor. Yet, fundamentally, Beiderbecke remained apart from them, alone.

He did, of course, have jazz-buff friends at the various colleges where he'd played and was revered by campus musicians at Princeton and Yale. When he went to see the Princeton Triangle Show—the student musical—he was touched to find that one of his breaks from "Riverboat Shuffle" had been written into one of the musical numbers. After the show, he joined the Princeton musicians for a jam session. He even agreed to take part in a recording session by the Princeton Triangle Jazzband, which was doing its best to get some of the Beiderbecke-Trumbauer-Challis sound. But on the day of the recording session, one of the Princeton musicians told me, Beiderbecke was too drunk to participate.[55]

It was easy enough to laugh off the excessive drinking, perhaps because it seemed to be a basic part of the jazz scene. But it had begun catching up with Beiderbecke. The fact that he began playing less open horn on his later Whiteman recordings is a tip-off. Muting his horn helped disguise the fact that his inimitable tone, which he had never before sought to hide, was beginning to deteriorate, that his breath control was starting to weaken.

The pace was proving too much for him. The Whiteman band's two-month-long tour in late 1928 meant a concert or two daily, and constant traveling. Beiderbecke kept mostly to himself, suffering from fatigue, nausea, weakness in his legs, and a cold that wouldn't let go. When the band arrived back in New York on December 10, 1928, his health gave out and he was hospitalized for two weeks with pneumonia. In those days, before wonder drugs, the only treatment was bed rest, to allow the body to heal itself. But Beiderbecke had few reserves upon which to draw.

When he was well enough to return to work, he found that he couldn't keep up with the other musicians. On the night of December 29, the Whiteman orchestra began a two-week run in the *Ziegfeld Midnight Frolic* at the New Amsterdam Roof. Whiteman simultaneously booked the band to play multiple shows daily for a week, beginning December 30, at the Palace Theater. Beiderbecke was hardly ready for a day-and-night performing schedule. He wound up missing shows, having to get substitutes. Weak, nervous, irritable, he never really got back on his feet. Whether his body had ever fully beaten the pneumonia is questionable.

As soon as the work for Ziegfeld ended, Whiteman took the band back out on the road. It was too much for Beiderbecke. On January 20, 1929, in Cleveland, he suffered a severe breakdown of some sort and smashed up a roomful of furniture in the posh hotel where the band was staying. Perhaps it was an attack of delirium tremens. After all, he was an alcoholic, in weak condition, who presumably had stopped drinking during his hospitalization. He had grown physically dependent upon large doses of alcohol, and what his body may have been reacting to was withdrawal. Or the overall pace of his life may have simply proven too much to bear.

Band members didn't know exactly what to make of his breakdown. Clearly, he was in no shape to keep touring, so Whiteman hired a male nurse to watch over him while the band continued on tour. Whiteman left Cleveland on the weekend of January 26–27, expecting Beiderbecke to return to Davenport and take a week or so to pull himself together.

In need of a cornetist, Whiteman called Jean Goldkette and bought the contract of a promising twenty-one-year-old, Andy Secrest, who was working in one of Goldkette's bands. Secrest idolized Beiderbecke, whom he had first heard with the Wolverines in 1924. Having modeled his own style and sound upon his idol's, he would provide listeners with a fairly good simulation of Beiderbecke's work.

The Whiteman band returned to New York on February 3. Some of the musicians promptly headed to the Forty-fourth Street Hotel and were startled to learn from the desk clerk that Beiderbecke was there. They found him in his room, bent over the sink, pressing a bloody towel to the lower part of his torso. His face was cut, and he was vomiting. It seems that he had come straight to New York from Cleveland, obtained some gin, and headed to a speakeasy. Exactly what happened next remains uncertain; years later different men were telling different stories.

Some said Beiderbecke had had a run-in with some sailors. Others said a hoodlum had come after him for moving in on his girl, or some such thing. Whatever it was, someone clearly had roughed him up. Some musicians said a broken bottle had been shoved into his gut; others said it was his groin. Still others suggested a bottle had been rammed up his rectum. In any event, the injury left him using a cane for awhile and walking with a limp afterward.

Whiteman didn't know what to do with his star jazz player. He put Beiderbecke on a train back to Davenport and told him that his chair would be waiting for him. But Beiderbecke's health never fully returned. For the rest of his life he had recurring complaints of weakness, irritability, nervousness. He caught lingering colds. He was on a downward spiral now, and he knew it. His ego, which had never been too strong, was further diminished by having to return to his parents' care in such awful condition.

Beiderbecke stayed in Davenport throughout February. Word of his presence got around, and a newspaper reporter went to interview him. As a cornetist with the famed Paul Whiteman, he was a local boy who had made good, now recuperating at home from an unspecified illness. The *Davenport Sunday Democrat* printed some of his observations about jazz on February 10, 1929. "Even in the hands of white composers," he stated, "it involuntarily reflects the half-forgotten suffering of the negro. Jazz has both white and black elements, and each in some respects has influenced the other. Its recent phase seems to throw the light of the white race's sophistication upon the anguish of the black." He didn't make the point that his own jazz, even at its most exuberant, was shaded by an undertone of his own anguish.

Beiderbecke returned to the Whiteman band on March 4, but he had to share solo work with Secrest—who came close enough to Beiderbecke's style that, to this day, jazz buffs dispute which of the two played certain recorded passages. Secrest, of course, didn't have the creativity of Beiderbecke, who was forever surprising his colleagues when he rose for a solo, leaving them to wonder if he'd be able to get back to the original melody.

The Whiteman band was now on the air weekly, sponsored by Old Gold cigarettes. Getting the radio show was supposed to have ensured the band's survival. There were hefty sponsor's checks coming in regularly, and Whiteman no longer had to worry about lining up tour after tour. Yet, as Bill Challis explained to me, in an unforeseen way the radio contract led to the decline of the Whiteman band. Old Gold wanted a continuing stream of new tunes, and they wanted more tunes per show than B. A. Rolfe and his orchestra were playing on the competing Lucky Strike program. Thus, the radio contract resulted in the band's playing more quickly written commercial charts, some of which even featured xylophones and accordions because Rolfe was using those instruments.[56]

Even after joining Whiteman, Beiderbecke had continued his recording dates with Trumbauer on the side, as well as recording numbers under his own name. These days, however, he could barely keep up with his obligations to Whiteman. He told Trumbauer that he was sorry he could no longer make his record dates. After April 30, 1929, Trumbauer no longer used Beiderbecke on his records. Trumbauer never seemed to sound as good without him.

By that summer, Beiderbecke was drinking heavily again. He didn't look well, and his playing wasn't consistent. The band headed west—Chicago, St. Louis, Kansas City, Denver, eventually to California. His mother traveled to California to see him, but she left rather quickly, no doubt uncomfortable with what she saw and with her son's unwillingness—or inability—to change his way of life.

The sensitivity and gentleness that friends recalled in Bix Beiderbecke is caught in this rare early portrait. (Author's collection. Courtesy of the Institute of Jazz Studies.)

The Wolverines, at the Gennett Recording Studio in Richmond, Indiana, 1924. Left to right: Min Leibrook, Jimmy Hartwell, George Johnson, Bob Gillette, Vic Moore, leader Dick Voynow, Bix Beiderbecke, Al Gandee. (Courtesy of Duncan P. Schiedt.)

The Jean Goldkette Orchestra, during its New England tour, September 1926. Back row, left to right: Dan Murray, Howdy Quicksell, Frank Trumbauer; front row: Ray Lodwig, Itzy Riskin, Spiegel Willcox, Doc Ryker, Bill Rank, Chauncey Morehouse, Bix Beiderbecke, Bill Challis, ? (bus driver), Steve Brown, Fuzzy Farrar. (Courtesy of Duncan P. Schiedt.)

This portrait of Bix Beiderbecke has become the standard image of him, even though it was taken in August 1921, when he was just eighteen, and does not represent the way he appeared during the years of his greatest success. (Author's collection.)

Bix Beiderbecke in 1926, as he was approaching his peak. (Author's collection. Courtesy of the Institute of Jazz Studies.)

The Jean Goldkette Orchestra, a favorite of the collegiate set, at the University of Pennsylvania's elaborately decorated Ivy League Ball, May 6, 1927. Standing, left to right: ?; Fuzzy Farrar, Howdy Quicksell, Steve Brown, Itzy Riskin, Spiegel Willcox, ?; seated: Don Murray, Frank Trumbauer, Ray Lodwig, Bill Rank, Bix Beiderbecke, Chauncey Morehouse, Eddy Sheasby. (Courtesy of Duncan P. Schiedt.)

On September 9, 1929, back in New York, Beiderbecke made what turned out to be his final recording date with Whiteman. His last issued Whiteman side was entitled, prophetically enough, "Waiting at the End of the Road." Beiderbecke's strength gave out as the band began recording the next number, and after the first take he relinquished his part to Secrest, going to sleep in a corner of the studio. Whiteman sent him home again to dry out. This time, seven months would pass before they'd see each other. Whiteman recalled later that he kept Beiderbecke on full salary for a couple of months, then on half salary for maybe four or five months more.[57]

At age twenty-six, Beiderbecke was just about washed up, although it took quite a while for that reality to become apparent to everyone. He still anticipated returning to Whiteman's orchestra once he regained his health. Records he had made with Whiteman were still coming out, still being played. (There was always a lag between when a recording was made and when it was released, and then an additional period in which sales might continue to build.) And via these records, he continued to exert an influence upon horn players who heard him, admired him, and had no idea that he had begun a final decline.

Trumpeter Doc Cheatham was one of those players. He wound up working in McKinney's Cotton Pickers in 1931, after touring in Europe for a couple of years with Sam Wooding's orchestra. His fellow trumpeters in the Cotton Pickers were Joe Smith and Rex Stewart, both formerly with Fletcher Henderson and well versed in Beiderbecke's work. "It was like a college of jazz," Cheatham told jazz writer Whitney Balliett. "But one of the teachers wasn't in the band, and that was Bix Beiderbecke. All trumpet players had been playing alike when Bix came along a year or two before and opened the gate. He was doing things we had never heard. He was a lyrical player, but he was also staccato and bright. He had a speaking, *trumpet* way of playing."[58]

Beiderbecke had his strongest stylistic impact upon such players as Red Nichols, Jimmy McPartland, and Andy Secrest. But his approach also affected, to varying degrees, other younger trumpeters of that era, even if he wasn't their main influence.[59] You'll hear echoes of him in recordings by Chicagoans of the late 1920s—for example, listen to Dick Feigie's cornet work on "Copenhagen," with Elmer Schoebel's Friars' Society Orchestra (1929). Benny Goodman also sounds Beiderbeckean in his alto sax solo on "Blue (and Brokenhearted)" (1928). And Charlie Teagarden often seems to show some Beiderbecke influence. Many bands, both black and white, played "Singin' the Blues" in the famous Trumbauer-Beiderbecke style; and

Speed Webb's band was playing "Sweet Sue" in 1929 much as Beiderbecke had recorded it with Whiteman (in fact, pianist Teddy Wilson wrote it out for the band from the record).

No discussion of Beiderbecke's general influence would be complete, of course, without mentioning Hoagy Carmichael, who often said he would not have made music his career except for Beiderbecke, his favorite musician. That Beiderbecke's phrasing colored Carmichael's thinking is evident in the curiously rising and descending notes that make up Carmichael's most famed composition, "Stardust." And the melody of "Skylark" also has definite Beiderbeckean echoes.

By late 1929, Beiderbecke's records were being collected by admirers, and his older out-of-print sides had begun rising in value. When a cash-strapped Bing Crosby heard that some Yale kids at the Astor Hotel were offering five dollars apiece for the Gennett Wolverines' sides, he sold his whole batch to them.

Meanwhile, out in Davenport, Beiderbecke was suffering pains in his legs and a general languor. Depressed, he saw virtually no one, living like a recluse with his family. He sensed, deep down, his inability to gain control of his life. His doctor wanted him hospitalized for treatment of his alcoholism.

Beiderbecke's drinking had become a source of pain and shame to his family. His parents were not proud of their broken-down "jazzer" of a son. On October 14, 1929, his brother drove him to the Keeley Institute in Dwight, Illinois, for treatment. Beiderbecke told the doctors of his bout with pneumonia and delirium tremens, adding that he had not regained his strength. They, in turn, noted that his overall condition was extremely poor. He stayed at the institute until November 18. The hard times following the stock market crash in October would affect everyone in the music business—even Paul Whiteman would be forced to scale down his orchestra—but right now Beiderbecke was fighting a private battle for survival.

From December 1929 through March 1930, Beiderbecke played occasional dates near home, working as a sideman in run-of-the-mill local dance bands where his musical creativity wasn't necessarily welcome. Cy Churchill, a contemporary of his who played in bands in the region, recalled: "Even though local bands weren't always thrilled to have Bix sit in because of his unusual style, they did know that he'd played with some pretty good musicians like Hoagy Carmichael, and with Paul Whiteman's orchestra for a while."[60]

Beiderbecke occasionally saw various childhood acquaintances, most of whom were now married and settled into the routine of Davenport life. He had little in common with them, however. Some remembered him saying he no longer drank, that he realized taking one drink was the same as taking 400. At some point, though, he quite clearly fell off the wagon. Les Swanson, a local musician, recalled going with him to Danceland, in Davenport, to hear a band. Some friends bought them a few drinks. Later that night, Swanson said: "I was driving Bix home and when we were about even with the Blackhawk Hotel, he started shivering and grabbing out and yelling, 'I have to have it! I have to have it! Pull over. I'll tell you where in a minute.' There was a bootleg joint in the next block. In about five minutes he was back with a sack. Bix pulled out a half pint of alcohol and said he was going to take it to bed with him."[61]

In early February, Beiderbecke visited Chicago, where he sat in with Wingy Manone's band at the Three Deuces. Art Hodes, who played piano that night, told me they played until the next morning. Hodes was struck by Beiderbecke's shyness, as well as by the quietness of his playing; he didn't have nearly as large a sound as Louis Armstrong did. In Chicago, Beiderbecke also rehearsed with Joe Haymes's band, with an idea of joining it, but his nerves were shot. Haymes recalled Beiderbecke stopping midway through his solo at the piano and stating that he was unable to go on because he simply felt too agitated.[62] Beiderbecke obviously knew he was going downhill. He had always been his own harshest critic, and he could tell his abilities, especially on the horn, were not what they once were.

In April 1930, he returned to New York City. When he could, he worked with Bill Challis on his piano compositions. He also told Whiteman he was not yet ready to rejoin the band. Beiderbecke was drifting now, uncertain about the future. Artie Shaw recalled seeing him in this period, "on the downgrade, a pitiable wreck of a guy, unable to control his drinking well enough to keep it from interfering with his trumpet playing." Jimmy McPartland told me: "I was working in this Broadway show called *Sons O' Guns,* and I was loaded with dough. I was also doing recordings in the daytime. And one night at Plunkett's—that was a speakeasy we all went to . . . —Bix came in. He was drinking so much that he just was not dependable, and people wouldn't hire him. He was ill, rather, more than anything else. I remember giving him a $100 bill. I had just gotten paid. And he wasn't working, couldn't play."[63] Beiderbecke told McPartland that he had a bad cold but insisted he would pay back the hundred as soon as he could. He had some college dates ahead; he'd settle up properly. But he never did.

Musicians who met Beiderbecke only in his final year were not apt to have been greatly impressed. Was this the man they had heard so highly praised? Some of the Young Turks who met him now, hanging out in a speakeasy, dismissed him scornfully as a "gin blower" who didn't have the wind to play more than two choruses. But he still had his moments—moments when his playing was as bright and clear and fresh and *innocent* as ever.

Beiderbecke got some pick-up dates in the spring at several colleges where, in the eyes of his fans, he could do no wrong. He played Princeton house parties in May, along with the Dorseys and Bud Freeman. Hoagy Carmichael used him for a successful Victor date on May 21, along with James "Bubber" Miley, Tommy Dorsey, Freeman, Benny Goodman, Gene Krupa, Joe Venuti, and Eddie Lang. The cuts included "Rockin' Chair" and a rollicking "Barnacle Bill the Sailor." Then on June 6, Beiderbecke made three recordings with Irving Mills and His Hotsy Totsy Gang. On these sides, the cornet work is so inferior to his earlier work that some Beiderbecke fans have refused to believe it's him.

Meanwhile, the makers of Camel cigarettes had decided they wanted an orchestra show to compete with the Old Gold show (with Whiteman) and the Lucky Strike show (with Rolfe). Nat Shilkret put together an orchestra that included some former Goldkette and Whiteman players, hired Challis to arrange, and got Beiderbecke on cornet. Soon there was talk of Beiderbecke hiding gin on the job. On August 6, 1930, *Variety* reported: "Bix Beiderbecke starting his own band. Formerly with Whiteman Orchestra and wants Whiteman to manage him." Bud Freeman told me Beiderbecke was rehearsing the band—the idea was to create an all-star white jazz ensemble and tour Europe with it—but got too ill to follow through.[64]

On September 8, using a band he rounded up at Plunkett's, Beiderbecke recorded three numbers under his own name: "Deep Down South," "I Don't Mind Walking in the Rain," and the touching "I'll Be a Friend 'With Pleasure.' " The next week, Hoagy Carmichael used him on a pick-up record date, having never lost faith in his friend. On "Georgia on My Mind," Beiderbecke comes through once again, the luminous notes unexpected—and unmistakably his in choice and placement. (The trumpeter heard first on the record, stating the melody with a bleating vibrato, is Ray Lodwig; Beiderbecke never sounded that unattractive.)

Having reached the point where he could drink straight alcohol flavored with just a few drops of lemon juice, Beiderbecke was making more mistakes, more frequently. Fellow musicians had the attitude, What a great player he would be if only he could stay off the booze. But would he have been as great, as creative, if he had never been a drinker, if he'd had greater self-control? I doubt it. The heavy drinking, the self-doubts, the distant, ethereal personality—they were all part of one package. A Beiderbecke who never drank to excess, whose ego was in greater control of his id, would never have given us the same haunting, brilliantly original music.

On October 8, 1930, midway through a solo during a Camel radio broadcast, Beiderbecke blacked out. Leo McConville finished his solo for him, and another trumpeter was hired to replace him in the orchestra. For the last time he headed back to Davenport. Callers were told by his parents that he couldn't come to the phone. Sometimes he sat by himself on the screened-in front porch, looking out on a world he was too weak to participate in, much as he had as an eight-year-old too ill to attend school. A few times he played with local bands.

In January and February 1931, Beiderbecke mostly hung around at home. He knew he didn't fit in, in Davenport. He told childhood friends, whenever he saw them, of the glamorous figures, from Paul Whiteman to Ziegfeld showgirls to Hollywood stars, he had met. He looked puffy, unwell. Lillian Leonard, a Davenport contemporary, remembered: "He came home during the last year of his life and I felt so sorry for him. He'd had pneumonia in New York and he'd have to lift his legs up with his hands when he first got up, and then he'd just shuffle along."[65]

Beiderbecke struggled back to New York that spring, to search for whatever free-lance dates he could find. One night he told Jack Teagarden he wanted to see the stiffs in the Bellevue morgue. The pair bribed a caretaker to let them in. Teagarden wondered later if Beiderbecke had not sensed his own impending death.

Eddie Condon recalled that Beiderbecke "wasn't being good to himself; he was cheating the cure he had taken. His feet were swollen and dragged when he walked; his thoughts were often muddled. . . . I never let him ask me for a drink; I offered it to him. It hurt me all over . . . but I knew nothing could help him. . . . He couldn't go back to Whiteman; he didn't have the stamina for the job, or the ability to concentrate. . . . When I heard Bix at the piano nothing seemed changed; he played with the same effortless, unbelievable imagination. It was only when I looked at his face and saw the absence there that things got cold and tight and I stiffened my drink."[66]

"Bix was complaining because he couldn't get any work," Bill Challis told me. "Once in a while the guys would get him a job, where they could, but it wasn't very often." Challis talked to Cork O'Keefe about Beiderbecke joining the Casa Loma Band, and everyone really liked the idea, except for Beiderbecke.

> . . . he wasn't so hot about going with them. I tried to talk him into it. I said, "Look, they play some of my arrangements. Some of those things you won't have to rehearse, you'll know what they are." Because that band was known for rehearsing a lot.
>
> I guess his money was running out, so he had us pick him up at NBC in Manhattan, to take him up to where the band was playing in Connecticut. We got as far as the opening to Central Park. He said: "Where am I going? What are we going to do?" He started asking questions, then he didn't want to go. He said, "You better let me out here," at the entrance to the park. And we did.[67]

Beiderbecke's parents were at a loss in trying to figure out how to deal with him. They helped as best they could, by sending him some money, probably sensing that nothing was going to change very much. He was so clearly on the way down, despite the brave front he tried to put up in his sporadic letters to them.

He began one letter, in March 1931, by saying he figured they would probably tear it up without reading it because they were so disgusted with him. The reason he hadn't written them lately—whether they wanted to believe him or not, he added—was that he'd been ill. He insisted—underlining the sentence—that he wasn't sick from drinking but from an annual attack of tonsillitis. He had grown so feverish that he believed he would have died except for Christian Science. He said he had talked himself out of being sick!

The letter went on to reveal that he had lost three dates due to his illness. One bandleader had paid him fifty dollars even though he'd been unable to work, suggesting he could work with the band on another occasion to make up for it. Then Beiderbecke apologized for not having sent his mother anything for her birthday on March 1; he had simply been too sick. He was all right now, he insisted, and was considering whether to go back to the Camel radio show or maybe do some motion picture soundtrack work. He doubted he would go back with the Casa Loma Band (which he had not really joined in the first place) because, he wrote in a transparent rationalization, he could pick up more work by doing radio shows and free-lance club dates. In fact, he added, he had some dates coming up at Princeton and Amherst. He promised to do his best to repay the money his parents had sent him when he needed it, as well as the "income money" (income tax money?) they had sent.

Beiderbecke's handwriting slants downward across the pages of the letter, perhaps reflecting his depressed spirits. The excuses, the apologies, the empty promises—his parents had probably heard all of that many times. The fervent denial of a drinking problem—in a vain attempt to maintain his self-respect and the respect of others—was, of course, part of his alcoholism.

On top of everything else, Beiderbecke could no longer count on fellow musicians, who were inclined to be far more tolerant, to overlook his constant drinking. For example, he got so drunk at a party after one Princeton job that Joe Sullivan angrily stopped him from playing piano. The Princeton students still felt honored to have him party with them—one recalled Beiderbecke playing a new piano composition called "Brooklets," which he had not yet put on paper[68]—but when Beiderbecke took out a flask of liquor one Sunday morning, in plain view of disapproving citizens walking to church, embarrassed youths hurried him indoors, away from public scrutiny.

There were moments, now, when Beiderbecke would reveal that even he was bothered by how much he was drinking. Pete Ehlers, a Princeton senior in the spring of 1931, recalled that Beiderbecke would sometimes visit the campus just to meet with acquaintances, not to work. He wasn't that much older than the Princeton students, and maybe hanging out with them let him share vicariously in the kind of life he had missed. But Ehlers remembered the plaintiveness in Beiderbecke's voice as he said, after another afternoon had been killed drinking: "Why are we doing this? I thought I'd come down here and we'd walk in the woods or something. . . ." Ehlers added: "I didn't know Bix was going to die . . . become a hero. I just took him for granted."[69]

Beiderbecke was suffering from circulation problems, sometimes having difficulty walking. Clearly, his time was running out. In May 1931, he changed his mind about joining the Casa Loma Band. "He needed the money," Challis told me. "He went up by train to where they were playing. It didn't work out. I guess they had bigger drinkers than he ever was. . . . I guess they told him, 'Let's go out and have a drink.' . . . I don't think it lasted much—a week, maybe two weeks."[70] A cooperative band, it couldn't afford to carry a member who didn't pull his own weight. And the precisely executed charts the band favored were no doubt too tough for him.

Beiderbecke must have realized that he couldn't control his drinking anymore. He also knew that the jazz world was passing him by. Guitarist Frank Victor recalled one night when Beiderbecke came to hear a band he was playing in, in Pelham, New York. The musicians all asked Beiderbecke to play, which he was reluctant to do. But they kept on asking. According to Victor: "The boys crowded around him, and after we had coaxed and handed him a horn, he began to play his chorus of 'Sweet Sue.' Well, it was an awful shock to us. He tried, but he just couldn't make the music he felt. It was one of the saddest moments I've ever experienced—Bix wanting to make his horn talk and not getting the response he'd always known."[71]

In late June or early July, Beiderbecke moved to an apartment in Sunnyside, Queens. He visited Hoagy Carmichael once that summer, bringing along a girlfriend who, like him, appeared to be somewhat of a lost soul. Carmichael got the impression that she was unaware of who Beiderbecke was, of how great he had been. Until recently, nothing else was known about this woman (or, for that matter, about the last couple months of Beiderbecke's life). But the discovery of an eight-page letter he wrote to his parents on June 16, 1931, adds some interesting nuggets of information.

Beiderbecke began the letter, as he had others, by making an excuse for why he hadn't written in so long. This time, he declared, his excuse was "pretty legitimate"—he'd gotten an offer to take a band on the road (New England and Pennsylvania coal mining regions) for several weeks and had no time to write while touring. He added, perhaps trying to impress his parents, that at times he'd worn swallowtails and had directed as well as played.

The main purpose of the letter, though, was to tell them about the woman he was seeing, a woman he hoped to marry. Alice was twenty years old, had red hair and blue eyes, and was of German-Irish background—her mother's name had been Weiss; her father's, O'Connell. (He must have figured that his parents, being of proud German stock, would approve of Alice's German background.) Having lived in New York all her life, he wrote, she had what seemed to his midwestern ears to be the most blatant New York accent. And, though he dreaded mentioning it—because of his mother's attitudes—the fact was that Alice was a Roman Catholic. She had dragged him (as he put it) to Mass several times in the hope that he might convert. He, in turn, had taken her to the Fifth Avenue Presbyterian Church—which she maintained she had liked, even as she protested that her brothers and sisters wouldn't accept the idea of her converting. He had met one brother, who seemed quite open-minded, and now sought to win the approval of Alice's sisters.

Beiderbecke wrote that he had told Alice he wouldn't marry her until he had saved up a couple thousand dollars (which at that stage in his life would have been an impossibility). She, in turn, had told him that he now *had* the money, and she showed him her bankbook.

He had nearly passed out. He figured that, counting her bonds and stocks, she was worth at least $10,000. Then, in a fervent, almost paranoid, request—penned all in capital letters—he asked his parents to tear up the letter. He did not want anyone to think he was after Alice's money. He swore—possibly protesting too much—that he had fallen in love with her *before* he had learned of her wealth. But considering how desperate his situation was, it's hard to imagine that her having money was of no concern to him. (Her parents, who had apparently been quite wealthy, had died when she was young, and she had spent nine years in a convent.)

Rather grandly, Beiderbecke added that he was now weighing two good offers to play at lake resorts outside New York (but close enough for him to pop in for record dates as offers came his way). Whoever bid the most for his services, he professed, would get him. But it was all an illusion; he wanted his parents to believe things were looking up for him. He was never to take any job playing at a lake. Nor was he ever to record again.

One final letter, begun perhaps on July 30 (the only address on it is "Thursday"), was never finished. What, he wondered, did his parents think of the photograph of Alice, taken in a Broadway Photomaton? He wrote that they were together constantly.

Beiderbecke had caught another cold and got to the point where he seldom left his apartment, except to buy liquor. He had no strength left, no ability to fight—or talk—his way back to good health. The building's rental agent took him for an occasional drive, during which he rambled on about musicians he had known, though he wasn't always coherent.

On August 6, 1931, Frank Trumbauer, playing in the Whiteman orchestra in Chicago, placed a phone call to Davenport. He had gotten word that his friend was seriously ill and urged the Beiderbeckes to go to New York. Beiderbecke's mother and brother were en route that same night when the cornetist suffered one final fit and died. Near the end, he was raving—trembling, screaming deliriously about Mexicans trying to kill him. Although he apparently died during an attack of delirium tremens, the death certificate listed the cause as lobar pneumonia. His friends all knew, of course, that it had been more than that.

The *Davenport Democrat* reported on August 7: "Davenport Youth, Famed As Master of Trumpet, Succumbs to Pneumonia / Dies While Mother and Brother Are Speeding to Bedside." The *New York Times,* which prides itself on reporting "all the news that's fit to print," did not report the death of Bix Beiderbecke.

Beiderbecke's family took his body back to Davenport. Alice O'Connell did not go west for the services. The pallbearers at the funeral were chosen by the family; none of them, significantly, was a jazz musician. The register of "Friends Who Called at the Services of Leon Bix Beiderbecke" lists just nine callers. Many more sent flowers, including (according to the register): "Paul Whiteman and Boys," "New York Friends," and "Alice O'Connell, N. Y." Most of the others appear to have been Iowa friends of the family.

Although the Beiderbeckes never really understood or appreciated the music their son had made—when jazz historian Marshall Stearns went to Davenport to interview them in 1935, they startled him by saying, "We never knew our Bix was famous"[72]—his fame snowballed after his death. The fact that the early jazz writers were nearly all Beiderbecke enthusiasts was significant. They placed him on a pedestal, establishing his position for later generations of jazz buffs.[73] The reissuing of his records started five years after his death and continues to the present.

Stories began to surface about Beiderbecke, one of the more persistent—if illogical, considering that he had passed away in August—being that he had died en route to a Princeton University prom; in another variation, he had supposedly gotten sick while driving in an open car to a Princeton prom in a snowstorm. One friend was told by a spiritualist medium a message that Beiderbecke had for "Helen." No one seemed to know of a Helen in his life, but the idea got around—and was printed as fact in his definitive biography—that the woman he had intended to marry in the final months of his life had been named Helen.

Other musicians offered their own interpretations of Beiderbeckean material, records that his admirers accepted as tributes. Red Norvo recorded "In a Mist" on xylophone in 1933. (He had first recorded it in 1929, but that version was never issued). Jess Stacy, who had been influenced somewhat on piano by Beiderbecke, recorded "In the Dark" and "Flashes" in 1935, and "Candlelights" in 1939. Red Nichols remade "Davenport Blues" in 1939. Bunny Berigan, who had played some college dates with Beiderbecke, paid tribute by recording five numbers in 1938. Swing bandleader Larry Clinton suggested to one interviewer that he'd gotten the idea of tackling classics from Beiderbecke. And Bobby Hackett got some attention in the late 1930s for playing some of Beiderbecke's work in Beiderbecke's manner.

Paul Whiteman accorded Beiderbecke near-legendary status. He spoke of him as an ethereal figure in an unfulfilled pursuit of beauty, one whose early demise had added to his mystique. For those who had enjoyed Beiderbecke during their college years, he would always summon up memories of their own youth. They would age; he would remain forever young, as in the one photo of him that was inevitably reprinted, showing him at age eighteen. Jazz buffs made special pilgrimages to Davenport, where Beiderbecke's brother grew used to having to point out the grave and answering endless queries. He even tried to familiarize himself with his famous sibling's music, with questionable results. Reportedly, he played for some listeners what he said he thought was Bix's best work—except that it was a Whiteman record featuring Henry Busse!

In 1938 *Metronome* magazine devoted much of one issue, written by George T. Simon, to Beiderbecke. In it, Whiteman is quoted as saying: "There's never been a soloist like him. . . . I'd give my right arm if I could hear another Bix."[74] The following year, England's *Melody Maker* carried an article by R. G. V. Venables that proclaimed Beiderbecke "the finest musician ever known to jazz." Venables quoted dozens of musicians, such as Hoagy Carmichael: "He was not only the greatest musician that jazz has produced, he was one of the grandest fellows I've ever known"; George Johnson: "Bix was the finest musician who ever lived"; Muggsy Spanier: "The greatest trumpet player of all time is dead"; Wingy Manone: "After Bix the others are just apes, for he had more ideas than the rest of us put together"; Paul Whiteman: "Bix was not only the greatest musician I have ever known, but also the greatest gentleman."[75]

One jazz buff reported to *Melody Maker* that one night he had queried Red Nichols, Pee Wee Russell, and other musicians at Nick's in New York City, and they had unanimously agreed that Beiderbecke was the greatest trumpeter of all time. "Red, Pee Wee and the rest of the musicians around the table looked at me and said, 'You should have heard Bix play in person—phonograph records give you just no idea at all.' "[76]

Rarely did anyone seem to sound a contrary note, although Jack Teagarden—trying to give his trumpet-playing brother, Charlie, a boost—once did. Jazz writer Les Lieber quoted him as saying in 1939: "You know I played with Bix and worshipped him. But I don't hesitate to say that my brother is greater than Bix. Bix is dead. That's why everybody is generous about glorifying him." Marshall Stearns also qualified his praise, observing in 1939, "There is no doubt that *white musicians* consider Bix the greatest artist of all time."[77]

Some white musicians *may* have been wearing blinders, unwilling to acknowledge that the greatest artist in jazz was black. Certainly, Beiderbecke was one of the all-time greats. Still, in 1939 it should have been obvious that Louis Armstrong was *the* greatest talent jazz had yet produced. Trumpeters like Manone and Spanier may have praised Beiderbecke to the skies, but they tried to emulate Armstrong and King Oliver. Armstrong's influence ran all through the swing era; he dominated an entire generation of musicians. By comparison, Beiderbecke's direct, readily perceived influence pretty much trails out once you get beyond players like Nichols, Secrest, and McPartland. There *were* others, of course—George T. Simon has noted, for example, that trumpeter/bandleader Billy Hicks played like Beiderbecke, and bandleader Ozzie Nelson featured a trumpeter named Bo Ashford who came up with some fine, Beiderbecke-like solos.[78] There were also many lesser known white cornetists playing in traditional jazz groups (both professional and semipro) who were at least partly influenced by Beiderbecke. All of them, however, were minor figures in an era when such musical heirs of Louis Armstrong as Harry James and Bunny Berigan were household names.[79]

Over the years, avid—almost fanatical—Beiderbecke fans have turned up additional sides on which they insist he played. Some cases seem fairly plausible. After all, we don't have accurate documentation of where Beiderbecke was every day of his life, and record companies didn't always keep accurate lists of who recorded what, when. Other cases are anything but plausible—as when one buff insisted in print that Beiderbecke, not Rex Stewart, soloed on Fletcher Henderson's first recording of "Singin' the Blues." It's hardly imaginable that Henderson's musicians could have forgotten whether Beiderbecke recorded that number with them.

Sides that have been misattributed occasionally bear witness to the influence that Beiderbecke had upon his contemporaries. Maybe those trumpeters who played like him were trying to do just that. For example, there are record collectors who thought they'd discovered Beiderbecke's presence in "Smiling Skies," recorded by Benny Meroff and His Orchestra in Chicago on December 9, 1928. What they didn't know was that Beiderbecke was giving a concert in Boston with Paul Whiteman's orchestra on that date. The trumpeter is actually Wild Bill Davison, who acknowledged, "I guess this was one time I was really trying to sound like him in a way."[80] He hadn't realized how much he had picked up from Beiderbecke until he listened to that early recording once again. Ordinarily, Davison had his own forceful style, reflecting his personal makeup. But in 1928, Beiderbecke—whom Davison had played alongside of at times—was simply too important a stylist to be ignored.

Andy Secrest could sound so much like Beiderbecke that Bixophiles have disagreed on whether it is Secrest or Beiderbecke on certain recordings—or even on certain parts of recordings. Was it Secrest who soloed on Whiteman's October 9, 1929, recording of "Nobody's Sweetheart," as is generally believed? Or did Beiderbecke and Secrest share the solo work, with Beiderbecke taking the first sixteen bars and Secrest the final sixteen? Could it be Beiderbecke, not Secrest, on Trumbauer's October 10, 1929, recording of "Manhattan Rag"? We can only make educated guesses in many of these cases, or play questionable recordings for surviving contemporaries and hope for some agreement.[81]

Bandleader Sunny Clapp claimed that Beiderbecke soloed on a recording he made of Hoagy Carmichael's "Come Easy, Go Easy Love" in 1931; it's been impossible to confirm that statement. Bandleader Joe Candullo and Red Nichols, who recorded often with Candullo, both asserted that Beiderbecke made sides with Candullo. Again, aural evidence is inconclusive. Various musicians have asserted that Beiderbecke took part in free-lance recording sessions in New York when he was a member of the Wolverines, which makes sense, though individual cases are hard to prove true. Record companies often issued sides under pseudonyms, and if Beiderbecke were playing in an ensemble, rather than soloing, identifying his presence would not be easy. Some of these questions are unanswerable; they simply taunt collectors.

Of course, we know that Beiderbecke didn't jam and record with every musician who has ever claimed to have jammed or recorded with him. People may exaggerate, wanting to link themselves to a legend. But it seems probable that he did take part in some recording sessions that have not yet been—and perhaps never will be—identified. Keeping accurate personnel lists for posterity was not a high priority of the record companies. And the better New York musicians were recording too often—usually commercial trash mixed in with jazz—for them to remember years later exactly who was present on every session.

For the record, here's an assortment of sides that various Beiderbecke enthusiasts have maintained sound like they might include him, though most serious collectors disagree: "Casey Jones" and "Steamboat Bill" by the Five Birmingham Babies (pseudonym for the California Ramblers); "I Can't Make Her Happy" by the Ipana Troubadors; "What a Day" and "Alabama Snow" by the Mason-Dixon Orchestra;

"My Man Is on the Make" by the Knickerbockers; "Lonely Little Cinderella" by the Rollickers; "Who Says They Don't Care?" by Al Lynch and His Orchestra; "So Long Blues" by the Biltmore Orchestra; "My Suppressed Desire" and "Just You, Just Me" by Pat Dollahan and His Orchestra; "Just Imagine" by Jean Goldkette and His Orchestra; "Happy Feet" and "I Like to Do Things for You" by Paul Whiteman and His Orchestra; "Why Do I Love You" and "Ol' Man River" by Lou Raderman and His Orchestra; "Dolores" and "Lila" by Bill Hawley and Puss Donahoo; "Little Did I Know" by Roy Carroll and His Orchestra; "Give Your Baby Lots of Lovin'" by Ed Blossom and His Orchestra; and "Keko" by the Andrew Aiona Novelty Four.

As the years passed, Beiderbecke became one of the godlike figures of jazz, a true immortal. The dwindling number of musicians who had actually been friends of his found themselves being endlessly asked, What was he like? or being told again and again what a tragedy his life had been. Bud Freeman pointed out that Beiderbecke's life "was completely filled with creating beautiful music. From that point of view, he lived a perfect life."[82] Eddie Condon talked a lot about him on radio broadcasts and in concerts, which helped keep his memory alive. In 1953 Jimmy McPartland recorded an album in tribute to his friend, and in the early 1960s, Herb Sanford and Yank Lawson put together a TV special about Beiderbecke (and were surprised to find out how much interest remained three decades after his passing). Beiderbecke's hometown of Davenport, which didn't much appreciate his talents in life, began an annual Bix Festival, which continues to this day.

In 1974 Beiderbecke's reputation received a significant boost with the publication of two books about him: *Bix, Man and Legend* by Richard M. Sudhalter and Philip R. Evans, with William Dean-Myatt—an exceptionally well researched, dramatically written biography; and the more impressionistic *Remembering Bix* by Ralph Berton, offering a sentiment-filled evocation of the man and the mid-1920s. Sudhalter has also championed Beiderbecke in assorted concerts, broadcasts, and recordings. Clearly, Beiderbecke's reputation has benefited from the work of some very dedicated, enthusiastic, and influential writers.

Today, the consensus of critical opinion places Beiderbecke in an elevated position, and rightly so—which is not to say that a few critics haven't expressed reservations over the years. Rudi Blesh wrote in 1946 that Beiderbecke "was and is a pervasive influence." But he found Beiderbecke's playing too restrained—that is, not hot enough—for his liking. John Hammond was of the opinion that "Beiderbecke's impeccable taste, liquid tone, and enormous sensitivity are present in all his solos. But he never had the forcefulness or drive to produce an integrated record, even in the rare instances when he controlled the recording dates and was able to choose the sidemen."[83]

Other critics have noted that Beiderbecke usually worked with stodgy rhythm sections, making his recordings sound more dated than those of the best black bands of the time. Musicians such as Louis Armstrong, Jelly Roll Morton, and Fletcher Henderson were foreshadowing the swing era by the late 1920s. And there's no avoiding the commercial nature of many of the Whiteman recordings, particularly those for Columbia. But such reservations—and there is some truth in them—do not diminish the gifts that Beiderbecke had, gifts that continue to win new admirers. You can listen again and again to his work and each time discover something new. Whether he's playing like a frisky pup on some up-tempo number or offering a plaintive sigh on a slower piece, he compels your attention, your involvement.

In Beiderbecke's best work, his soul seems to be exposed. You can sense both his elations and his sorrows. He may not have been strong enough, thick-skinned enough, to survive in this world. But in his relatively few, often troubled, years he gave us some unforgettable music. He may not have created a style that everyone tried to copy. Indeed, what he created could not easily *be* copied. A trumpeter would have to have his particular psychological makeup, as well as his technical abilities (including his idiosyncratic fingering habits), to improvise passages with the subtle, quicksilver mix of feelings he had. And as for the particular, lyrical gift he had, the facility for instantly inventing passages of curious beauty—how could anyone have copied that?

Bix Beiderbecke was one of a kind, an original. And in any art form, how few true originals there are.

4

JOE TARTO

New York Jazz

"When we'd get through with a job, we used to go to Roth's restaurant, across the street from the Roseland Ballroom, which was on Broadway between Fifty-first and Fifty-second Street. And we'd all meet in there and have coffee after the job: Red Nichols, Miff Mole, Bix. . . . They were all a bunch of good guys. They were lovely people and I miss them. I mean it." Joe Tarto takes a sip from a tiny glass filled with soda. He's eighty-two now, living for the past year or so in a recently built addition to his daughter and son-in-law's home in Boonton, New Jersey. It seems kind of odd to find Tarto here, tucked away in this sleepy suburb. You wonder if the people in the town have any idea of the rich and varied career their neighbor has had.

Joe Tarto—playing tuba and string bass, and also arranging—was an integral part of the New York jazz scene of the 1920s. You listen to an old 78 on which he's featured, such as "There'll Be a Hot Time in the Old Town Tonight" (Miff Mole's Molers) or "I Must Have That Man" (Joe Venuti's band) or "Hot Heels" (Eddie Lang's orchestra), and perhaps you conjure up an image of smoke-filled speakeasies. Jazz record collectors know Tarto's name from the many sides he recorded for the likes of Miff Mole, the Dorseys, Joe Venuti, Eddie Lang, Phil Napoleon, Benny Goodman, Sam Lanin, and Frank Signorelli. But the name they first associate with Tarto is probably Red Nichols, for Tarto played with that ever-working bandleader on records, in Broadway pit orchestras, and on radio shows.

Nichols is best remembered as the leader of the Five Pennies, although the records he made under that specific billing were only a small part of his prodigious output. Pseudonyms such as the Red

Heads, the Charleston Chasers, Red and Miff's Stompers, and the Alabama Red Peppers were used to cover his recording groups on various labels. When collectors speak of Five Pennies–type recordings today, they're referring to all of those Nichols combinations which, regardless of the billing used, drew from the same pool of players.

Records by Red Nichols and His Five Pennies usually carried the sounds of more than the five musicians the billing implied; eleven or twelve weren't unusual. And one, "Sally Won't You Come Back," recorded May 20, 1929, employed no less than nineteen musicians, Tarto included, plus vocalist Scrappy Lambert. Tarto refers to himself as the last of the Five Pennies. He says: "Red Nichols played trumpet—he's gone; Jimmy Dorsey played clarinet—he's gone; Tommy Dorsey or Miff Mole, they alternated on trombone—they're both gone; Eddie Lang on guitar and banjo—he's gone; Stan King, drums—he's gone; and Frankie Signorelli, piano—he's gone. I'm the only one left."

Tarto was always in demand in the twenties and thirties. In fact, there were so many theater and dance hall gigs, jazz and pop record sessions, radio variety shows, motion picture and even cartoon soundtracks that no one could ever come up with a complete accounting. He worked, at one time or another, under the batons of such well-known leaders as Paul Whiteman, Paul Specht, Jean Goldkette, Cass Hagan, Vincent Lopez, Ted Lewis, Ben Selvin, Bert Lown, Meyer Davis, Carl Fenton, Irving Mills, Matty Malneck, Will Osborne, Jan Garber, Art Jarrett, Leo Reisman, Freddy Rich, Buddy Rogers, B. A. Rolfe, Roger Wolfe Kahn, and George Olsen—a veritable who's who of the white orchestra world of the era. And even though bands were not racially mixed in those days, Tarto did write some arrangements for the bands of Fletcher Henderson and Chick Webb.

Over the years, Tarto worked on records, films, or radio shows with such diverse talents as the Boswell Sisters, Mildred Bailey, Burns and Allen, Eddie Cantor, Maurice Chevalier, Russ Columbo, Perry Como, Bing Crosby, Morton Downey, Cliff Edwards, Ruth Etting, Annette Hanshaw, Georgie Jessel, Helen Kane, Billy Jones and Ernie Hare, Nick Lucas, Irving Kaufman, Ethel Merman, the Mills Brothers, Dick Powell, Lanny Ross, Bill Robinson, Hazel Scott, Frank Sinatra, Kate Smith, Sophie Tucker, Ethel Waters, Lee Wiley, and Ed Wynn, not to mention others whose names would probably only be recognized by specialists. To young jazz buffs today, Bix Beiderbecke is a legendary figure. But to Tarto, he wasn't a legend; he was simply a fine musician Tarto knew, someone with whom he did a little work.

Who were Tarto's favorite jazz age trumpeters? "Well, during the period of working with all these fellows," he recalls, "I liked Red

Nichols, and Manny Klein, and another fellow, Leo McConville, and then [Sylvester] Ahola . . . I owe him a letter now. . . . He did a lot of good things. We used to call him Holy. . . . In England he was quite a favorite." As for Bix Beiderbecke, Tarto answers casually:

> I thought that he played good, you know. And that I was always trying to compare him with Red Nichols. And they said that Red Nichols patterned himself after him, but it's not so. If you listen to Red Nichols and you listen to Bix, Bix played more of a melodious jazz. It was a different, altogether different—and I couldn't see where people were saying that Red Nichols copied from Bix. And I don't think so. Because it's two different styles. Manny Klein, I would say, would be close enough to Red Nichols. . . . Manny Klein would be the one who would be the closest to Red Nichols. But I liked Manny. When he'd take a chorus, boy, he really used to go. He used to lift the band right up. He was a great player.

Tarto has framed, autographed pictures hanging on his wall of some of the greats with whom he has worked. "I want to have some for remembrance," he says. "They were all wonderful people, that's all."

Joe Tarto—originally Joseph Tortoriello—was born on February 22, 1902, in Newark, New Jersey. "I got started playing with the Italian bands," he says. "And then when I enlisted in the army in World War One—I was fifteen, I told them I was eighteen—we organized a little jazz band in our group. . . . And then after I was discharged in May of 1919, another fellow and I organized a Dixieland band and we worked around Jersey, oh, for about a year or two. Then I went to New York. My first job was with 'Ukelele Ike,' Cliff Edwards." During that audition, Tarto remembers, Edwards started "calling different tunes out":

> . . . They had no music; I had to fake it. And the last thing he asked me to play, if I knew "St. Louis Blues." And I said, "Sure." So we started playing. And about halfway through, he stopped; he says, "I like the way you play. Would you like the job? I'll pay you $75 a week"—that was good money at that time. And he said, "You start right today, at the City Theater on Fourteenth Street. Bring your tuxedo and the horn, and we'll go on at two o'clock." And I said to him, "I don't own a tuxedo." He says, "Ya don't? . . . Well, you're my size. I'll give you one of mine." And that's how I started with him. And we

played vaudeville for about nine months. And it was *after* the band broke up that I made some records with him that are collector's items.

While touring with Edwards in perhaps 1920 or 1921, Tarto says, he made records under the leadership of Joseph Samuels, Harry Reser, and others. However, he believes he was perhaps as young as seventeen or eighteen when he made his very first recordings. He remembers getting into an argument with a man at Thomas Edison's studio in New Jersey during one early recording date (he can't recall the name of the band he was with).[1] The man told him to put out his cigarette, and he rebutted that the man was himself smoking a cigar and that others were chewing tobacco. The man argued that only pansies smoked cigarettes; men, he insisted, smoked cigars. Tarto learned from one of the other fellows on the recording date that the man who had been admonishing him was Edison himself, who personally supervised the recording session. The band recorded into a single large horn (a system Edison used up until 1925).

Tarto joined the Paul Specht Orchestra at Loew's Theater in Newark in 1922 and stayed with the group for a little over two years. "We were doing vaudeville and then we went to the Astor Roof. We wound up at the Alamac Hotel. I made all the records with them and also the records with the Georgians." He remembers sheet music hanging from the ceiling while the band recorded, there being no room in the cramped studio for music stands. His first confirmed recordings were made on June 24, 1922, with Specht: "A Dream of Romany" and "In Rose Time." His first hot side, "You Can Have Him, I Don't Want Him," was recorded with Specht five days later. As vintage jazz buff Steve Hester has observed, Tarto was thus on record before such early jazz notables as King Oliver, Louis Armstrong, Red Nichols, Bix Beiderbecke, and Muggsy Spanier.[2] Tarto also started his arranging career while with Specht.

In 1923 or 1924, Specht's drummer, Chauncey Morehouse, urged Tarto to go with him to see another band. Tarto, Morehouse, and clarinetist Johnny O'Donnell went; the band they heard included a young bass sax player by the name of Adrian Rollini. Tarto recalls with excitement: "When I first heard Adrian, when I heard that bass sax, I said, 'Oh boy!' And I had a bass sax; I was trying to play it. You know what I did the next day? I went down the bushes and got rid of it. I said, 'I'll never catch up to that guy.'"

In 1923, Tarto began his recording work with Phil Napoleon and the Original Memphis Five, as well as the band's many variants:

Napoleon's Emperors, the Hottentots, the Broadway Syncopators, the Cotton Pickers, the Tennessee Tooters, among others. (Throughout the twenties, the same basic personnel would record on a variety of labels under many different names.) Proudly, he also recalls Christmas 1923 at the Alamac, when Lee DeForest, the developer of the radio, gave all the members of Specht's band crystal radio sets as presents.

Tarto joined Sam Lanin at the Roseland Ballroom in 1925. "And that's where I met up with Red Nichols and those fellows there. While I was with Sam, I was making records with everybody. I was in demand. I was the only one that played string bass and tuba. That's what made me valuable, see." Tarto notes that Lanin got as much recording mileage as possible out of each number.

> Most all the things that I recorded for Sam Lanin were recorded at different times with different studios. Sam would say, "Now here's two orchestrations. I want you to make a different introduction on each one, they're both to be different. Then what you do in the last chorus, put first in this one. Reverse the whole thing around, so it doesn't sound the same, because we're going to do one at OKeh, and we're going to do one at Columbia." The same thing, the same band, but under a different name. So that's the way we'd do those things. And then the arrangements were mostly like a guide because then the guys would improvise on it, you know.

In the second half of the 1920s, cornetist Red Nichols was undoubtedly the busiest jazzman in terms of contracting players for recording dates. He didn't always use a tuba player—he came to prefer using a bass sax on his small group sessions, Tarto notes—but when he did, it would most likely be Tarto. Tarto recalls getting to solo on numbers such as "Ja-Da," "Hot Time in the Old Town Tonight," "Bill Bailey," and "Darktown Strutters Ball" with Red Nichols or Miff Mole combinations. More commonly, as on "Nobody Knows and Nobody Seems to Care" and "Smiles," Tarto would be pumping away in the rhythm section rather than soloing.

In those days, there was *always* work around for a good tuba player. In the mid-1920s, it was common practice for jazz bands to include both banjos and tubas, and since Tarto was unsurpassed on the tuba, he stayed busy, free-lancing. He was known for his strong, moving bass lines, as well as for his occasional solos. He even had an instructional book published, by Alfred and Company: *Hot Breaks and Modulation Techniques,* for tuba, string bass, bass trombone, and mellophone.

Paul Specht's orchestra gathers for a recording session at the Columbia Studio, in the Gotham Bank building on Columbus Circle in New York City, 1922. Front row, left to right: Russell Deppe, Chauncey Morehouse, Johnny O'Donnell, Harold Saliers, Paul Specht; back row: Frank Smith, Frank Guarente, Arthur Schutt, Donald Lindley, Russ Morgan, Joe Tarto. Prior to the invention of electrical recording, musicians clustered closely around the recording horn (which is over Guarente's head in this photo). Note the sheet music suspended from the ceiling near the recording horn; there was no room for music stands. (Author's collection. Courtesy of Mrs. Charles Kenney.)

In 1923 Lee DeForest, who perfected the radio, gave crystal sets (note the earphones) as Christmas presents to the members of Paul Specht's orchestra at the Hotel Alamac. Left to right: Johnny O'Donnell, Artie Schutt (at piano), Elwood Boyer, Arch Jones, Russell Deppe, Dick Johnson, Chauncey Morehouse, Joe Tarto, Harold Saliers. (Author's collection. Courtesy of Mrs. Charles Kenney.)

Joe Tarto backed the Boswell Sisters on records and on their CBS radio program of the early 1930s. Tarto is visible between Connie Boswell, seated on the piano, and Vet Boswell, who stands to the left. At the far right is orchestra director Bob Haring. The guitarist, according to Tarto, may be Eddie Lang. Note that the musicians are holding bars of Baker's Chocolate, the program sponsor. Tarto was still in touch with Vet Boswell more than fifty years after this photo was taken. (Author's collection. Courtesy of Bryan Nalepka.)

Paul Lavalle conducts while Joe Tarto solos on the world's only eight-foot tuba, which Tarto had custom-made for himself years before, for the Broadway show *Rain or Shine*. (Author's collection. Courtesy of Bryan Nalepka.)

And there was always arranging to do. "I have scores that I just found a couple of weeks ago of the waltz medley I made for Fletcher Henderson. I used to make all his waltzes. He used to do all his jazz, and I used to do all his waltzes. See, I got acquainted with Fletcher when I was working in the Roseland because we alternated; they played a half hour and we played a half hour. And that was a band that he had! Louis Armstrong was in that band. That was really a terrific band. Yeah." Henderson's band, at the time it played opposite Lanin's, included Coleman Hawkins, Don Redman, Buster Bailey, and Kaiser Marshall.

Tarto's recollections of having arranged waltzes for Henderson is particularly noteworthy since many younger jazz fans seem to assume that jazz orchestras like Henderson's played hot music all the time. But Henderson's men had to be able to please the various patrons who came to Roseland to dance, and in the 1920s many of them—particularly the older patrons—still liked to waltz. (Even pure jazz records, such as those by the Louis Armstrong Hot Five, were advertised as dance records—you could fox-trot to them. Jazz and dancing were inextricably linked in that period.) Henderson also recorded at least one hot composition by Tarto: "Black Horse Stomp" (1926).

After his stint with Lanin, Tarto recalls, Vincent Lopez called him and asked if he were interested in going to Europe, to England. "When we came back to the States—we were gone three months—he asked me if I would like to stay on. So I stayed with the band for quite a while." He continues:

> Then later on, Red Nichols formed a band for Don Voorhees, and we went into the theater and we did a musical called *Rain or Shine*. Yeah. Yeah. Oh boy! That was some orchestra: Joe Venuti was there, Eddie Lang, Frankie Signorelli, Arnold Brilhart, Jimmy Dorsey, Fud Livingston, Red Nichols, Manny Klein, Fuzzy Farrar, Dudley Fosdick—the greatest mellophone player during that period; he was great, nobody ever followed him. He was on a lot of records with Miff Mole and His Little Molers—and, I think, "You Took Advantage of Me." I remember that because he and Miff did a duet thing, it was terrific. Chauncey Morehouse was on drums. That was really some band. Musicians used to come just to listen to the band, even though it was a pit orchestra.

For *Rain or Shine*, Tarto had a custom-made eight-foot tuba, which he subsequently used in every Broadway show (and in many other gigs) that he played. He still has that tuba; in fact, it's become something of a trademark for him.

During the year the show ran, Tarto says, musicians from the pit orchestra often cut jazz records on their own:[3] "For instance, Joe Venuti would say, 'Hey Joe, here's two numbers. Make the arrangements. The vocal—what's-his-name will do the vocal, and the vocal will be in such-and-such a key, OK?' So he'd give me the numbers, and I'd make 'em. I've got the records of them someplace. In one of those records, I had Tommy Dorsey change from trombone to trumpet. And so then in half of the last chorus, Tommy, Manny Klein, and Fuzzy Farrar were playing a thing in there. But Tommy's got the lead on trumpet." (The number, he says, may have been "The Good Old Sunny South.") "Tommy plays a chorus on trumpet, and in one spot, between he and his brother, Jimmy, he's playing, do-do-do-dee, la-da-do-dee, la-da-do-*dee—that* note Jimmy plays on clarinet, because Tommy couldn't go that high. And when you hear the record, you can't tell that it was a clarinet that played it, it still sounded like the trumpet."

Tarto's only confirmed recording date with Bix Beiderbecke and Frankie Trumbauer occurred in September 1927, when the group recording as The Broadway Bell-Hops cut "There's a Cradle in Caroline" and "There Ain't No Land Like Dixieland."

Sometimes late at night, after their jobs, musicians would gather at someone's apartment to listen to records, talk, and drink. Tarto recalls staying out late, not letting his wife, Helen (nicknamed Goodie), know when he might be home. His hours, he admits, must have been tough on her. "I felt so sorry for my wife. I didn't realize, you know. I didn't call her. Tommy [Dorsey] had gotten some new records from somebody and he says, 'Let's go to my place and play some of these records,' and we all went up and listened to these records and the first thing you know, when I got home it was a little after 5 o'clock in the morning. And here my wife was sitting out there on the patio, waiting for me to come home, and she sort of bawled me out a little." That was the last time he stayed out like that, he says.

The frenetic pace of the jazz age did not continue unabated, of course. Tastes in music were changing. Jazz faded as a public attraction. And by the early 1930s, almost all bandleaders had gone from using banjo and tuba to using guitar and string bass. Tarto was tops on the tuba, but there were younger players coming up in the jazz world in the early thirties with more advanced ideas on string bass.

Tarto played tuba in Rubinoff's orchestra on radio's top variety show of the early 1930s: Eddie Cantor's "Chase and Sanborn Hour."

At the time, the orchestra included Fuzzy Farrar and Leo McConville on trumpet, Tommy Dorsey on trombone, and Benny Goodman on clarinet and alto sax. "Rubinoff used to take us out to lunch every now and then," Tarto comments. "So one day, Rubinoff was at the end, and Benny Goodman was over here, and I was over on the other side of the table. And out of a clear sky, Rubinoff came out and started saying, 'You know Benny, when you play that clarinet, it's so beautiful, but when you play your alto sax, it's just like flushing a toilet.' " Tarto laughs at the recollection, adding, "Rubinoff, I want to tell you, was funnier than Cantor!"

In addition to the radio work, Tarto continued to make records. "We made one, 'Life Is Just a Bowl of Cherries,' and Vic Young was the music director and he made the arrangements. And on that record—it was a big one—on that record was Bing Crosby, the Boswell Sisters, the Mills Brothers. And that's the first record that Tommy Dorsey started playing high register." He was also on the classic 1931 recordings by the Joe Venuti–Eddie Lang All-Star Orchestra, such as "After You've Gone" and "Farewell Blues."

Tarto stayed busy throughout the Depression, recording for motion pictures—everything from Betty Boop cartoons to Maurice Chevalier musicals at Paramount—and doing more and more radio work. If tubas were falling from grace in jazz, they were always in demand in the more "legitimate" orchestras. Through the years, Tarto also played in orchestras on recording dates, backing such "serious" singers as John Charles Thomas, Lawrence Tibbett, Richard Crooks, Lily Pons, and Jan Peerce.

From early 1935 through 1936, Tarto enjoyed playing tuba in what he terms a super band led by Red Nichols on the "Kellogg's College Prom" radio show. Gradually, though, he found himself getting fewer jazz-related gigs. He played on "Hit-of-the-Week" recordings of pop songs (which were made on laminated cardboard—the first flexible records—and sold for fifteen cents at newsstands), in Broadway—and even some opera—pit orchestras, in hillbilly bands and polka bands, and on Bill Gale's "Borden's Country Fair" radio show. As record dates tapered off, he filled his days with studio work at NBC, in the 1940s, and later at ABC. Sometimes he played at Nick's in the Village, with Dixieland groups led by the likes of Phil Napoleon, Muggsy Spanier, Bobby Hackett, and Lee Castle. He also played in Lionel Hampton's augmented orchestra at Carnegie Hall in 1945.

From time to time, Tarto took jobs with Paul Whiteman, sometimes playing tuba, sometimes string bass. (Whiteman was one bandleader who retained a fondness for both the banjo and the tuba.) Tarto estimates he was associated with Whiteman, off and on, over perhaps a quarter of a century, up through the radio broadcasts late in Whiteman's career in which Glenn Osser was actually doing much of the rehearsing and conducting. He also settled in for an association of perhaps fifteen years with Paul Lavalle and the Band of America, which performed on radio, a year on TV, and at the 1964–65 New York World's Fair. Lavalle's brand of "beautiful music" was usually far removed from the jazz world, but Tarto—billed as the Tuba Ambassador and playing his eight-foot-high tuba—was prominently featured.

There were frequent appearances with the New Jersey Symphony, and Tarto also lent his rich bass notes to the pit bands of far more Broadway shows over the years than can be listed here, including *The 9:15 Review* (with Nichols and Mole), *Flying High, The Earl Carroll Vanities, Anything Goes, The Boys from Syracuse, South Pacific, Peter Pan, Gypsy, How to Succeed in Business,* and *Oliver.*

In the mid-1960s, Tarto decided he no longer wanted to drive into New York daily. Since then, he's taught and taken occasional gigs, from straw-hat type places to country clubs. He has a group of his own that plays "legitimate" music in concerts, billed as the Essex Brass Ensemble, and jazz music, as the New Jersey Dixieland Brass Quintet: two trumpets, a french horn, a trombone, and a tuba, all playing 100 percent Joe Tarto arrangements. Often they perform at assemblies in public schools. In 1980, shortly after his wife died, Tarto played tuba in a TV movie, *Sunshine Is on the Way,* and in 1984 he was a special guest at the Breda (Holland) Jazz Festival.

Periodically, Tarto is visited by people who ask him to listen to old recordings and identify the personnel. (The job of sorting out who played on all of the recordings from the golden age of jazz is far from complete; Tarto himself has been omitted from discographical listings on some dates that he played.) And every day he works on arrangements. For a jazz band in Holland, he has been revising an arrangement of "Muskrat Ramble" that he did for Paul Whiteman in the 1940s. "This is the kind of stuff they want in Holland, and in the foreign countries. They don't want new stuff. They want the old things," he says. A sampling of Tarto's work may be heard on the album *Joe Tarto: Titan of the Tuba* (Broadway Intermission Records 108), with painstakingly researched liner notes by Steve Hester.

Joe Tarto no longer plays string bass, but he still plays his tuba. He enjoys working with banjo artists such as Cynthia Sayer and Eddie Davis and trombonist Rocco Paterno, and he welcomes getting calls to work. "Mostly, all these little banjo bands call me," he says softly. "You see, I know all the tunes.

5

BUD FREEMAN

Hear That Music

Bud Freeman's saxophone playing has often struck me as *delightful.* Now there are plenty of excellent saxophonists around, but exceedingly few for whom the word "delightful" would seem just right. Some play stronger, bolder lines than Freeman. Others play more sultrily. No one else plays quite like Freeman.

There's often something fanciful about Freeman's work, as if he is looking at things from a slightly different angle than everyone else. Those unexpected twists and turns his solos take. (You doubt, at times, if he's ever going to be able to get comfortably back to the theme. But he always does. Or almost always does.) The way he'll state a theme strongly and then seem to back off from it a bit. That sense of wonder he can project. The slender but impressive sound he gets. Surely Freeman's is one of the most individual, immediately recognizable of all jazz voices. And that individuality is one of the hallmarks of a true jazz great.

Freeman has long been a favorite of mine. He was one of the very first jazz soloists I was able to recognize from his style. As a boy, checking out old Tommy Dorsey records, I got a kick out of discovering sides that included solos by that Freeman fellow. So you can imagine my pleasure when I arrived at the 1985 Conneaut Lake Jazz Festival and producer Joe Boughton told me Freeman was a surprise guest. I enjoyed soaking up his music and talking with him then. One of the main reasons I repeated the nearly 500-mile trip to Conneaut the following year was to see Bud Freeman again.

Freeman's conversations are much like his sax solos. They take unexpected twists and turns. They wander far from the theme and then return to it. They're filled with periodic questions and qualifications. And they're usually delightful. He also tends to accent unexpected *words* for emphasis; the very rhythm of his speech is distinctive.

During our talks in 1985 and 1986, we covered the waterfront. I learned a bit about everything from the Austin High Gang, of which Freeman was a charter member, to Zen Buddhism, which he has studied in more recent years. At one point or another, he recommended specific books and movies and offered his views on nuclear arms, race relations, and various Greek gods. The list of things that interest him is a long one. He still makes frequent concert appearances in the United States and abroad, as well as occasional lecture appearances. Not bad for a gent in his eighties.

On most anybody's list, Bud Freeman would be rated as one of the all-time great jazz tenor saxists.[1] He was, along with Coleman Hawkins, one of the two major jazz saxophone stylists to emerge in the 1920s.

Now Freeman didn't grow up in a vacuum; no one does. As a teenager in Chicago in the early twenties, he was fortunate enough to have witnessed firsthand the greatest jazz then being produced in America. He heard young Louis Armstrong, Bix Beiderbecke, and others when they were all in Chicago. Certainly, he was in the right place at the right time.

Freeman freely admits that many performers had an influence upon him, that he enjoyed—and learned from—gifted instrumentalists, singers, and dancers. And yet, Freeman's is as wholly original a musical voice as can be found in jazz. We cannot say, as we can with most jazzmen, that he initially sounded like so-and-so and then gradually developed his own identity. Quite simply, no one was playing tenor sax like Bud Freeman before Bud Freeman. He essentially blazed his own path.

Compared to most jazzmen, Freeman did not take up his instrument until rather late. Even after he first began playing professionally at age eighteen, it took him some years before he made up his mind that he really wanted to make music his career. He loved music, but he loved a lot of other things, too. All he and his younger brother, Arny, initially knew was that they wanted to be artists of some kind. Both savored the jazz they heard as teens, but they were also avidly interested in literature, painting, classical music, and drama. Arny, who listened to the same hot jazz that Bud did, made acting his life's work, going on to appear in many plays and later on television.

Bud Freeman is a natural raconteur whose recollections of his early years provide an intriguing portrait of an artist as a young man—an artist who might well have gone into another field besides jazz. In fact, when Lawrence F. "Bud" Freeman was born on April 13, 1906, the word "jazz" hadn't yet entered the public vocabulary. Americans began to grow jazz conscious only after the success of the Original Dixieland Jazz Band in 1917. "When I was a boy," Freeman says, "ragtime was the music one heard. So, we were all influenced by that. But I didn't become a musician until I was about eighteen years old." That's when he did his first *professional* gig.

Perhaps Freeman's earliest musical experiments were at drumming. As a boy, he played with a pair of drumsticks his father had brought home years before, a souvenir from the Spanish American War. He would beat them on a chair, accompanying his mother or others when they'd play the family piano. Later, after his father bought the family's first Victrola, he would drum along with recordings by singers such as John McCormack and Enrico Caruso and by then-popular orchestras led by Paul Whiteman and Isham Jones. His interest in drumming, however, was not deep or long-lived.

When Freeman was fourteen, he got into the habit of going to the huge Senate Theater on Sunday to watch movies. They were silent, of course—talkies had not yet been invented—but they were accompanied by a pit orchestra, conducted by Paul Biese, a highly paid regional celebrity. Biese, who led orchestras in movie palaces and hotels, owned a diamond-studded saxophone that glittered in the spotlight of the otherwise darkened theater. The sound and the shininess struck Freeman, who was at a most impressionable age, and he decided he would certainly like to have a saxophone. But he wasn't yet thinking of becoming a jazz musician.

I suspect that Freeman was at least as much impressed by the glamor as by the music (Biese was not a jazz player), for there is a streak of the dandy in him. He is always smartly dressed and contends that he has loved good clothes since he was twelve. Even when he was a scuffling, up-and-coming young musician, he recalls, he sported fifty-dollar shoes. And he and his brother both had the same boyhood idol: the Prince of Wales (who later became Edward VIII). The prince seemed the epitome of elegant sophistication and the two brothers started dressing as he did: dapper, with a carefully tied Windsor knot and neat peg-top trousers. They copied his walk, his mannerisms, even his speech. Freeman, a confirmed Anglophile, still speaks with something of a British accent.

The Freeman brothers enjoyed seeing *Journey's End,* a popular British drama about the Great War. In one scene, a heavy-drinking captain is asked by a cook in the trenches if he would like a nice plate of sardines. The captain replies slowly: "I should *loathe* it." That line slayed the Freeman boys. It became their pet response to anything they didn't care for: I should *loathe* it. When he was perhaps fifteen, Bud saw an English touring production of *Macbeth.* Although he didn't understand what all of the words meant, he was fascinated by the sound of them.

Something else happened to Bud Freeman when he was around fifteen that profoundly affected the direction his life would take: he became friends with a group of boys near his age who were avidly interested in music; and he got a C-melody saxophone, a now-extinct but then-popular instrument.

"We met in high school, Austin High School," he says of the group that would go down in jazz history as the Austin High Gang. "Jimmy McPartland, the cornet player, played before I did. [Frank] Teschemacher played the violin and later the clarinet. Dave Tough [the drummer] played professionally before all of us. He was at Oak Park High, but he had a girl at Austin, so he used to come over." The McPartland brothers, Jimmy and Dick (who played banjo and guitar), lived on the same street, Superior Street, as the Freemans. Jim Lanigan, the tuba and later string bass player in the group, loved jazz but eventually went on to play symphonic music. Dave North was the pianist.

Freeman could not read music; in fact, his initial contribution to the group consisted of swinging on the single note he knew how to play. Later, Dick McPartland taught him chords so that he could jam with them. The Austin High Gang played initially for their own enjoyment and then at high school socials. "I was really lucky," Freeman says, in recalling those friends of his youth. He became particularly close to Tough, who was two years his junior but looked older. Tough had already been out on the road drumming professionally, and he became an important overall influence on Freeman.

The professional band that the group initially favored in 1922 was the Friars Society Orchestra, which shortly thereafter became better known as the New Orleans Rhythm Kings. Freeman's friends first heard recordings by the band at a soda shop where they hung out after school. Because they were so impressed by what they heard, they formed their own group and named it, in homage to their inspirers, the Blue Friars. Freeman says he admired C-melody saxophonist Jack Pettis of the Friars Society Orchestra, whom he heard live at Mike Fritzels' Friars Inn, as well as on records.

The Chicago-based Friars Society Orchestra was the second important white band to emerge in the history of jazz, after the pioneering Original Dixieland Jazz Band. Like the ODJB, the Friars were offering their interpretation of the jazz played by black bands of New Orleans (although their playing was rhythmically freer, more spontaneous than that of the ODJB). Freeman would soon be exposed to the genuine article, however. And once he heard the far more powerful, far more emotional jazz of King Oliver, he lost his initial enthusiasm for the Friars.

Looking back, Freeman doubts that he would have become a professional musician had he not been exposed to King Oliver's Creole Jazz Band. Oliver opened at the Lincoln Gardens, a huge black dance hall in Chicago, on June 17, 1922, and soon sent for twenty-two-year-old Louis Armstrong, who came up the following month from New Orleans to join him as second cornet in the band. At that time, there was no better jazz band in the country than Oliver's, which included Lil Hardin (soon to be Armstrong's wife) on piano, Honore Dutrey on trombone, Bill Johnson on banjo, Baby Dodds on drums, and Johnny Dodds on clarinet.

It should be noted that Oliver's success was still of the local, not national, variety. Back in 1922 there was no network radio (which in the 1930s would rapidly develop national reputations for bands), and there were no remote radio broadcasts, even on local stations, to bring King Oliver's music to the attention of people beyond the physical confines of the dance hall. Oliver's band would not cut its first records until April of the following year. But in the meantime, the band's fame spread via word-of-mouth as it played nightly to enthusiastic, nearly all-black crowds.

Dave Tough, the first of the Austin High Gang to discover King Oliver, soon had the whole group hanging out at the Lincoln Gardens. Freeman recalls that they were all knocked out by the great beat the band had. And, he adds, by the simple fact that Oliver and Armstrong were geniuses.

> When I was sixteen, King Oliver and Louis came to town. They were playing at a place in the black section of Chicago, and we heard about it, and we went out there. And once we heard that music, we said, "If we're going to become musicians, that's the way we want to play." Because there was so much freedom of spirit in the music . . . it was a happy kind of music.
>
> . . . if it had not been for that kind of music, [I] would have been some kind of artist. I mean, maybe a sculptor, maybe a painter, a writer—I've always loved words. Maybe, you know—we loved the theater, the cinema, something in

the arts. So we were very lucky, really, to have had this environment of music.

Hearing that music altered the course of Freeman's life. He sensed that he was picking up an invaluable education at the Lincoln Gardens. He was learning a lot, he believed, from his involvement in the jazz world—not just about music, but about living life fully. And he remains grateful for the understanding that his father, a garment cutter, showed. The average Chicago parents would hardly have looked favorably on the idea of their sons hanging out until all hours at a dance hall—a black dance hall, no less—listening to jazz when they could be cracking the books or getting jobs and bringing money into the house.

My parents—well, Mother died when I was sixteen [and] my father never troubled me about this, never asked me why don't I go to work or why don't I go to school, because he was glad that I didn't belong to a gang and that I was doing something creative. And he loved artists anyway. He was not an artistic man himself—he worked very hard—but he loved the idea that he had two sons who were artists.

We lived in a very lovely area called Austin, a suburb of Chicago. And the people in the neighborhood used to have meetings, and they'd call up my dad and they'd say, "Mr. Freeman, why don't your boys do something? Why don't they go to school? Why don't they go to work?" And Dad would say, "You don't understand. My boys are artists. They're different. They're crazy. They're different than we are. And you're going to hear about them one day."

He was a wonderful father. Without my father we could not have done it, you see. Because we never paid any rent. He never took anything from us. And he always used to say, "Boys, there'll always be something to eat here for you, no matter where you go." We'd roam off somewhere and come back and he was just—he was a very sophisticated man. Lovely man.

And I'll never forget . . . after having been brainwashed by the community about our doing something, my father dared to come into our bedroom one morning at 7:30! A cardinal sin, as we had been out all night, listening to King Oliver and Louis and the black musicians on the South Side, because that was our music. *We had to hear that music as one had to eat.* We really loved it, you know, and felt it. That's the point—feeling the music—you can't teach that.

Now, Dad came in and shook my brother, and my brother

> sat up very indignantly. And Dad said: "You boys are going to get up! You're going out into the world. You're going to get jobs. And you're going to live as do other normal people!" Whereupon my brother, in stentorian Shakespearean fashion, said, "Sir, how *dare* you wake us before the weekend!"
>
> And so Dad walked out very sheepishly, because he didn't know—he felt that he had done a terrible thing. He felt very guilty about it. And that was the last we were ever to hear of that. My brother was sixteen then, and I was eighteen. He had just broken into the theater, and I had just begun to play professionally.

School held minimal interest for Freeman. He was bored there. Indeed, he *loathed* it. In grammar school, he had flunked some classes and been left back. Yet, he had also put on a play, "The Jack of Hearts," which he cast, directed, starred in, and even performed a dance routine in—to the great surprise of one teacher who had previously known him only as another poor student. Today, no doubt, Freeman would be labeled a "gifted student," but back then he was mostly a puzzle to his would-be educators. How could a presumed dullard stage and star in a play?

Freeman thought most of his classes were childish—they certainly weren't stimulating—and he didn't do all of the work assigned to him. But he did read a lot—books of his choosing, not the school's. He wanted an education, he explains, but not the trivial one he felt he was being fed. As a teen, he was impatient to get on with his life, to *be* somebody. He didn't know if he would become a writer, sculptor, actor, dancer, poet, musician, or what—but he knew that he didn't want to be ordinary.

"I was in and out of high school quite a lot," he remembers. He was still in high school, in fact, when he first began working professionally.

> The education I wanted was a tutelary education, which I was to get, because I loved books, as I do today. Reading is, outside of women, my chief hobby. And the books that we wanted to read, that we were cognizant of as kids, were esoteric, disallowed books. You could get kicked out of school for reading the books that we read . . . Rabelais, Theofil Gautier, all the French school, the Russian school. And you take Flaubert, I mean *Madame Bovary*—we were reading [it] when we were children, you know. . . . the principal found out about it

> and had my Dad come down to the school. And Dad said, "Well look, I think it's wrong that you take this view. They're not getting anything immoral out of the book; it's just beautiful writing." Because Dad was a reader, too. And he beat the principal down in the arguments. . . . They wanted to kick us out of school. But they didn't *really* want to kick us out of school, you see, because they needed the students, because if a lot of students leave a school, who is to blame? The dean or the principal. They say, "What's wrong with the school?"
>
> Anyway, we were destined to get a tutelary education. I've had so many professor friends around the world. And if I wanted to learn a language, I studied it. If I wanted to learn something, I did.

Of the Austin High Gang, Freeman notes, "We were all readers." If they discovered Greek mythology, for example, they were reading about it out of sheer interest, not because some teacher assigned it or because they were striving for some degree. Davey Tough, in particular, was a valuable mentor. Freeman respected his judgment and recommendations, whether they were about literature, music, or painting. "Here's how I learned about painting," Freeman recalls.

> . . . Dave Tough called me up one day—I was about sixteen—he said: "Bud, the Louvre has sold all of its Cézanne to the Chicago Art Institute. Let's go over and have a look at it." So I went over and saw this first painting of Cézanne, you know, the fruit on the table, and it looks as though it were just waiting to be plucked. And I said to Dave, "I wish I could say something about this magnificent thing." And Dave said: "That's the best thing you'll ever say about it. There are no words for these things. They're magical." And Dave knew all about it. So it was through Dave that I developed an interest, sort of a third eye.
>
> And then, of course, now when [I was] about eighteen, we were listening to the modern composers, the Stravinskys, the Debussys, the Shostakovichs, the Prokofievs, the Gustav Holsts—you know, we were listening to all of that. And it was not until maybe ten or fifteen years ago that I went to Beethoven and Mozart and Brahms and Bach and Haydn. We started with the modern ones. And when so-called bebop came along [in the 1940s], I was not impressed with it, although I was impressed with Dizzy [Gillespie] because he was a masterful musician and impressed with Charlie Parker because he was

some sort of genius, and I loved Bud Powell's playing—he was a magnificent player. Because I had *heard* all the rich harmonies, you know, the whole-tone scale, the augmented fifths, and the harmonies of the great—of the modern composers of my childhood. And so what the so-called beboppers were doing was not new to me.

It was the music at the Lincoln Gardens, however, that most fully captured Freeman's interests. He immersed himself in it, gaining an exposure not just to black music but to black culture in general that the average white youth of his generation certainly never had.

The black people lived in their area. And because of the prejudice, the stupid conditions that existed, they were not allowed to come into the white man's area. But we were allowed the privilege of going into theirs, and they welcomed us with open arms. We could go into their clubs, and we never had any trouble. In fact, there was a big fat doorman, a black doorman—the guy must have weighed 400 pounds. And we'd all come up, all well dressed from high school, and he'd say—and he was so nice: "I see you're all out here to get your music lessons tonight." Now that was a sage thing for him to say. He knew.

Not only were Freeman and his friends hearing the finest music they'd ever heard, but they were seeing an entirely different way of life. His eyes are bright, his voice filled with a gentle enthusiasm as he recalls those times. He enunciates his words distinctly.

Here were these people who had nothing—and yet had such a beautiful spirit of living! The way they danced, the way they felt, the joy they had when they were out—and they could tell you they had nothing! So we learned from that. The man who is greedy, who wants to be a millionaire and everything—there's no way you're going to get that without hurting somebody else. So we learned as artists that—yes, we wanted to make a living in our art, [and] as we did, we went on to become world-renowned. We were very lucky, of course. But we were *dedicated*. . . . That part of my life was a beautiful life, because I was learning. And I was living.

Freeman became friends with Armstrong and other musicians whose playing he admired so much. And unlike the typical white youth of his generation, he paid no attention to the "color line." He comments:

> Now, for instance, if some black friends came into my home, we'd be sitting around in the living room, somebody'd be playing the piano. Louis [Armstrong] would be sitting there, talking and telling stories, and my father would come home from work. And he'd just look at everybody and say, "Hi, fellows," and he'd go on into his reading room. And all the black musicians would say, "Gee, your dad sure is a cool guy." And I said, "What do you mean?" He said, "Well, he didn't even pay any attention to us." I said, "Well, my dad doesn't. My dad's—he just believes in, you know, people are people." So, you know, I didn't go into it, because that would have been condescending. That would have been stupid. And then I'd—we'd go out and I'd go to Louis's house. And Louis had a chef, and he used to cook us red beans and rice. . . .

It is important to Freeman that proper credit be given in any discussion of the origins of jazz. "All white musicians who are worth their salt know that the black man started, created this music," he says. "The music comes from, as far as I'm concerned—I used to go to the black churches to hear it, and they used to swing better than most bands." There's a kind of hush in his voice, a sense of wonder, as he speaks. "This soulful singing. Bessie Smith was a church singer. She was the greatest blues singer that ever lived. Ethel Waters. They all learned that in their churches."

Freeman's first professional gig came when trumpeter Wingy Manone arrived in Chicago from New Orleans and got a ballroom job. Teschemacher and Freeman worked with him three nights a week while Freeman was still attending high school. Then they began getting jobs with unknown bands in dives, mostly on the South Side. Jazz was hardly recognized as an art form in America. As often as not, the real jazz Freeman wanted to play was found in low-life places.

Freeman was rather green when he first began working as a C-melody saxophonist. One of his early gigs (1924) was at the Calumet Inn in Sheboygan, Wisconsin. Dave Tough had been working there with an elderly vaudeville pianist named Lyman Woods. Woods liked Tough's work enough to accede to Tough's insistence that Freeman be hired. (Tough said he would quit if Woods hired anyone else.) Woods often got drunk—to numb himself, he said, to Freeman's inexperienced playing—and when Tough finally left to take a better job, Woods told Freeman he'd kill him if he didn't leave immediately. As a musician in Chicago in the 1920s, Freeman says, he wound up playing in plenty of mob-controlled joints, but Woods's was the only death threat he ever received.

Taking a moment to reminisce about working in mob joints, Freeman comments:

> I was about nineteen years old and I got a call from one of Al Capone's henchmen. Now I never knew Al Capone; I never saw him. I didn't socialize with those people. I didn't call them by name. One didn't do that. It wasn't healthy. But they were all very nice to musicians, anyway. I played in all their places. So I went over one day to look at his place, and here were these guys standing around with collars turned up, very sinister-looking guys with black hats and guns on the other side. And I felt a little frightened of all this, and I said, "Tell me, I don't think I want to work here. You see, I'd like to finish my education and I want to live long enough to do so." Whereupon he put his arm around me and he said, "Buddy, I don't want youse to worry about nobody in this here joint, because nobody in this here joint'll hurt you unless he gets paid for it."

Prohibition, it should be remembered, was a tremendous boon to organized crime. Before the introduction of the Volstead Act in 1919, gangsters had done some business in gambling, prostitution, and (on a small scale) narcotics. But Prohibition enabled them to supply something nearly everyone seemed to want: liquor. Although it could not be sold openly, it was sold readily in speakeasies, to which people flocked. That, in turn, provided employment for plenty of musicians. It also made the mob rich and powerful. By 1927, in fact, Al Capone, who had consolidated control in the Chicago area, was earning profits of about $60 million annually, mostly from sales of beer. From the mob's point of view, Chicago was a great town.

"And you know," comments Freeman on mob violence, "I never saw anything. With all these bullshit moving pictures and television shows about the gangster era, we never saw anything like that! Chicago was a safe place to live, as it is today. I could walk with a girl at 4:00 in the morning through the park. Nobody ever bothered—because they [the gangsters] were the control. They didn't want any trouble, you see, because it was bad for their businesses. The government would come down and would close them up. Do you understand? So the last thing they

wanted was trouble. And when you worked for them, you got paid."
Does that mean there weren't shootouts in the clubs?

> Oh, nonsense! I mean, they had them out in Cicero—you know, it was bound to happen—but never in a crowded nightclub. These men, these bandits, used to hang out in nightclubs all the time. They wouldn't get up and—once in a while, a guy on drugs, which was a rare thing in those days, might shoot up a place, but he was careful just to shoot at the lights. Because, you see, they were business people.
>
> I was never frightened in those days because those people never bothered anybody but themselves. They were in competition for territorial rights to sell booze. They weren't into drugs and all that, in those days. It was beer and wine and bourbon that they probably made themselves, or they might have had a deal with a legitimate firm. It's a strange thing that during Prohibition, more people drank in the world than ever during repeal.

Freeman worked often with his Austin High compatriots, the Blue Friars, as well as on his own, as opportunities arose. Eventually, Husk O'Hare took over the Blue Friars, presenting them (circa 1924–25) under the billing of the Red Dragons and then as Husk O'Hare's Wolverines, after the demise of the original Wolverines, which had featured Beiderbecke.

In April 1925, Freeman got his first tenor sax and realized this was the instrument for him. He had decided that the sound of the clarinet and cornet were too "obvious" but that the tenor conveyed a certain subtlety. One tenor man Freeman liked was Prince Robinson, who played with McKinney's Cotton Pickers. The often whimsical Frank Trumbauer, who played C-melody sax, also exerted a general influence on many young saxophonists—Freeman included—in the mid-1920s.

From time to time, Freeman took jobs in commercial (nonjazz) bands, such as Herb Carlin's at the Hollywood Barn, Art Kassel's on tour, Jack Gardner's theater pit orchestra, and Spike Hamilton's at the Opera Club—the latter being a band whose music he found so puerile and commercial that he hired a replacement for himself and went over to sit in with Thelma Terry's band instead, at the Golden Pumpkin. The plethora of commercial bands, playing unimaginative stock charts (as was common in the period), was the bane of the true jazzman's existence. The best jobs, in the hottest bands, never seemed to last very long.

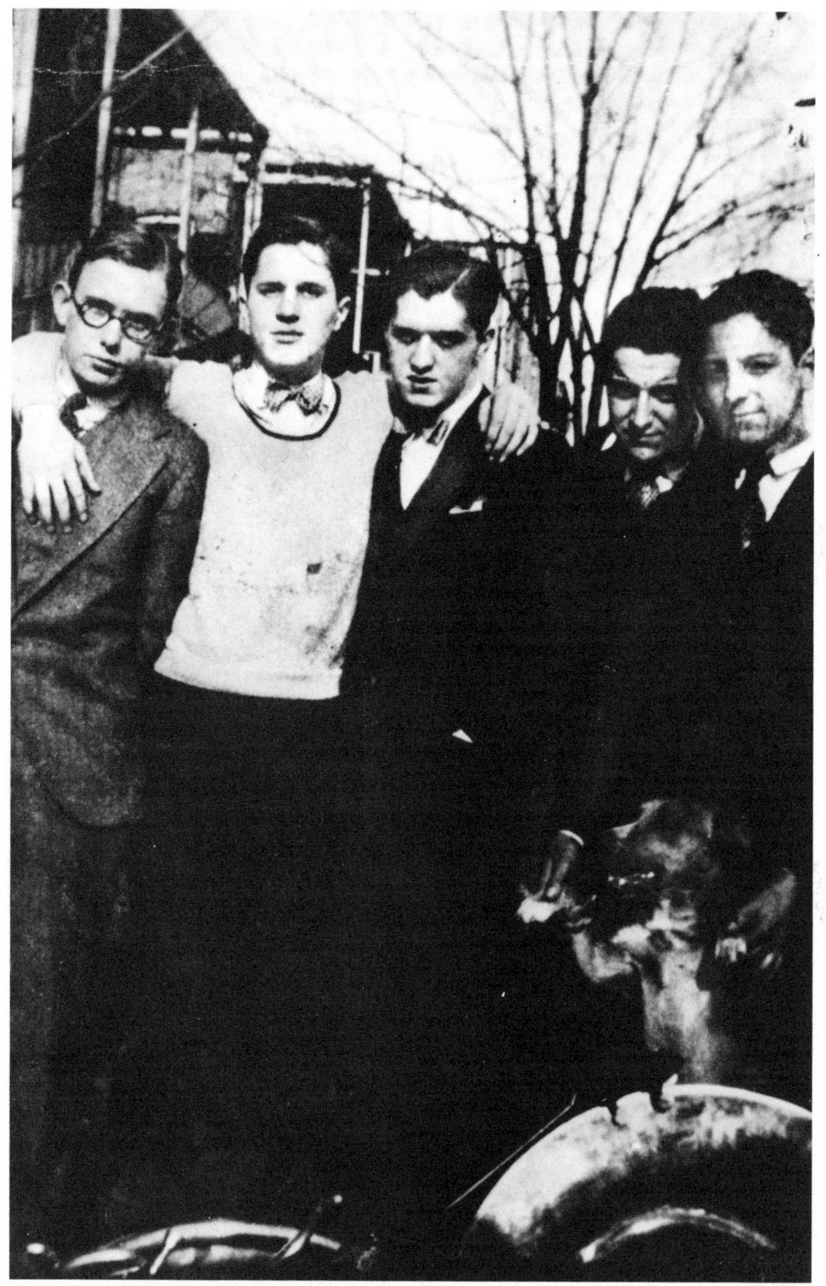

Four Austin High Gang members in Chicago, circa 1927. Left to right: Frank Teschemacher, Jimmy McPartland, Dick McPartland, and Bud Freeman, along with Freeman's brother, Arny, who became an actor. (Courtesy of Duncan P. Schiedt.)

Pee Wee Russell, Jack Lesberg, Jimmy McPartland, and Bud Freeman, probably in the early 1960s. The year isn't too important, though, because players of Chicago-style jazz like Freeman were forever getting together. (Author's collection. Courtesy of the Institute of Jazz Studies.)

The World's Greatest Jazzband of Yank Lawson and Bob Haggart, at the Roosevelt Grill in New York City, 1969 or 1970. Left to right: Ralph Sutton, Bob Wilber, Bud Freeman, Bob Haggart, Yank Lawson, Billy Butterfield, Gus Johnson, Jr., Lou McGarity, and Carl Fontana. (Author's collection. Courtesy of the Institute of Jazz Studies.)

Bud Freeman, caught in a characteristically playful pose, at the 1985 Conneaut Lake (Pennsylvania) Jazz Festival. (Photo by Chip Deffaa.)

Freeman was playing, briefly, in Art Kassel's band at the Graystone Ballroom in Detroit (1926) when he first encountered Coleman Hawkins. (Hawkins was in Fletcher Henderson's band, which was playing opposite Kassel's.) From hearing Hawkins, who was essentially the first tenor sax jazz soloist—the player who would exert a profound influence on most tenor saxists of the next two decades—Freeman realized that the tenor sax could be a strong solo voice. But he worked out his own idiosyncratic style.[2]

So who were important influences upon Freeman musically? "Now there's an interesting thing," he reflects.

> I heard Hawkins when I was about nineteen years old. I was not influenced by his playing, but I was influenced by the idea that a man could play with such powerful authority. Because the tenor was sort of an accompanimental instrument in a jazz band. You see, I played—in the so-called Chicago style they threw out the trombone, and I played—I used to weave in and out between the clarinet and the cornet lead. Now, of course, Hawkins was always a big band player, and he became a powerful soloist. And I was just amazed, because I hadn't become a soloist yet. So it was on the strength of having heard Hawkins's authoritative voice, and the power, that I became a tenor player. But I never tried to play like Hawkins. I wanted to do my own thing.
>
> If I [was] influenced by anybody, it was black dancers of my childhood—Buck and Bubbles, you know, John Bubbles and Baby Lawrence and all of the great black dancers. Bill Bailey. . . .[3]
>
> And then, probably the greatest influences in my life: Louis Armstrong and Bix, as horn players. But the truly great influences were the pianists. . . . there was James P. Johnson, who was Fats Waller's mentor. Fats Waller was another. Willie "The Lion" Smith. And Luckey Roberts. Now Luckey Roberts—now all of these guys were great accompanists to singers. Ethel Waters used to say, "If you couldn't sing, these people, these great pianists made you sing." So there were powerful influences out there. Then, of course, I would say that I was influenced by several of the clarinet players: Jimmie Noone, Benny Goodman, Buster Bailey, Johnny Dodds.
>
> But then as I came on and started to become my own being, as it were . . . this strange style that I play is mine. You see, I have been faithful to that way of playing, although I

admire what other people do. I admire Eddie Miller's lovely sound, and Scott [Hamilton], and I admired Hawkins and Lester Young.

Lester Young, of course, I thought had the best taste, was the best jazz tenor player I ever heard. I thought he was the best. Yet he started to play eight years after I did. And there was an odd thing that everybody says we sound a little bit alike. Now I'm not going to sit here and say that Lester Young was influenced by me, but Lester Young told a lot of people that he used to listen to those things that I made with [Tommy] Dorsey [1936–38]. . . . I must have made over a hundred sides, maybe a hundred sides. Now, that's all right with me, but you cannot say that a man that great was influenced by anybody. If he was, he was influenced by Louis Armstrong, as I was. Very powerful. And he was influenced by Bix, too, real strong by Bix. Lester and I were very good friends. And he was also very strongly influenced by an Indian by the name of Frank Trumbauer. You can hear the influences. Having had the same background of influence sometimes makes Lester and me sound a little bit alike.

But there was one chorus—a guy played a record that I made with Tommy [Dorsey] on a thing called "Everybody's Doing It" [1938]. And the guy said that Lester Young told him that he used to play my chorus of that all the time. And I was very flattered because, you see, in that style that Lester played, there was nobody that could touch him. Think of how powerful he was. Hawkins was the hegemony, the big tone, and everybody was copying him. You know, he was the powerful player. Everybody tried to play like him. I didn't try to play like him, but most players did, with the big tone. And Lester Young came along with this little tiny tone and just took over the whole world. There's an amazing thing about power. It can be very timid—timorous—and quiet, can't it? Real power.

Louis Armstrong, of course, was a major influence on nearly all musicians who came up in that era. Freeman comments: "I realized when I heard Louis play—I realized that I was hearing a true, truly religious music. I was not a religionist, you see. I believed, when I was quite young, that if a man is a decent man and lives his life as a decent, loving man, that's as close to God, any god, as you can ever get. All the rest of it is just terribly commercial. It's very difficult for us to be decent and loving all the time because man's nature is not good. Time has taught us that tigers and lions are much better creatures."

Bix Beiderbecke, who showed that jazz could be played with subtlety without losing impact, left his imprint on Freeman as well. Beiderbecke was a member of the Wolverines when they played in Chicago (late 1923–early 1924). He returned to Chicago in the spring of 1925 to play for several months in a house band at the Rendezvous Cafe; and he later came through, after he had made the big time, as a featured member of the Paul Whiteman Orchestra. Freeman says of Beiderbecke: "Oh, we were very dear friends. . . . He was one of my idols. He and Louis were the true geniuses. Now, there's one thing about Bix. He didn't know, neither did Louis—they didn't know they were geniuses. They were just nice guys, you know. And Bix had a drinking problem, but not when he played. You cannot play that beautifully if you're drunk. He used to get pretty stoned when he wasn't playing, but when we played—every time I played with him we were cold sober. But, you know, he destroyed his body." Beiderbecke took three "cures" for his drinking, Freeman recalls, but he was unable to solve the problem.[4]

Freeman also marveled at the great blues singers, many of whom he heard in clubs as well as on records. "Oh, I heard them live. Bix, the great Bix, took me [and Teschemacher] to hear Bessie Smith in a little bit of a place—I can't remember the name of it now. Jimmie Noone had the group, a little quartet, and ohhhhh, it was just magnificent! And Bix would get drunk and throw all his money at her. Oh yeah. He felt that music so deeply." Bessie Smith's singing was like a symphony to Freeman, and she more or less spoiled him for other singers. After having heard her in her prime, it has been hard for him get thrilled over other singers.

A list of who influenced him would not be complete, Freeman notes, without including

> . . . my dear friend Dave Tough, who was a powerful influence on me in everything, you know—education and love for the arts, and, of course, music. Dave Tough was so great a drummer that all of the so-called avant-garde drummers you hear today—*all* of them, all the black drummers—were influenced by Dave Tough. And they'll tell you that. They'll tell you that themselves. Dave Tough is a little white guy, a little Scot, but he understood the black man's music, as I did. We lived it, see. And, of course, we never had any of that

> stupid, you know—I don't know if you know this, but people are taught prejudice. [Freeman's voice is so gentle here.] We're not born with it. If a child is taught that another ethnicity is beneath him, then he's going to grow up believing that. We never had that. My father always said, "Always remember that everybody has a life to live." And if you grow up understanding that, and feeling that, you'll never have any prejudice, and you will love your fellow man.

Thankful that he was raised with those values, Freeman acknowledges that he would not have become the musician he did if he had been taught the racial prejudices most people he knew had been taught. He adds: "I don't know if you have noticed that theatrical people are very sophisticated. They're worldly. They don't have that [prejudice]. They're beyond that. And I don't recall any of it ever happening with jazz musicians. They all loved one another." Here Freeman is idealizing a bit, for some of the white jazzmen of that era, who obviously drew heavily from black musicians stylistically, nevertheless retained their share of racial prejudice. But certainly Freeman and Tough showed no signs of it. They moved freely within black culture, had romances with black women, and so on. They were rebels, set apart from conventional society, creating their own music and living life the way they wanted to. They were also set apart from many jazz musicians, whom they found boring. Freeman and Tough were both interested in all the arts—theater, writing, and so on—while the average musician they met seemed interested in little more than music.

Freeman still didn't think of jazz as something one could make a living playing, though it was clearly important to him. He and his friends immersed themselves in it. Once or twice each week there would be a new 78 issued by Armstrong or Beiderbecke or James P. Johnson or Ethel Waters or Fats Waller, and the gang would get together to have a party and play the 78 all night long. And, of course, Freeman always loved improvising, rolling off in his own direction while a band played behind him. The prospect of making some satisfying jazz records on the side intrigued him. But much of the music he actually had to play to support himself was routine. It was far from obvious that Freeman would ever be able to make a living primarily by playing the music he enjoyed.

Clarinetist Milton "Mezz" Mezzrow, who sometimes gigged with the Austin High Gang in the 1920s, suggested one day during a slow spell that they drive out to Hollywood and get Freeman into the movies. (Freeman notes that he always had a flair for the dramatic.) So they piled into Mezzrow's $3,000 Marmon, which he had bought on a $28-down type of deal, and headed west. Before they had gotten very far, though, the car wound up being repossessed. Undaunted, Freeman hocked his horns for $125 so they could buy a Ford and continue. When they ran out of money in Kansas, they wired home for more. Mezzrow came out of the Western Union Office beaming, waving $250 in cash at Freeman, Freeman's brother, Arny, and drummer Josh Billings. But right behind him was the Western Union clerk, highly agitated because he had misread the money order, which turned out to be for $25. Fate did not intend for Bud Freeman to go to Hollywood.

In Chicago in the mid- and late 1920s, Freeman jammed with the likes of Bix Beiderbecke, Benny Goodman, Tommy and Jimmy Dorsey, Gene Krupa, Joe Sullivan, Eddie Condon, and trombonist Floyd O'Brien. At one such jam session, at the Three Deuces, he connected with singer Red McKenzie. That, in turn, led to Freeman's recording debut on December 8, 1927, on the OKeh label. The septet with which he recorded was billed as McKenzie and Condon's Chicagoans, but members of the Austin High Gang formed the nucleus. The group included Jimmy McPartland, cornet; Frank Teschemacher, clarinet; Bud Freeman, tenor sax; Joe Sullivan, piano; Eddie Condon, banjo; Jim Lanigan, bass; and Gene Krupa, drums. They recorded "Sugar" and "China Boy"; eight days later, they cut "Liza" and "Nobody's Sweetheart." All four sides pulsed with a nervous excitement.

The two McKenzie-Condon Chicagoans sessions were of landmark importance. They effectively displayed what would soon become known as Chicago-style jazz. All of the soloists on these records would go on to become famous individually. And, after breaking the ice with this first recording date, it became much easier for each of them to get others. In subsequent years, the players worked frequently with one another.

The early New Orleans bands had stressed ensemble playing, collective improvisation. But the Chicagoans, typically, would start a number with the whole band and then go into a series of solos. The band would join in again for a couple of bars at the close of each solo, to give the next soloist an exuberant send-off, before wrapping things up with a well-thought-out (usually by Teschemacher), intricate ensemble finale. The band would push the beat strongly in both ensemble and solo passages, with the rhythm section kicking things along hard.

Freeman soon got an invitation to join Ben Pollack's band, a superb, jazz-oriented twelve-piece orchestra that went into the Little Club in New York City. When Freeman came on board in the spring of 1928, the band included fellow Chicagoans Jimmy McPartland, Benny Goodman, and Gil Rodin. Glenn Miller, initially featured on trombone, was replaced shortly thereafter by the far more imaginative Jack Teagarden. While with Pollack, Freeman began playing one number that has remained an especial favorite of his: "You Took Advantage of Me." He took part in only two Pollack recording sessions, on April 6 and 26, 1928; at both, the band recorded takes of "Singapore Sorrows" and "Sweet Sue, Just You." Freeman left Pollack after only a few months, which he soon concluded was a mistake.

Preferring the freedom of small-group jazz work to playing in big bands, Freeman opted to reunite with fellow Chicagoans Teschemacher, Krupa, McKenzie, and Condon. Unfortunately, their hot improvisational style failed to wow New York audiences, for most listeners still favored a smoother, more commercial style of playing. The Chicagoans found employment backing a dance team at the Palace. *Variety* proclaimed them "the worst band ever assembled" and *Billboard* reported that "the dancers didn't even bow to their accompaniment." After reading the reviews, Freeman didn't stick around long enough to get paid. Dave Tough had gone to France, and Freeman opted to pay him a visit. He and fellow tenor saxist Babe Russin earned their passage to Europe by playing aboard the liner *Ile de France.*

Back in New York after two weeks abroad, Freeman gigged as he could. He did some dates with a Meyer Davis society band and worked for the more jazz-oriented Roger Wolfe Kahn and others. He also began getting more and more jazz record dates. (In the 1920s, record companies issued plenty of sides by jazz groups put together just for recording dates.) For example, Wingy Manone led a sextet that included Freeman and Gene Krupa on a September 4, 1928, session that produced "Downright Disgusted" and "Fare Thee Well." Freeman's first record date under his own name came on December 3 of that year. He assembled eight musicians, including Chicagoans Krupa, Dave North, and Floyd O'Brien, to record an instrumental, called "Craze-O-Logy," and "Can't Help Lovin' Dat Man," with Red McKenzie on vocal.

In 1929 Freeman got in on a date with Benny Goodman's Boys, a seven-player group that included Wingy Manone and Joe Sullivan; they cut "After Awhile" and "Muskrat Ramble." That same year, Freeman was one of Mills's Merry Makers, an eleven-piece group organized by Irving Mills for a record date. The band included Jimmy McPartland, Jack Teagarden, Jimmy Dorsey, Pee Wee Russell, and Ray Bauduc and cut sides such as "12th Street Rag" and "After You've Gone."

More important to his career was the work Freeman did in 1929–30 with Red Nichols. Nichols was about the busiest contractor for jazz record dates in New York, and his sides enjoyed great popularity. When he began using the Chicagoans on records and for some live performances, on tour, it meant they had really arrived. On June 11, 1929, a Nichols group, recording as the Louisiana Rhythm Kings, including Teagarden, Pee Wee Russell, Joe Sullivan, Dave Tough, and Freeman, cut "That Da Da Strain" and "Basin St. Blues." The next day, recording as Red Nichols and His Five Pennies, the same players, plus some others, cut "Who Cares?" and "Rose of Washington Square." On August 27, 1939, Nichols used Teagarden, Freeman, Krupa, Goodman, and four others to record "By the Shalimar," "Carolina in the Morning," and "Who," which included a brief but engaging sample of Freeman's free-wheeling solo work.

Freeman made the date on May 21, 1939, when Hoagy Carmichael and His Orchestra (including Beiderbecke, Goodman, Krupa, Joe Venuti, Eddie Lang, Tommy Dorsey, and Bubber Miley) cut celebrated sides of "Rockin' Chair" and "Barnacle Bill the Sailor." And he was there on September 15, when Carmichael and company (including Beiderbecke, Teagarden, and Jimmy Dorsey) recorded "Bessie Couldn't Help It" and "Georgia on My Mind." Freeman was also in on Beiderbecke's final session under his own name, on September 8, 1939, when "I Don't Mind Walking in the Rain" and "I'll Be a Friend with Pleasure" were recorded. The Dorsey brothers used Freeman for a session on November 7, in a twelve-piece pickup band that included such mainstays of the New York white jazz recording clique as Glenn Miller, Eddie Lang, Joe Tarto, and Charlie Margulis.

Then, on October 30, 1930, the two greatest tenor saxists of the era—Freeman and Hawkins—were brought together for one of the first racially mixed jazz recording session, under the nominal leadership of Red McKenzie; the septet also included Goodman, Condon, Josh Billings, and Fats Waller. But the sole side recorded with both Freeman and Hawkins, "Girls Like You Were Meant for Boys Like Me," was not issued at the time. It made its first appearance, decades later, on an LP.

It should be noted that virtually all of the bands recording or appearing in clubs, dance halls, and theaters in those years were racially segregated. Thus, posterity has been denied hearing the leading white and black musicians working together. Even if they admired and respected each other in life, and jammed together when opportunities permitted, they could not freely record together. For example, Freeman was a good friend of Louis Armstrong, but they did not have an opportunity to record together in this period. Freeman and Fats Waller recorded together just once during this time, even though they, too, were friends. "I was always visiting Fats Waller," Freeman recalls.

The issue of racial equality is important to Freeman. He made a point of telling one late-1930s interviewer that if he were big enough, he'd have a racially mixed big band of his own, and he predicted that racially mixed bands were the coming thing, since musicians of both races could learn from each other. On his second recording session under his own name, on December 4, 1935, Freeman used both white musicians, such as trumpeter Bunny Berigan, pianist Claude Thornhill, and guitarist Eddie Condon, and black musicians, such as bassist Grachan Moncur and drummer Cozy Cole. Racially mixed groups became more common as the 1930s wore on, with small recording jazz groups becoming integrated before big bands did.

"When I lived in New York, I had a girl in Harlem," Freeman comments.

> Oh sure. See, the Cotton Club show—most of the gals had white boyfriends. They were beautiful. They were black models, beautiful gals. Not that they were beautiful, it was just that they were lovely, lovely girls. And it was a natural thing that in time to come, the whites and the blacks were going to get together. . . .
>
> I'd have a girl, say, from the Cotton Club or some other black revue, and I'd take her into a white nightclub. And people would—prejudiced people, bigoted people—see, people don't really want to be hateful, they're taught that. How else could they become that way? And silly. Or I might be staying at some black musician's household, and I'd tell my white friends about it, and they'd say, "What are you, an *n*—lover?" [He can't bring himself to use the term "nigger," even in quoting someone else.] And I'd say, "Yeah! Especially the women!" [He laughs.] And they looked at me—they didn't know what to make of me, because they didn't know. And they became curious. They'd say, "Well are they different?" And I'd say, "No, they're just woman. They're just people." They'd say, "You mean to tell me they're not, not—you know, better in bed?" I said, "For Chrissake man, you have the same problem with all women. If you're a

man, you're going to have problems with a woman. What the hell's the matter with you?"

I say this because there's so many people who don't understand. The only hope this world has is that all people begin, as of this very moment, caring about one another. Because if they don't, we're in trouble.

Freeman says that Chicago, where he now lives, is "a sort of prejudiced town. But it has—just the fact that there is a black mayor [the late Harold Washington] is very healthy. He gave me an award, by the way."

Freeman's greatest musical kicks may have come from playing pure jazz in small groups, but from 1928 through 1938, he earned most of his income playing in big bands, not all of which were very jazz-oriented. He was always available for small-group jazz record dates and also got into after-hours jazz jam sessions from time to time. But the big band work was what paid his bills.

With the Depression, record sales fell off sharply. There were fewer recording dates generally, and far fewer in hot jazz, which in the early thirties was much less popular than sweet music. (Hot music enjoyed a resurgence with the breakthrough of Benny Goodman's big band in 1935.) In 1931 and 1932, Freeman did not record any jazz sides, but he had better luck in 1933, when he got to record sides with bands led by Jack Teagarden, Eddie Condon, and Joe Venuti. The Condon sessions, with such players as Max Kaminsky, Floyd O'Brien, Pee Wee Russell, and Sid Catlett, produced two classic Freeman recordings: "The Eel" (a number Freeman is still playing—and if you've heard "The Eel," you've heard the essence of countless other Freeman solos) and "Home Cooking." The Venuti sessions, which included Benny Goodman, Adrian Rollini, and Joe Sullivan, yielded such fine sides as "Jazz Me Blues," "In De Ruff," and "Doing the Uptown Lowdown."

In 1934 Freeman cut jazz sides under the leadership of Rollini, Wingy Manone (with a band that included such notable players as Dicky Wells, Artie Shaw, Jelly Roll Morton, John Kirby, and Kaiser Marshall), and Mezz Mezzrow (with a ten-piece band that included Kaminsky, Reunald Jones, O'Brien, Benny Carter, Willie "The Lion" Smith, and Chick Webb), recording such numbers as "Sendin' the Vipers" and "35th and Calumet." The following year brought us "New Orleans Twist," recorded under the leadership of arranger Gene Gifford, with a band including Manone, Bunny Berigan, Matty Matlock, and Claude Thornhill; and, under Freeman's own leadership, "Keep Smilin' at Trouble," "The Buzzard," and "Tillie's Downtown Now," the latter two with Freeman on clarinet. Free-lance jazz recording work in 1936 included sides with bands under the nominal leadership of the three Ts (Jack Teagarden, Charlie Teagarden, and Frank Trumbauer), Mezzrow (whose septet included Frank Newton and Willie "The Lion" Smith), and Berigan.

During this period, Freeman was almost certainly the greatest white tenor sax player on the jazz scene. Some may have preferred Eddie Miller's playing, but his style derived heavily from Freeman's. Prominent (and controversial) French jazz critic Hugues Panassie in 1936 called Freeman "one of the greatest hot musicians of all time." He insisted that no white player came close to Freeman and that, among black tenor saxists, only Coleman Hawkins could be placed on the same high level.

> Bud, from the purely hot point of view, is one of the most perfect of all musicians because his style is completely simple, is of a superb intelligence, and never suffers as a result of sheer instrumental virtuosity. . . .
>
> To my way of thinking, a tenor saxophonist wishing to learn to play hot would study Bud's style more profitably than that of any other musician. . . .
>
> Not enough justice has been done Bud Freeman. He is a far greater musician than is generally realized. I owe him some of the greatest musical enthusiasms of my life. Anybody who doesn't know or fails to appreciate Bud's work in "Nobody's Sweetheart" and "China Boy" by McKenzie-Condon, in "Sendin' the Vipers" and "Apologies" by Mesirow [*sic*] is deprived of one of the greatest joys that the hot style can give. I shall never cease to marvel at this admirable halfchorus in "Nobody's Sweetheart" where Bud, using very few notes, creates, by means of very short phrases each clearly separated, a hot architecture of unique perfection. It is striking how Bud draws hot effects from the simplest combinations. Milton Mesirow was the first one to remark about it to me—in 1929 when he was in Paris. He said to me, "Listen to the final eight measures of Bud's chorus in 'China Boy' and see what Bud obtains by a simple repetition of notes." It is, as a matter of fact, a marvelous passage which should always be cited as a typical example of the PURE hot style.

> In the slow numbers, such as "Home Cooking" and "Can't Help Lovin' Dat Man," Bud is extraordinary in his depth, his balance, and his repose.[5]

Some jazz buffs will question Panassie's placing Freeman above all black tenor saxists except for Hawkins. But remember that, at the time, Lester Young had not yet made his recording debut and was not widely known. Other noteworthy tenor saxists included Chu Berry (then with Fletcher Henderson), Dick Wilson (then with Andy Kirk), and Ben Webster (then with Cab Calloway), whose greatest work was still ahead. In mid-1936, then, Freeman was a major figure with rather few rivals.

On the small-group jazz sides that earned Freeman his reputation among jazz devotees, he and his colleagues were generally aiming to please themselves. They wanted to make the best music they knew how, and they didn't expect the records to become commercial hits. However, the big bands Freeman worked in were generally far more commercially oriented. In their pursuit of the elusive smash hits, they played and recorded an awful lot of quickly forgotten slop. As a member of Joe Haymes's big band, for example, from sometime in 1933 until early 1935, Freeman was required to play section parts on innumerable pop tunes of far from lasting value. He participated when the band recorded songs with such memorable titles as "I've Got a New Deal in Love," "The Bathtub Ran Over Again," "Under a Beach Umbrella with You," "Oh! You Sweet Thing," "Ten Yards to Go," "Oh Leo! (It's Love)," "Cross-Eyed Kelly (From Penn-Syl-Van-Eye-A)," "Rock and Roll," and the aptly named "It's All Forgotten Now."

Early in 1935, Freeman joined Ray Noble's splendid new orchestra, which was organized by Glenn Miller and opened at the Rainbow Room in New York. With players including Pee Wee Erwin, Charlie Spivak, Will Bradley, and Claude Thornhill, the band could offer a convincing brand of hot as well as sweet music. Freeman was in the Noble band when it recorded some of its best sides, including "Down by the River" (February 9, 1935), "Chinatown My Chinatown," and "Way Down Yonder in New Orleans" (both June 10, 1935), "Bugle Call Rag" and "Dinah" (both October 9, 1935).

In the spring of 1936, Freeman joined what would be his most important big band: Tommy Dorsey's. The Dorsey band recorded close to 150 sides during Freeman's two-year stay, and because Dorsey really appreciated what Freeman had to offer, he was given frequent solo opportunities.

When Freeman joined up with Dorsey, the latter had been leading his own band (after quitting the Dorsey Brothers' Orchestra) only since the previous September, but he was making frequent personnel changes and improving his band steadily. He had recently brought Davey Tough in on drums, which made the band especially inviting to Freeman. Max Kaminsky was the hot trumpet soloist; others featured during Freeman's tenure included Bunny Berigan, Pee Wee Erwin, and Johnny Mince. Dorsey also had a small jazz band, the Clambake Seven, within his big band, which ensured Freeman additional solo space.

From the start, Dorsey focused attention on Freeman. One side, cut at Freeman's first recording session with Dorsey on April 15, 1936, began with a Tough drumroll and vocalist Edythe Wright announcing: "Introducing our new addition to the Clambake Seven, Bud Freeman and his tenor sax, 'At the Codfish Ball.' Take 'em away, Davey!" Tough showed his stuff on the drums, followed by the whirling sax of Freeman before the rest of the group joined in. It was unprecedented for Dorsey to give a new member of the band an introduction like that, for sidemen came and went frequently. But Dorsey wanted the public to know that he had made an important addition to the band in hiring Bud Freeman.

In that period, Dorsey's band played many of its up-tempo instrumentals in a Dixieland style.[6] Freeman felt right at home. He was in the Dorsey band—and often heard to good advantage—when it recorded such sides as "Ja Da" (April 15, 1936), "That's a-Plenty" and "San Francisco" (both June 9, 1936), "After You've Gone" (October 18, 1936), "Marie" (January 29, 1937), "Stop, Look and Listen" (an especial favorite of Freeman's; April 15, 1937), "Beale Street Blues" (May 26, 1937), "Little White Lies" (December 6, 1937), "Yearning" and "Everybody's Doing It" (both March 10, 1938; Freeman's final session with Dorsey). He also turned in some great solos on plenty of forgettable pop tunes.

Freeman did one vocal during his period with Dorsey: a mockery of various saccharine, Mickey Mouse bands entitled "Am I Dreaming (Or Are All My Favorite Bands Playing)?" in which he pretentiously declaimed the words of a ridiculous bit of pop fluff the band had recorded straight with Edythe Wright that same day. The mocking version, which is still fun to listen to, was released anonymously. Does Freeman enjoy listening to the sides he recorded with Dorsey? "Not very much," he answers. "I like to feel that I was really just learning to play."

Looking back upon his big band years, Freeman has mixed feelings: "The big band era for me lasted about ten years [1928–38]. I must have played with a half a dozen name bands, namely, oh, Roger

Wolfe Kahn, Joe Haymes, Zez Confrey, Paul Whiteman, the Dorsey brothers, then Tommy Dorsey, Benny Goodman. Of course, I was lucky, I worked in the bands as a soloist—that was the only reason I was there. But I hated the life, because we were always living on the road." Not much interested in big band section work, particularly under the dominance of often egotistical bandleaders who were usually his inferiors in terms of creative ability, Freeman needed to be able to express himself as a soloist. Dorsey always allowed him that. Freeman recalls that the Dorsey band he joined had not yet achieved great popularity for its leader. Dorsey's big breakthrough came in early 1937, following the release of a 78 with "Marie" on one side and "Song of India" on the other.

> . . . We got our hit record from a band that was playing an arrangement of "Marie"—a black band, in Philadelphia. And I remember, I went to the leader of the band—I knew all the guys—and they were playing the pit. It was a black theater, the Nixon's Grand, and Tommy's band, a white band, would sell it out. And they had a wonderful chorus and some wonderful comedians. I enjoyed that one week we were there. And this band had this wonderful arrangement of "Marie," taken from a Don Redman idea. Or he might have created the idea of using these voices singing riff phrases behind a given theme: "On a night like this . . . we go pettin' in . . . ." And it swung, you see. . . . this phrasing behind the melody of "Marie" was so natural. "On a night like this . . . [Freeman snaps his fingers to the beat] you go pettin' in the park. . . ." You know, it just fit so beautifully.

"Marie" proved to be a smash for Dorsey. Jack Leonard sang the lyrics in his pure, earnest style, while the other members of the band called out riff phrases behind him, ending with a shout of "Mama!" Berigan followed that with a trumpet solo that became a classic. The general public could scarcely have imagined that this arrangement, which became permanently linked with Dorsey's name, had first been played by an obscure black band in Philadelphia. Follow-ups "Who," "Sweet Sue," "Yearning," and others were all eventually recorded by Dorsey in the same manner, with riff phrases behind the straight vocal, but none duplicated the great success of "Marie."

According to Freeman, after "Marie" became a best-seller, the band members "all started to make some money. Then Tommy got his own [radio] show, and I enjoyed that in a way, excepting the one-nighters. When we played the hotel, I liked that because we'd get through at midnight. You had some sort of social life. But before we became successful, we'd be on the road in broken-down cars or buses."

Dorsey, of course, featured his own sweet trombone prominently—no trombonist got a better sound—but he also gave ample room to other soloists in the band. He loved Freeman's playing and often encouraged him to take one chorus after another. In live performances, Freeman could stretch out as he never could on records (there was only room for about three minutes' worth of music on one side of a 78), and Dorsey mentioned Freeman by name often enough in broadcasts that the general public came to know who he was. Dorsey was a domineering, temperamental man, in the view of many of his musicians, but Freeman remembers him appreciatively, for Dorsey helped make him famous.

After two years with Tommy Dorsey, Freeman left to join Benny Goodman, making his first recording with Goodman on April 8, 1938. Davey Tough had recently joined the band, and Freeman was glad to be reunited with him. Although they had both known Goodman (who was three years younger than Freeman) since he was in short pants, Goodman did not treat any of his sidemen as buddies. It was *his* band; *he* was the star—and he wasn't crazy about sharing the spotlight. Freeman was given little to do, which was demoralizing. He looks back upon his decision to join Goodman—who he freely acknowledges was a great artist—as a big mistake.

Freeman has to strain a bit to come up with anything good to say about the eight months he spent in Goodman's band. Finally, he acknowledges that at least the band did not travel in broken-down cars or buses: "When I went with Benny Goodman, he had his own parlor car on the Twentieth Century—that great train that ran from New York to California. So that was OK. But I really—I still wasn't doing what I wanted to." With the band when it recorded such well-known numbers as "I Let a Song Go Out of My Heart" (April 22, 1938), "Big John's Special" and "Wrappin' It Up" (both May 28, 1938), he felt—correctly—that his talents were being wasted. When Tough left the band, Freeman's interest waned. He went off on a drinking binge for several days and was fired.

Freeman had continued doing free-lance jazz recording work throughout his stays with Dorsey and Goodman, often in the company of fellow Chicagoans. He had recorded sides, for example, under the leadership of Eddie Condon in 1937 and 1938, along with Bobby Hackett, Pee Wee Russell, Jess Stacy, George Brunies, and George Wettling. He took part, too, in 1938 dates accompanying singers Maxine Sullivan and Billie Holiday. And he had an opportunity that year to work with Louis Armstrong, Fats Waller, Jack Teagarden, and others on a radio show. He also indulged his flair for histrionics by recording a take-off on Noel Coward's *Private Lives,* called "Private Jives," playing Coward's part to Minerva Pious's Gertrude Lawrence.

Freeman made some fine trio recordings, with Stacy and Wettling providing the rhythm, such as "You Took Advantage of Me" and "I Got Rhythm" (January 17, 1938), "Keep Smiling at Trouble" and "At Sundown" (April 13, 1938), "Three Little Words" and "Swingin' without Mezz" (November 30, 1938). He used eight musicians (including Hackett, Russell, Condon, Stacy, and, on some cuts, Tough) for a session on July 12, 1938, that produced "Tappin' the Commodore Till" and "Memories of You." And in 1939 and 1940, Freeman (along with Max Kaminsky, Joe Bushkin, Wettling, and others) played on a memorable series of Lee Wiley recordings, including "'S Wonderful," "I've Got a Crush on You," and "But Not for Me."

After working for Dorsey and Goodman, Freeman could have gotten a high-paying job in just about any big band. But he had been soured by his experience with Goodman and, his confidence shaken, vowed never to work in anyone else's big band again. His first love had always been small-group work with pure jazzmen. Now, he had the opportunity to do occasional gigs with jazz groups organized for private parties. Could he make it financially playing only jazz, maintaining an organized group like the ones with which he had made so many memorable free-lance jazz records? It was certainly worth a try.

The band was billed as Bud Freeman and the Summa Cum Laude: eight players, including Russell, Kaminsky, Condon, pianist Dave Bowman, and valve trombonist Brad Gowans. They proved a great hit in 1939 at Nick's, a prominent jazz joint in Greenwich Village. For fans of this type of music, it was a dream band, playing hot jazz without compromise. Best of all, Freeman no longer had to do section work on mindless current pops. And his new band was receiving attractive recording offers. He told one 1939 magazine interviewer:

> When I worked with big bands, all I ever thought of was pay-day. I wasn't happy in my work—I never felt inspired—I never had a chance to do the things I wanted to do, but now I'm happy for the first time in many years. Now I'm doing exactly the things I feel and like to do, and it's truly wonderful! . . .

> I would rather work for less with a small band and be happy, because happiness means infinitely more to me than money. Nowadays, I feel much more inspired—more energetic. I practice every day, and quite often all day long. Maybe, someday I will be able to master my instrument, although I feel that I still have a long way to go. When I think of those rehearsals with the big bands—how they used to bore and depress me! But now I'm eager to get to rehearsals. It doesn't seem like work anymore.[7]

Playing in this band reminded Freeman of his early years in Chicago, when he and his friends had made joyous music without any commercial considerations.

The Summa Cum Laude held forth at Nick's for seven months. They could have stayed on much longer, but they accepted an offer to go into a lavish musical stage production entitled *Swingin' the Dream,* a jazzed-up version of *A Midsummer Night's Dream,* featuring Louis Armstrong and Maxine Sullivan. That decision proved to be a mistake. The show died a quick death and the musicians never got paid for their work. In the meantime, another band had settled in at Nick's. The Summa Cum Laude, joined by Davey Tough, whom Freeman considered the world's finest jazz drummer, relocated to a midtown joint frequented by underworld types. The band next took a booking at Chicago's Sherman Hotel but did not do well there.

Before the Summa Cum Laude came to an end in 1940, it had made some excellent recordings, including "China Boy," "Sunday," "Big Boy," "Oh! Baby," "Sensation," "Fidgety Feet," "Copenhagen," "Muskrat Ramble," "That Da Da Strain," "Shim-Me-Sha-Wabble," "At the Jazz Band Ball," "After Awhile," "Prince of Wails," and Freeman's showcase specialty, "The Eel." It's interesting to note that none of the above titles—which the band recorded in 1939 and 1940—were new tunes; almost all dated back to the 1920s.

In the early 1940s, big bands were America's preferred musical format, enjoying wider public acceptance than did seven- or eight-piece jazz groups. So for the next couple of years, until he was inducted into the army in June 1943, Freeman spent most of his time leading big bands, playing society parties and country club dates in and around Chicago. He always had smaller jazz units within his big bands, to ensure himself sufficient musical kicks; and he sometimes reunited with his old friends for special occasions, such as a Carnegie Hall concert in 1942 with Eddie Condon, Pee Wee Russell, Max Kaminsky, and Fats Waller. He also made a couple of small-group V-discs with Ray McKinley, Yank Lawson, and others. On one, "The Latest Thing in Hot Jazz" (a spoof), he took the speaking part of a know-nothing jazz critic.

The army sent Freeman to the Aleutians, where he led a big band for most of his twenty-two-month hitch. After his release, in the spring of 1945, he served briefly as house bandleader for Majestic Records, before it folded. He got to record some satisfying jazz sides while he was there. Especially intriguing is "The Atomic Era," with only drummer Ray McKinley accompanying him. He also made appearances leading a quartet at Eddie Condon's Club, for example, in late 1946–47. And there were various concert bookings, including some that mixed both the old guard in jazz—such as Freeman, Joe Bushkin, Hot Lips Page—with members of the new guard—notably, Dizzy Gillespie. In addition, Freeman recorded small-group sides for Keynote and EmArcy records, using the likes of Wild Bill Davison, Billy Butterfield, Charles Shavers, Peanuts Hucko, Joe Sullivan, and George Wettling.

But jazz was changing, and Freeman wasn't quite sure where he fit in anymore. The jazz world seemed to be dividing into two armed camps. During Freeman's tenure in the army, bebop had begun to emerge. The beboppers were now proclaiming themselves to be in the forefront of jazz, rebelling against the past.[8] Freeman wasn't interested in playing bebop, but he didn't want to be lumped with hidebound traditionalists, either. He had always thought of himself as something of a rebel.

Like Freeman, Davey Tough found himself in an uncomfortable position. He got offers to work in traditional jazz joints, like Nick's and Condon's, and he accepted them when he could. But he also made public statements to the effect that he thought a lot of that scene *was* reactionary—aimed at nostalgic, middle-aged Republicans seeking to recall their youth. Tough deliberately sought out other gigs with more "progressive" players. In 1944–45, he powered Woody Herman's First Herd, then in the forefront of modern orchestrated jazz. He was the oldest musician in the crew. Afterward, he free-lanced with both modernists and traditionalists. But despite the universal praise he received for his playing, up until his death in December 1948, he worried that he wasn't "modern" enough to keep up with the beboppers. It was a crisis of self-confidence.

Freeman was similarly questioning himself. He didn't fit in with the Charlie Parker–Dizzy Gillespie–Miles Davis scene. But he could see that some of his contemporaries had begun to stagnate, playing the same tunes night after night at Condon's or Nick's in exactly the same way, usually in an alcoholic stupor. For a stretch in the late 1940s and early 1950s, he made no recordings under his name. In fact, for a few years he gave up playing entirely. It no longer seemed important to him. In 1952–53, Freeman lived quietly in Chile and Peru, focusing his energies on the woman he was with. Musically, it was a fallow period for him.

Back in the United States, Freeman became intrigued by one of the leading modernists, pianist Lennie Tristano, whose recordings he found brilliant. Tristano was stretching the harmonic boundaries in jazz improvisations and had an almost cult following among some of the progressive younger players, such as Wayne Marsh, Billy Bauer, and Lee Konitz. Freeman telephoned Tristano and asked if he could study with him. Tristano was considered a radical thinker in jazz, but he made it immediately clear that he appreciated Freeman's playing just the way it was; he had no interest in trying to "modernize" Freeman's style. They worked together for several months, simply reviewing fundamentals of music. Yet the words of appreciation from this key member of the avant-garde helped renew Freeman's confidence. In subsequent years, he often seemed to take delight in discovering one or another of the young bebop-oriented players who dug his style, as if their appreciation also helped validate his worth.

After he returned to performing, Freeman still felt something was missing in his life. He explored psychotherapy, on and off, for about ten years. While it helped to improve his overall outlook, he was still somewhat disenchanted, demoralized. He eventually explored Zen Buddhism, intently for about four years, and maintains an interest in it to this day. He got into it, he recalls, after the death of a woman he loved. Broken up, in mourning, he poured out his troubles to a total stranger, a black taxi cab driver, who surprised Freeman by responding, "Your problem is you're thinking of yourself." He suggested Freeman read Lao-tzu. Freeman did just that, and went on to read other works, including *Zen and the Art of Archery*. Zen gave him calmness. He no longer was rattled by a critical review or a personal insult.

Freeman's senior years have been quite productive. In fact, he might be considered a model of the gracefully aging elder jazzman. He has stayed true to his own way of playing, without becoming a cliché or a caricature of himself. He most frequently performs as a soloist with a rhythm section. Through the years, however, there have been periodic get-togethers in larger group formats, both on records and in person, with his contemporaries. On one 1957 album, for example, Freeman resurrects the Summa Cum Laude name, reuniting with Pee Wee

Russell, Jimmy McPartland, George Wettling, and Jack Teagarden to record new versions of such oldies as "Sugar," "Nobody's Sweetheart," "Prince of Wails," and "At the Jazz Band Ball." He was even brought together, by George T. Simon, with Coleman Hawkins for a recorded challenge between the master tenor saxists. But most of the time, he has gone his own way, beautifully. Now in his eighties, his work still shimmers with life.

In reviewing Freeman's musical output, it is interesting to note how many times he has recorded different versions of the tunes he especially liked. Always agreeable to recording new material, including originals he composed, he has nonetheless had a core repertoire of tunes, mostly from the twenties and thirties, that he has favored through the years. In 1958, for example, he made trio recordings of such numbers as "'S Wonderful," "Limehouse Blues," and "California Here I Come." "Crazy Rhythm" was a highlight of a 1960 live concert album, and in 1963, accompanied by guitarists George Barnes and Carl Kress, he dug into "Sweet Sue" and "The Eel's Nephew," along with a batch of new things. In 1964 he made quartet recordings of such tunes as "Dinah" and "'S Wonderful," followed in 1966 by quartet recordings of "You Took Advantage of Me," "The Eel," "Sunday," "Three Little Words," "I Got Rhythm," and "Sweet Sue." He also cut a quintet version of "'S Wonderful" and a sextet version of "California Here I Come."

From 1968 to 1974, Freeman was member of the World's Greatest Jazz Band of Yank Lawson and Bob Haggart (whose other members originally were Billy Butterfield, Carl Fontana, Lou McGarity, Bob Wilber, Ralph Sutton, Clancy Hayes, and Morey Feld). He got to do his thing on current pop tunes like "Mrs. Robinson," as well as on old favorites like "The Eel," "At Sundown," "Jazz Me Blues," and "California Here I Come." One of his specialties with the band was "That D-Minor Thing," his own variation of traditional blues. Then, in 1969, backed by the rhythm section of the World's Greatest Jazzband, Freeman made a solo showcase album entitled *The Compleat Bud Freeman,* which included "Dinah," "Exactly Like You," "You Took Advantage of Me," and "I Got Rhythm"; Wilber joined him on "That D-Minor Thing."

In 1974 Freeman made trio recordings with Jess Stacy and Cliff Leeman of "I Got Rhythm," "Somebody Stole My Gal," and "'S Wonderful." That same year he made quartet recordings, in London, that included "'S Wonderful" and "You Took Advantage of Me." Ted Easton's band backed him for a 1974 album that included "You Took Advantage of Me," "That D-Minor Thing," and "Dinah." In Italy, in

1975, he recorded quintet versions of "Exactly Like You" and "Just One of Those Things"; and, with a nine-piece band, he recorded "Sugar," "That's a-Plenty," and "Wolverine Blues." In London that year, Freeman recorded "Keep Smiling at Trouble," "That D-Minor Thing," "The Eel's Nephew," and "Stop, Look and Listen."

And so it continued, through his digital recordings in the 1980s. Freeman had no interest in trying to change with every new trend in music; nor was he interested in falling into the deep ruts some of his contemporaries had. He just wanted to keep playing—and he's done that, never sounding stale or bored. As for bebop, Freeman reflects:

> I would not have played like it anyway because I had to be honest with myself, and play what *I* felt and what *I* do. I think that if an artist is going to make it in any of the fields of art, he has to become his own man. Influence can only go so far, and then you've got to become yourself, or you're just not going to be. You might be a good technician, but you're never going to be a real artist. And that is the great problem with music today. All the young guys are technicians, but they don't say anything. Now you take a player like Eddie Miller or you take Scott Hamilton—these guys play. They tell a story when they play. They're magnificent players. It's all so simple and yet so hard to do.

After leaving the World's Greatest Jazzband in 1974, Freeman settled in London, where he was based until the early 1980s, when he returned to Chicago to live. He has become almost exclusively a concert and festival artist, rarely accepting club engagements. He paces himself, he says; he likes to offer half-hour sets because he doesn't have the stamina he once had. He also believes there is such a thing as giving an audience too much music.

With advancing years, there is customarily some decline in a musician's technical facility. But Freeman never emphasized impressing listeners with dexterous, high-speed fingering or other displays of technical virtuosity in his youth, so whatever decline may have occurred is less evident than it would be for many musicians. (He has suggested, for example, that he cannot play the intricate "Eel" as he once could.) The fact is, there have been some compensatory gains. Freeman's work has a greater depth today than it did in his youth. On lively tunes, his playing has a quicksilver vitality; and on slow numbers, he offers a breathy sensitivity. He comments: "I've been playing for sixty-one years, and I would rather hope that I—if I'm going to go on living—that I get *better* as I play, because I play the horn about an hour every day. I want to get a better sound if I can and have better facility. There are many players who get old and they sort of rest on their laurels. And there's no such thing as that for me. If I can't play well, I'll just stop."

I ask Freeman if he believes he's playing stronger than, say, ten years ago? "I like to feel that I'm playing in better taste," he answers. "Yeah. Stronger may not be the word. I would rather hope that I'm playing more easily. I like to think that I can handle a ballad better than I could, say, twenty years ago. And playing a ballad is probably the most difficult thing. It takes taste, it takes control, it takes a pretty good knowledge of music. And improvisation can be one note, if you know where to put it."

Freeman describes his life today as "so much happier and less complex" than it was in his youth.

> . . . I think that life is far better now than it ever was for me. I have the freedom to select the jobs I want. If a man calls me and he has a job that I don't feel pays enough money, and yet he sounds a decent fellow and genuinely wants me, and says, "This is what I can pay," I think about it. I say, "All right, I like the way you talk; we'll do it." Sometimes I've been disappointed, found that I was working for some monster and I shouldn't have done it. Then, if a guy sounds a little on the pernicious side, then the fee is doubled. Sometimes a guy'll say, "Jesus, I can get another famous tenor saxophone player for a couple hundred dollars less." I say, "You get him! Call him up right away!" And the guy gets nervous. I say, "No, you get him. If money's your problem, I don't want to work for you."

Freeman is by no means a rich man; indeed, he lives modestly in a Chicago residence hotel. But he has enjoyed being able to devote so much of his life to his art and says he wouldn't trade places with any of the well-heeled patrons he has played for. "The millionaires who have no talent have to buy what we have so they can be around it," he comments. "And we're thankful for that." You're apt to spot him chatting freely with his many admirers before any of the concerts or festivals in which he is to play. He's not a drinker—he lives rather an ascetic life-style—but you might find him standing near a bar, regaling listeners with anecdotes of Hoagy and Bix and old-time Chicago. He's an amiable fellow and, one suspects, maybe a bit lonely.

Freeman makes it clear that music is not the whole of his life. In his free time, he is far more likely to listen to symphonic music than to jazz, and his friends include actors, writers, and painters, as well as musicians. I ask him what sorts of things he enjoys doing when he's not playing. "Well, of course, I adore women," he answers. "I adore women. And I love going to the theater. I love the cinema. I spend a great deal of time reading. There's a book, a new book you must get—it's a must for you, it's called *Flaubert's Parrot.* I read it twice." He also urges me to see the film *Prizzi's Honor,* which he has seen twice.

Freeman says that he has been doing some lecturing in recent years. "I've got three of them coming up in the fall. And I'll be doing more of those as I go on. I did a two-hour lecture at the Field Museum, and the people just loved the stories. So that's a lot of fun, and obviously I'm a very gregarious person." I tell him I love his spirit; it's almost as if there's a light inside of him. "Well, that has to be," is his response, "because a lot of people go to sleep at my age. . . . I hate to hear a man say that having women, that's in the past. . . . That makes me ill. Because to me, life without a woman would be death. I've been married twice. They were lovely women, and we were good friends and all that, but I'm not cut out to be a husband. And I guess I like too many different women."

Ever the optimist, Freeman makes little of the fact that he has recently had two operations for a malignancy. He would have been much more worried, he insists, if he were a younger man. But people his age, he declares, actually have a better prognosis with this type of cancer than do younger people.

Bud Freeman seems truly at home onstage. At the Conneaut Lake Jazz Festival, he lets the band play several numbers without him before making a late entrance. He receives pent-up applause from an audience that is eager to hear him. He tells a little story about how George Gershwin, whom he describes as egotistical and unsmiling, used to hate the way Freeman and his friends jazzed up Gershwin songs. He jokes that when Eddie Miller first started coming up, Miller seemed so threateningly good that he tried to hire some of "the boys" in Chicago to kidnap Miller—but when they heard Miller play, they decided they preferred Miller's playing to his own.

At one point, Miller and Scott Hamilton, who is young enough to be Freeman's grandson, join Freeman on an improvised jump blues and then on his much-loved "Crazy Rhythm." The three play the theme together on the latter, with Freeman spinning out additions of his own as they near the end of each phrase. Later, drummer Ray McKinley establishes a tempo for him. "Good tempo, Ray," Freeman assures him. He says he loves to play on the solid beat McKinley lays down.

Freeman bubbles in the spotlight, his patter a distinctive and engaging part of his act. He draws the audience closer to him and confides that the saxophone he uses once belonged to Miller, now seventy-five, who stands alongside him smiling softly. "You know, Eddie's horn plays so easily. I tried to play it once and it just didn't work, because I'm used to things that don't work, you see." The audience laughs. His timing is just right. "But this is Eddie Miller's horn. I was playing a concert with the World's Drunkenest Jazzband [the audience laughs louder] in some little place near Idaho, and in the middle of a ballad my horn fell apart. We called Eddie and Eddie very graciously sent this to me. You know, I got this in four days. He wanted to give it to me, but I talked him into letting me pay for it."

"Anyway, it's a *wonderful* horn. I don't know how it sounds, but it doesn't matter. . . . You see," Freeman's voice drops low, "it's just Eddie Miller's horn." His affection for Miller is touching. But before the sentiment gets too strong, he continues, "So I'm always dropping Eddie's name. What do you have to say about me lately, Eddie?" The monologue takes unexpected twists, as do his solos. There is much audience laughter now, and applause. Contented, without any introduction, Freeman begins playing "Lady Be Good."

6

JIMMY McPARTLAND

The Austin High Gang

"What better thing can a person do in life than do something he enjoys . . . like trying to blow a cornet? Or music? And get *paid* for it. It's amazing! It always has been to me," Jimmy McPartland says, between spoonfuls of grapefruit and orange sections at his snug Long Island home. He has been blowing his cornet professionally now for well over sixty years. As a key member of the Austin High Gang, he long ago earned a permanent place in jazz history, and his recollections would be valuable even if he had done nothing more in his career than play lead horn on the famed recordings that put Chicago-style jazz on the map.

One of New York City's busier jazzmen in the late 1920s, McPartland worked multiple jobs concurrently, and recorded prolifically. He quickly earned big bucks—and spent them just as quickly. For a stretch in the following decade, however, he pretty much dropped out of sight. Then, his career took a sharp upward turn after the war. He entered into a marriage with pianist Marian McPartland that had a positive effect upon his life. He eventually gave up drinking, which had thoroughly destroyed a number of other jazzmen.

Leonard Feather has observed that McPartland "remains one of the best performers in a Bix-inspired, neutral jazz style that he prefers not to hear described as Dixieland."[1] Certainly, McPartland appears to be one of the less-complicated jazzmen. A bluff, rather affable man, he plays his cornet with the aim of producing music that swings and is pleasing to his own ear. And that's about it. He's never striven to make his mark as a composer or to combine jazz with classical music (or anything else). He hasn't sought to produce radically new sounds;

nor has he pondered for long if he might have been better off in another field of art altogether. He's not one for pondering. Today, he is one of the last active survivors of the jazz age of the 1920s. His occasional appearances at jazz festivals are a real link to those years. He can still come across with sassy, vigorous work that drives a band.

McPartland has often been described as a dedicated follower of Bix Beiderbecke. He *did* think the world of his friend, personally and professionally, and he can evoke Beiderbecke better than most trumpeters around today. But he's not out to copy Beiderbecke. He doesn't produce those crystalline, somewhat tense passages; nor is there evidence of the same fragility in his work. And McPartland has a bit of Louis Armstrong's strong, flowing swing in his playing as well. In his youth, McPartland's style was closer to Beiderbecke's. As he's aged, his playing has grown darker, more astringent. Marian McPartland will tell you Jimmy is too modest when describing the individuality of his style, which she noticed the first time she heard him. He could imbue even hackneyed standards with a cocksure vitality that reflected his own personal makeup.

In contrast to Bud Freeman, McPartland doesn't feel that he was destined to become some kind of an artist. In fact, if he hadn't gotten into jazz, he believes that he may have wound up a criminal, for he was a feisty youth, always ready for a scrap. He grew up tough—and fairly bitter at the blows life had dealt him. He was stealing things and getting into trouble with the law before he reached his teens. He says he's lucky that he fell in with the jazz-oriented Austin High Gang.

It's not surprising that both of the McPartland boys—Jimmy and older brother Dick—were pretty good scrappers. Their father had been, among other things, a professional boxer, and he made sure his boys knew how to handle themselves in a fight. A professional baseball player and a professional musician, he also taught his sons how to play ball and, beginning when each reached age five, how to play the violin.

The McPartlands lived at Lake and Polina streets, part of a poor racially mixed neighborhood on the west side of Chicago. Blacks, whites, Italians, Poles, and Irish all lived together. Jimmy, who grew up without racial prejudice, remembers his mother impressing upon him that she never wanted him to use the word "nigger," as some of his friends did. She told him that colored people no more liked being called "niggers" than he liked being called a "shanty Irishman" (his father was Irish; his mother, Scottish).

McPartland recalls that he was five or six (which would have been around 1912–13) when his parents got divorced. His father drank; his mother apparently couldn't cope. The judge placed all three children (Jimmy, Dick, and Ethel) in the Baptist Orphanage in Maywood, Illinois. Jimmy didn't understand legal questions of custody or why the judge made the decision he had. All he knew was that his parents seemed to be abandoning him and that the world was a far from friendly place.

An angry child, McPartland grew understandably angrier when his sister and brother left the orphanage while he was forced to remain. Ethel was taken in by a relative, while Dick, who had been left with a weakened heart after a bout with rheumatic fever, was taken in by his mother. Jimmy stayed behind for what seemed to be an eternity. Looking back, he figures he was in the orphanage a total of maybe two and a half or three years. He felt unwanted, on his own, and he's sure the experience affected him for the rest of his life. He can still recall strongly those childhood feelings of abandonment and of being mad at everyone. He acknowledges having had a chip on his shoulder.

McPartland began causing trouble at the orphanage. One night a matron punished him for his conduct by locking him in the attic, after telling him that tigers were going to get him. He remembers pounding on the door, frightened and crying, until he finally fell asleep. When the matron let him out the next morning, he was still scared and very bitter. Then the orphanage superintendent's son (whose name, Art McGilvery, will remain lodged in McPartland's memory forever) pushed him or said something abrasive to him, and that set him off. He knocked the kid through a glass door. The superintendent branded McPartland "dangerous" and sent him packing. His clothes wrapped in a paper bag, given three cents for carfare, he was taken outside, while it was snowing, and put on a streetcar to his father's place in Oak Park, Illinois. The final indignity was having the boy he had knocked through the glass door help carry out his belongings.

The experiences of those years made a loner out of McPartland, at least on the inside. Eventually, his parents got together again, and his father started a music school. But the McPartland boys grew up a bit on the wild side. They had a gang, the Hermitage Gang, and would steal just about anything they thought they could get away with stealing.

McPartland recalls one exception, when they had an easy opportunity to steal but chose not to. He and his brother encountered eight blind black men making music on the street. They were singing spirituals, accompanying themselves with maybe a couple of guitars, a mandolin, a banjo. The music was really swinging. McPartland and his brother flipped. There was "jazz" in that music, he says; he had never heard anything quite like it. (Jazz, McPartland believes, resulted from the wedding of African feeling for rhythm with European interest in harmonies and melodic lines.) They loved the music and began passing the hat for the men, giving them every cent—a sign of just how much the music meant to the McPartlands.

McPartland recalls that he was put in jail when he was twelve or thirteen. In court, the judge insisted that Mrs. McPartland get her sons out of their rough neighborhood and into a better environment. The directive had a far greater impact than anyone could have foreseen at the time. The family moved to Austin, a socioeconomically "better" part of Chicago, and McPartland fell in with a whole new crowd at the high school. He was soon introduced to the world of jazz and became so eager to be a good cornet player that, as he recalls, he no longer had time to think about getting into trouble.

Music, of course, wasn't new to McPartland. He had played violin first and then peck horn in his father's band (which did marches and ragtime at picnics). But he had never been much interested in the serious music his father had tried to teach him on the violin, and he considered ragtime corny. The jazz he discovered when he was sixteen, though, excited him as no music had before.

Born on March 15, 1907, James Dougald McPartland was younger than the other guys in the Austin High Gang.[2] He had a forceful personality, however, and could comfortably boss around older friends. Before he ever thought of playing music professionally, he had picked up a trade, operating a printing press and making letterhead and business cards for local shops. But when he and his friends discovered jazz, it took over their lives.

"There was a place called the Spoon and Straw, where we'd go after Austin High School," McPartland recalls. "We used to go every day, have a malted milk and a sandwich or something. There was a gang of us. We were all musicians to begin with. Teschemacher, my brother, and I were violinists. Bud Freeman was not, however. He was a good Frisco dancer. He'd do these fantastic dances, you know . . . jumping around. He had great rhythm." The Spoon and Straw had a combination lamp and phonograph machine, with an assortment of records strewn on a table. Customers could listen to the popular dance bands of Paul Whiteman, Art Hickman, and Ted Lewis.

One day in 1922, according to McPartland, some new sides by the Friars Society Orchestra, on the Gennett label, came in, with numbers like "Farewell Blues," "Discontented Blues," "Bugle Call Blues" (all recorded on August 29, 1922), and "Tiger Rag" (recorded on August

30, 1922). The orchestra, which would soon change its name on records to the New Orleans Rhythm Kings, included Paul Mares on cornet, Leon Roppolo on clarinet, and Jack Pettis on C-melody sax. The Austin High kids had found little to get excited about in the comparatively sedate dance band sides, but they stayed until perhaps eight that night playing these new records. This was *it.* This was *jazz.* They decided on the spot to form a band and try to play like the Friars.

Each one chose a different instrument. McPartland picked cornet because it was the loudest; his brother chose the banjo and guitar; Lanigan opted for string bass; Freeman for C-melody sax; Teschemacher for clarinet.

> . . . And away we went! My father was a music teacher, my brother and I had already played violin, so we were familiar. We heard these records in the Spoon and Straw, and we copied the numbers off the records. Played 'em the right tempo. And we'd get the numbers and started rehearsing. And we got good.
>
> My father taught all the instruments anyway. He was a professional baseball player. He was with Anson's Colts, who became the Cubs eventually. An athlete and a musician. And he became a professional musician; he had his own bands—they used to play at picnics, bandstands in the parks. We'd just go and watch him. So we'd had a musical training since we were five years old. So my brother wanted to play the banjo and guitar, and I wanted to play the cornet. And we told Bud to get a saxophone, and he took lessons from my dad. Teschemacher was already a violinist. And then Jim Lanigan—who was going with my sister, Ethel; he became my brother-in-law—decided to take the bass violin and the bass horn. He was already a violinist.
>
> And we rehearsed. Every day after school we'd say, "Let's have a session today." A jam session. Learn the numbers [two bars at a time] off the record. Each guy'd pick his notes, so we got the right harmonies and everything. We developed ourselves, because you were allowed to copy anything from the record of the ensembles, but you had to play your own solo. Each guy had to play his own solo his own way, not the way the guy did it on the record. Without realizing it, we were developing our own style. We just said, "That's not fair, you can't copy a guy's music." Improvising. We just kept that up. Somehow or other, I got pretty good fairly quick.

It took only a few weeks for the guys in the group to learn their first tune, "Farewell Blues," and a few months to master a handful of tunes. Because most of them had a background in music, and because all of them were so enthusiastic, they learned their instruments in just a few weeks. Freeman was the only one who hadn't had any musical training, and Teschemacher sometimes wanted to kick him out because it took him so long to play well.

After school the gang would meet at the home or apartment of one of the members. They'd jam until dinner, go home to eat, then go to a different home and practice from eight-thirty until ten or eleven at night. They supplied music for charity meetings, high school fraternities, and the like. Once, when they played a social at the Austin High gym, a drummer from Oak Park High School named Davey Tough sat in. Tough, who had modeled himself after Baby Dodds, the drummer in the Lincoln Gardens band, became a key member of the Austin High Gang. Dave North, who never did become a name jazz musician, joined them as pianist.

Jimmy McPartland would stomp off the tunes and lead the group, which his brother had named the Blue Friars, after the Friars Society Orchestra.[3] "We got all those numbers [played by the Friars Society Orchestra] and then we got the Louis Armstrong–King Oliver numbers: 'Chimes Blues' [1923], etcetera. We rehearsed every day." He was sixteen when he first heard King Oliver and Louis Armstrong live at the Lincoln Gardens. (The two would sit with their high school–age fans, and Armstrong, who was then twenty-one, would call them "my boys.") The Austin High Gang was so inspired that they did nothing but play music from then on, and they gradually got farther away from the records upon which they had modeled themselves.

McPartland's father liked jazz, but—being of an older generation—was more interested in ragtime, which the gang members found corny. They felt music had to flow, the way King Oliver's blues did. To them, ragtime was kind of jerky. It was also set music. If someone asked for, say, the "Maple Leaf Rag," the pianist or the band played the number exactly as written. Jazz, by contrast, demanded improvisation. When they heard the Wolverines' records in 1924, they were excited anew. McPartland found Bix Beiderbecke's tone to be perfect; and his articulate phrasing left its mark on Teschemacher and Freeman, too.

McPartland had to hustle to get the band work. "I was running a tea dansant at Columbus Park. A dance, 3:00 in the afternoon, and my girlfriend at the door collecting tickets. I was more or less the instigator of the whole thing, like the leader. I was a gangleader type guy. Any fights come up, why I'd handle 'em. I think I was the youngest of the group, but a cocky, very cocky, intolerable asshole, you know—really, now that I look back on it—because I wouldn't stand for any screwing around. So we did this tea dansant, and I gave myself the leader's money and the guys scale or whatever it was."

According to McPartland, it was with very good reason that the group came to be known as the Austin High *Gang:* without a doubt, they could handle themselves in a scrap. He, in particular, took pride in his ability to fight as well as to make music. In fact, with the rough childhood he'd had, he was always ready for a fight. His older brother, he recalls, used to call him Cocky. If there was trouble, his brother would say something like, "Cocky, you want to go?" And they'd go at it.

The band played at every opportunity—on the street, at fraternities, anyplace. One time when they were playing for a fraternity, a listener piped up that their playing stunk. McPartland told the heckler to come closer and say it again. Then, he looked at his brother, who gave an encouraging wink, and started brawling. After that happened a few times, word got around that you didn't dare tell them you didn't like their playing, because they'd beat you up if you knocked them. They were a *gang, the Austin High Gang.*

McPartland says he first met Benny Goodman, who was two years his junior, around 1923. "I worked for Murphy Podalsky, who had Benny Goodman in his band. Benny heard about us and came out and heard us one day. He was just a kid in short pants, and I told him, 'Why don't you get some long pants, Ben?' He says, 'Well, I don't know what to do.' So I says, 'Come on with me.' We went down to Marshall Field's. I got him long pants." McPartland was so knocked out by Goodman's playing that he invited him to hang out with the gang. Goodman wound up playing—for free—at the tea dansants McPartland ran.

Soon good enough to get periodic free-lance gigs as a sideman in various other bands, McPartland was only a sophomore in high school when he began playing gigs with the Maroon Five at the University of Chicago. He also worked with them that summer at Lost Lake, a resort in northern Wisconsin. He looked up to the college men, and they treated him as an equal. They even pledged him to Delta Tau Delta, their fraternity, with the idea that he'd become a real member when he enrolled at the university. McPartland dreamed of getting a good education and maybe becoming a doctor. But fate had other plans for him.

In the fall of 1924, Bix Beiderbecke decided to leave the Wolverines. McPartland, who loved Beiderbecke's playing—his ringing sound, his balanced phrasing, his lyricism—wound up replacing him. He wasn't the band's first choice, however. They initially approached Paul Mares, who turned them down but suggested Joseph "Sharkey" Bonano. They gave Bonano a tryout at the Cinderella Ballroom but dismissed him within a couple of hours. Cornetist Fred Rollison—who later recalled that the Wolverines had head arrangements of well over 100 tunes—didn't satisfy them either. So Wolverines drummer Vic Moore suggested the seventeen-year-old McPartland, whom he'd heard one night.

McPartland didn't quite believe it when he received a telegram, signed by Wolverines leader Dick Voynow, that asked: "CAN YOU REPLACE BIX BEIDERBECKE WITH THE WOLVERINES? $87.50 A WEEK. WIRE YES OR NO. WE'LL SEND TRANSPORTATION."

He considered the Wolverines one of the greatest bands in the country, and he figured the telegram was probably a gag, somebody putting him on. But with the guys in the band egging him on, he wired his answer: "YES. SEND TRANSPORTATION." The $32.50 for train fare to New York was promptly wired back, and all of his friends—Freeman, Tough, Teschemacher, Goodman, Lanigan—saw him off at the South Street station. He was the first from their crowd to make the big time.

"And away I went," McPartland recalls:

> . . . I had never traveled. And I get to New York, and to the Somerset Hotel, and call up this Dick Voynow. And he says, "Get some rest and we have a rehearsal this afternoon at 2:30 over at the Cinderella Ballroom."
>
> I came over to rehearse all the numbers that they had recorded. And I knew everything off the records—I hadn't seen the band live before then—and it was great. And all the fellows said, "That's great. Do you know any other tunes?" Sure, I knew everything. "Running Wild," all the numbers that they recorded, I knew 'em in the correct key and everything else. The same routine. And so those guys were happy as a bug in a rug. "Hey! Great! You're in," the guys said. I'd passed the test.
>
> After the thing was over, I said, "Where's Bix? I'd like to meet him. I enjoy his playing so much." And they said, "Well, he's sitting right out there." And he started to walk across the ballroom floor, and he came up, and man, I was so happy to meet him. I didn't know he was there.

As cocky as McPartland was, he would have been damned nervous if he had known Beiderbecke was listening to his tryout. To someone who'd just quit high school after only two years, Beiderbecke, at twenty-one, must have seemed worldly. "And he says, 'I like ya, kid. Ya sound like me but ya don't copy me. . . .'" It's a line McPartland repeats proudly and often. It may have been a casual comment on Beiderbecke's part, but it carried a great deal of weight with McPartland who took it as praise from the master. (Marian McPartland reflects that the simple affection in those words, "I like ya, kid," meant a lot to Jimmy, who seems to have received so little affection from his parents.)

McPartland recalls that Beiderbecke was soon giving him pointers. "Dick Voynow said, 'I'll tell you what Bix's going to do. He's going to show you the other numbers that we haven't recorded, that we have little arrangements on. You know, intro or an ending or an interlude or whatever. Key change. So forth.' Well, Bix and I moved in together then. He played with the band a couple of nights, I think it was, and then he was going to take off. So he showed me all the numbers, and I'd write things down, remember little arrangements that they had." Before Beiderbecke left to go with Jean Goldkette, he picked out a good horn for McPartland, a Conn Victor, which McPartland paid for on the installment plan.

"I made one record, one side with them," McPartland notes, "'When My Sugar Walks Down the Street' [recorded on December 5, 1924]. Bix wasn't on it, just me. And the banjo player, I know, wanted to make a key change on the thing. Christ, he wanted the key of D concert, which is murder on the cornet. You used to play C, F, and G, but this was in D. The clarinet player couldn't find the notes in that key; he couldn't read. So he says, 'You take it, kid.' And the kid got it. So I played a solo. . . . I just fit in very well, did a good job. They were all happy." He played on one other side with the Wolverines, "Prince of Wails," recorded on December 12, 1924. (In the fall of 1927, he played cornet on four sides issued under the billing of the Original Wolverines, but by that time none of the musicians, except for Voynow, were original members of the band. Without Beiderbecke, the Wolverines no longer had the same appeal.)

The band stayed on in New York for perhaps six or eight weeks and then in December 1924 headed to Florida. "We all went down for a job at the Biscayne Bay Country Club, where we were supposed to open. Opening night we came to the door with our instruments to get set up. Had hired a house and everything. I got a picture of it. Cripes! We get there and this joint was closed because of Prohibition. They'd been selling alcohol," McPartland notes, and federal agents had just raided the place. "We couldn't get a job in Florida. I starved. Man, I had to get a job, just to eat, because all the other guys in the Wolverines faded away quick. They all either got jobs or had enough money to live."

Unable to get back to New York, McPartland hitched a ride over to where a railroad was being built in the Everglades and pleaded to be hired as a laborer. The foreman took him over to where some men were digging to put the tracks through; snakes were coming up out of the damp ground. The foreman said McPartland was too young, that the work was too rough, but he gave McPartland a dime, which bought an O'Henry candy bar—his first meal in three days.

McPartland finally got a job playing music at a party. He was as hungry as he'd ever been in his life. The hosts permitted the musicians to drink whatever they wanted from the bar but offered no food. When he got paid, McPartland hurried to a restaurant and ordered a fish dinner. He started wolfing it down—and threw up. After three days of no food, his body couldn't handle it. He had to settle for soup.

In the end, McPartland had to send home for train fare. A couple members of the Wolverines stayed on in Florida, but the rest went up north and tried to play some dates with substitutes before finally breaking up. The name was too well known, however, particularly in the Midwest, for Voynow to simply abandon it. Eventually, he and McPartland reorganized the Wolverines, using the Austin High Gang. Bud Freeman came in on tenor sax, Frank Teschemacher on clarinet, Davey Tough on trombone, Dick McPartland on banjo and guitar, Jim Lanigan on bass, and Floyd O'Brien on trombone. Only Dave North—the pianist of the Austin High Gang—couldn't be accommodated, since Voynow also played piano.

"We went out on the road, doing one-nighters. Then we'd do two or three days at a theater, and played dances and collegiate proms all over Indiana and Illinois and Michigan, and come back," McPartland recalls. In addition to playing his cornet, McPartland sang, which he continues to do. On the bill with the Wolverines in one vaudeville theater was Bill "Bojangles" Robinson, who later became one of the most famous of all tap dancers. Robinson taught McPartland a dance step that he would do while he sang his featured number, "Oh Boy, What a Girl." McPartland moved around as he sang and broke up the audience. He also learned to mug to prompt even greater audience reactions.

Before long Voynow got an offer to work as an A&R man, supervising recording sessions, for Brunswick Records. He turned the leadership of the Wolverines over to McPartland, who brought in Dave North on piano. Now the Wolverines consisted entirely of the Austin

High Gang. Husk O'Hare, who booked a variety of orchestras in the Chicago area, booked the band and billed it as Husk O'Hare's Wolverines, under the direction of Jimmy McPartland.

"We did very well," McPartland notes. "O'Hare booked us into Des Moines, Iowa, the River View Park—an amusement park—ten cents a dance. We'd play like one chorus or something like that." In Chicago they worked at the White City Ballroom. The band was really swinging now, McPartland recalls, and top musicians were coming to hear it.

> Even Louis Armstrong used to come—he'd listen from behind the bandstand at night because we started earlier than he did. He was over at the Sunset Cafe, and he didn't start till nine or ten, or something like that, at night. And he used to come over early, even when we were rehearsing, and listen to us play back there. He liked our band and liked us—because we loved him!
>
> And I remember Bix was now with Frank Trumbauer and his orchestra, at some place down at Indiana, and on their way into Chicago they stopped by and heard us—and liked the band, you know. It was a swinging band—Jeez! Criminy!—and a good one, well rehearsed and everything. And we'd all go and hear Louis Armstrong together. It was nice.

Chicago was rich in music in the late 1920s. The members of the Austin High Gang worked, at various times, with such Chicago-born contemporaries as Muggsy Spanier, Joe Sullivan, Benny Goodman, Gene Krupa, and Mezz Mezzrow. They also played with musicians from other cities who came to Chicago for long-enough stays to qualify as Chicagoans musically, men like Eddie Condon, Pee Wee Russell, Wild Bill Davison, and Jess Stacy.

Bud Freeman had commented that, in all of his years working in and around Chicago, he had never witnessed any gangland violence. Naturally, I wondered if McPartland had. He recalls one gig, when he was still quite young, at Eddie Tancil's joint, near the racetrack in Hawthorne. "And Al Capone wanted to break up this joint because they were infringing on the Hawthorne racetrack and Capone's territory. With selling alcohol and all that kind of stuff. One night, Capone's men came in, and a guy came up right in front of the band—one of them—there [were] about six or seven of them—and held a gun on us and said, 'You guys just keep playing and you won't get hurt.' And we kept playing 'Rose of the Rio Grande' till it came out our eyes. We all knew Capone was moving in. Word had gotten around."

McPartland never forgot the face of the mobster who held the gun on the band. Much later, he adds, he was playing a gig at another club in Chicago when Capone himself came in, along with the same henchman.

> . . . And he looked at me on his way to the men's room and, you know, gave me a good look. And I looked at him and kept playing. He came back from the men's room, went back to the table with Capone, and I was watching him. And he was talking to Capone and pointing to me. So Capone sends him—the guy comes up to the bandstand with a $100 bill. He says, "Al wants you to play 'My Gal Sal.'" I said, "Great." And he says, "Do you know me?" I says: "No. I never saw you before in my life. Who are you? No. Thanks a lot for the hundred." I put it in the kitty. And Al nodded on his way by, going to the men's room, with the cigar in the mouth, says, "How are ya kid?" You know, that was all.

For McPartland, things began to fall into place, professionally, in 1927–28. In rapid succession he took part in a number of significant recording sessions. With McKenzie and Condon's Chicagoans (including Frank Teschemacher, Bud Freeman, Joe Sullivan, Eddie Condon, Jim Lanigan, and Gene Krupa), he recorded such briskly exciting sides as "Sugar," "China Boy" (both on December 8, 1927), "Nobody's Sweetheart," and "Liza" (both on December 16, 1927).

McPartland joined Ben Pollack's orchestra, staying with the group from late 1927 to late 1929. He had been brought in by Benny Goodman. His first session with the band, on December 7, 1927, yielded "Waitin' for Katie" and "Memphis Blues." (Fellow Chicagoan Bud Freeman joined the band the following spring.) January 28, 1928 saw the recording of two sides by Benny Goodman's Boys with Jim (McPartland) and Glenn (Miller): "A Jazz Holiday" and "Wolverine Blues." On June 4, 1928, "Benny Goodman's Boys (including Miller, Tommy Dorsey, Fud Livingston, and Ben Pollack) laid down "Jungle Blues," "Room 1411," "Blue," and "Shirt Tail Stomp."

By this time, the Pollack band had landed in New York and McPartland was getting rapidly caught up in the New York free-lance recording scene. He found plenty of work. In 1928, for example, he recorded sides for the Broadway Broadcasters and the Ipana Troubadours (both Sam Lanin groups), Joe Candullo and His Orchestra,

Eddie Condon and His Footwarmers, Jimmy McHugh's Bostonians, and a Victor Records all-star orchestra. He also did a slew of sides for Irving Mills. But his main employer was Pollack—smartly played dance music with hot jazz solos.

In New York, McPartland roomed with fellow Pollack band members Benny Goodman, Harry Goodman, and Gil Rodin. He considered Benny Goodman a great guy, a real pal—a frugal fellow, admittedly, but one who always took good care of his parents. (McPartland is one of few jazz musicians to speak warmly about Goodman as a person.)

McPartland remembers Glenn Miller as a taskmaster. He says, for example, that Miller refused to rewrite an arrangement that he thought was needlessly tough to play; rather, Miller insisted that McPartland practice until he mastered it (which he did). Miller's hard-driving, competitive personality also came out when he and McPartland would play tennis. McPartland, who was not much of a tennis player, says that Miller hit every ball hard. One time they played for money, and after McPartland won the first game, Miller got madder and madder, and he began hitting the ball increasingly harder. But he kept hitting into the net or over the line, and McPartland kept winning.

Miller was an excellent band musician, a fine technician, in McPartland's view, but he was not a gifted jazz improviser. One night Pee Wee Russell phoned McPartland and Freeman and urged them to go to a speakeasy on Fifty-first street and Broadway to check out a man he insisted was the greatest trombonist he had ever heard. They were both skeptical but went anyway—and met Jack Teagarden. When he took his horn out of its simple cloth case and began playing "Diane" for them—with no accompaniment whatsoever—the tone, the lazily relaxed, imaginative phrasing awed them. Soon Teagarden was the trombonist in the Pollack band and Miller just did the arranging.

Besides playing cornet, McPartland also periodically got to sing with the Pollack band, as did Dick Morgan and, on occasion, even Pollack himself. "But Benny Pollack was terrible. An excellent drummer, a nice guy, a horrible singer," McPartland declares. Pollack once used Dorothy and Hannah Williams, a song and dance team, as vocalists on a record. In McPartland's judgment, they were very good; they could really swing. And they caught the eyes of plenty of fellows, McPartland included. He fell hard for Dorothy Williams, whom he eventually married.

The full twelve-piece Ben Pollack band played written charts, and there was a smaller jazz band within the big band that featured Pollack on drums and Goodman, McPartland, and Teagarden—the three highest-paid sidemen in the big band—in a dynamite front line. Pollack had the hottest white orchestra around in 1928–29. McPartland remembers:

> We played in a nightclub; Lillian Roth was singing there. Then we got the job at the Park Central Hotel. And we started to do *lots* of recording. And the Park Central Hotel job was for over a year. And then while we got that, we got to double in a show called *Hello Daddy,* with Lew Fields, an old-time comedian. We played *Hello Daddy* for six, eight, nine months; I don't know, a year maybe. So much money. We were busy recording every afternoon, and then matinees at the show, then play at the theater at night, and then come back and double at the Park Central Hotel. Even in those days, I was making $400, $500, $600 a week—which is like a couple of thousand now.

When his long workday was officially over, McPartland and his buddies would often head up to Harlem to jam. McPartland, in particular, enjoyed his scotch and his marijuana—or "tea," as he referred to it. He asked various doctors about marijuana, and they told him it wasn't addictive. Because it dried his mouth out too much, he wouldn't smoke it while playing, but after a gig he'd enjoy taking a few whiffs. He felt it was superior to liquor.

McPartland recalls a night when he was playing in Pollack's band at the Park Central. Louis Armstrong had just opened in the show *Hot Chocolates,* and they got together after their jobs so they could go up to Harlem and sit in with pianist Willie "The Lion" Smith at Pods' and Jerry's. (According to McPartland, during the taxi ride Armstrong taught him a brand new song he had introduced in his show: "Black and Blue." They sang it together in the taxi.) When the night came to a close, Armstrong asked if McPartland had any "tea." McPartland answered that clarinetist Mezz Mezzrow—a reliable supplier—had just gotten him a whole cigar-box-full and suggested Armstrong drop by later.When Armstrong went to McPartland's apartment, it was Mrs. McPartland (who had come to visit her son) who answered the door. She said, in her most hospitable voice, "Louis, will you have some tea?"—prompting a rather startled Jimmy McPartland to rush out from his room to make sure Armstrong understood his mother was offering only a friendly cup of tea.

In McPartland's opinion, Louis Armstrong was, of course, a master musician. What did he think of cornetist Red Nichols, whose records were so overwhelmingly popular in the late 1920s? "He was all right, but he didn't have it, really, didn't have a real good beat like the—didn't have a good swingin' beat, you know? He was interested in getting phrases together; it didn't come too spontaneous. He was a good musician, like a band player, you know, a high school band type. Red was a good musician."

As for the Dorsey brothers, they were "fabulous musicians. And nice guys. . . . [But] they were always fighting. Fist fights too." McPartland explains: "I tried to stop them from fighting once—they both hit me. They both clunked me. And I said, 'Fuck you guys. That's the last time. No more. Kill each other. I hope you do!' [It was] at Jimmy Plunkett's, which was a speakeasy. That's where everybody'd congregate after either recording sessions in the afternoon or morning or a theater or a dance job at night. All would come into Plunkett's and get loaded." This was back when the Dorseys were still sidemen, maybe with Paul Whiteman, before they had formed their own big band.

McPartland considers Whiteman, with whom he later did some radio shows, "a dear man. He liked me because I sounded like Bix." And how does he remember Beiderbecke? "He wasn't too talkative," McPartland answers after a pause. "A rather serious-minded guy that really had a drinking problem, which I also had. That was the only thing to do, it seems like." He recalls:

> Musicians would all get together after the gig in a speakeasy and drink. A lot of times you had to get up early the next day for a nine o'clock recording session, and that's what made an alcoholic out of me. You'd have a terrible hangover, maybe get the shakes. All you had to do was take a couple swigs of whiskey and you were in business again, you'd calm down. You needed that whiskey. . . . [But] that isn't the way to do it, I found out. So eventually I went into AA. And it's been some thirty-odd years now since I've had a drink of alcohol. And I'm very happy for that. [According to Marian McPartland, he's overstating how long it's been since he gave up drinking. It may have been half that many years.]

For quite awhile, McPartland says, things went along fine for him in the Pollack band. "But then Ben Pollack didn't want to play drums anymore. He'd just stand up and lead the band and he was terrible. And all the guys got down on him." Pollack stopped acting like just another musician in the band and became more of a hard-nosed leader type. Some sidemen were griping that it would be an ideal band if it weren't for the boss. McPartland remembers: "And one day [in late summer 1929], Benny Goodman and I were playing handball up on the roof of a theater over in Brooklyn. And we had a show to do and our black-and-white shoes got dirty. Pollack saw my shoes after the show and fired me. Benny Goodman was standing there, and Benny Goodman says, 'You just fired Jimmy?' He says, 'Yes, I did.' Benny says, 'I quit.' And Goodman quit. Miller stayed on."

McPartland was a strong, versatile player, so he wasn't out of work for long.

> Manny Klein, who was one of the great trumpet players in New York, got me this job in the pit band of a Broadway show, *Sons o' Guns,* with Jack Donahue and Lilly Damita, a good-paying job. And I went with the leading lady, Lilly Damita, became good friends.
>
> But Dorothy Williams, who I had been going with before that, came back in town and we had to get married—a baby on the way. . . . My mother came in, and her mother. We had a wedding. [The only child McPartland would ever have was named Dorothy, after her mother.] She was born in 1930, and everything was fine. We got an apartment. . . . I wasn't hurting for money. I used to do a lot of recording dates with different bands in the afternoons and then play the show. Had a nice place and had the baby and went along for three or four years like that.

Most of McPartland's work was commercial now. Chances to cut even a moderately jazzy record were few and far between since the 1929 stock market crash. His only hot recording in 1930 was with Jan Garber and His Greater Columbia Recording Orchestra: "Puttin' on the Ritz" and "When a Woman Loves a Man." He also did some motion picture soundtrack work for Paramount. The music wasn't always interesting, but as long as he was able to support his wife and daughter, he was happy enough. Even Benny Goodman had to compromise, taking a job in Rubinoff's orchestra. Jazz musicians knew they had to do that if they wanted to earn a living. Hot music was simply not selling in the early 1930s.

McPartland remembers a job he got with Russ Columbo, the crooner, violinist, and bandleader.

> . . . We recorded, went on the road. And he started going with Hannah Williams [Dorothy's sister]. They were in love. Dorothy and I were already married. Russ Columbo and Hannah . . . they didn't get married. She turned Russ Columbo down and it just tore him apart. He couldn't play or sing.

> We tried to close down the show. We were on the road, in Cincinnati, playing these picture houses, where they have a picture and a stage show, and he just couldn't make it. He couldn't sing. He was heartbroken over Hannah. So he went back home to California.

Hannah Williams had broken Columbo's heart, and Dorothy would soon break McPartland's. He got a job in the pit band of Billy Rose's Broadway show *Crazy Quilt,* featuring Fanny Brice, George Jessel, Ted Healy, James Barton, and Hannah Williams. When Hannah married bandleader Roger Wolfe Kahn, her place in the show was taken by Dorothy. But when the show was set to tour after concluding its Broadway run, Dorothy said she wanted to stay in New York with the baby. McPartland and the rest of the orchestra went on the road.

Eventually, McPartland returned to New York and found that the two sisters had gotten together and decided to divorce their husbands. Dorothy was planning to marry some quite wealthy fellow. A crestfallen McPartland took a job in Smith Ballew's band, which then included Glenn Miller and Ray McKinley, working in New Orleans. Some months later, when he was back in New York, he learned that Dorothy had remarried and gotten custody of their child. McPartland broke down.

"She married somebody else, and I just didn't give a damn what happened to me," he recalls. Unable to cope with the loss of his wife and daughter, he no longer felt like playing; nor did he eat much. Drink, which had always been part of the scene, was no doubt even more tempting in this period. He took a few jobs around New York and played in Harry Reser's band on South American cruises, but he was no longer recording and no longer a factor of any importance in New York jazz.

Finally, his brother offered him a job in his Chicago quartet, the Embassy Four, which was playing at the Palmer House. But Dick McPartland's group was too commercial for Jimmy; it played hotel music, not the real jazz he preferred. Still, it paid the bills for a couple of years (circa 1934–36). Then Dick switched from being a full-time musician to being a booking agent who only played occasionally, and Jimmy again began leading small bands under his own name (1936–41).

In April 1936, McPartland cut his first jazz sides in six years: "Eccentric," "Original Dixieland One-Step," "Panama," and "I'm All Bound Round with the Mason Dixon Line." His eight-piece band included brother Dick on guitar, George Wettling on drums, and Rosy

McHargue on clarinet. He didn't make any more jazz records until 1939, when, leading a septet that included brother Dick and brother-in-law Jim Lanigan, he cut four oldies dating from the 1920s and before: "Jazz Me Blues," "China Boy," "The World Is Waiting for the Sunrise," and "Sugar." He had passed through the 1930s almost unrecorded as a jazz musician.

McPartland got a job leading his band at the Three Deuces, downstairs at 222 North State Street in Chicago. "Our band singer was Anita O'Day," he recalls. He became good friends with Art Tatum, who, at one point, was intermission pianist at the Three Deuces. McPartland used to go to Tatum's hotel room to read to him. (Tatum's vision was severely impaired by congenital cataracts.) He led the house band at the Panther Room of the Hotel Sherman for awhile and also emceed the show—dancers, a magician, and Fats Waller as the headliner.

In 1941 McPartland joined Jack Teagarden's big band. His old buddy from the Ben Pollack days was glad to hire him. But McPartland's star had lost a lot of its luster in the past decade. He wasn't playing at his best, and his name didn't mean much to young swing fans who considered Harry James, Ziggy Elman, Roy Eldridge, Cootie Williams, Bunny Berigan, and other to be the big stars now among trumpeters.

In late 1942, McPartland joined the army. Although it was customary to assign musicians of his caliber to bands, he asked instead to be assigned to a regular combat unit. He was something of a "drunken patriot," he says, gung ho about becoming a fighting man. He also figured that the service bands didn't play his style of music.

After finishing basic training, McPartland found himself on a troop ship bound for Scotland, where his late mother had been born. In his childhood, his mother had taught him a song she had often sung as a choirgirl: "Blue Bells of Scotland." Now, as the ship approached the shore, he took out his cornet to offer a remembrance for his mother. He played the first chorus pure and pretty, the second jazzy. From the shore, which had been quiet until then, came enthusiastic hollers of approval; some even answered him on bagpipes.

The realities of combat quickly sobered McPartland. He was a member of a real fighting unit, he notes, the 462nd AAA Automatic Weapons. "I came in D-plus four—Normandy, Omaha, and Omaha Beach—and went all the way through, all the way up to Germany, to Belgium, right across." His fervor to fight for his country vanished as he saw colleagues dying in combat and realized how much his own life was at risk. He wound up asking for, and being granted, permission to serve as a musician.

In Eupen, Belgium, McPartland met a British pianist named Marian Page, then just twenty-four years old, who was touring to entertain the troops. He recalls: "I was the emcee of the USO camp shows. I had my own band, choice of picking any men I wanted. And I became the emcee of the show at the theater there, and all the different acts would come in. Marian came through, and that's it. She was an English citizen, on lend-lease to the USO camp shows." Initially, he wondered if she could be any good—a *female* jazz piano player, and British to boot. Although her first number didn't thrill him, he noted her feel for harmony and asked her to play a ballad with him. They blended together well. "She was playing piano," he says, "and she was a killer. She was just something. She knocked me out. And so we got together."

Marian had never heard of Jimmy before, but other musicians assured her he was a legendary Chicago jazzman. He seemed kind of rough-hewn, yet he could charm anyone when he wanted to. He was drinking heavily in those days, and the war seems to have made him somewhat ornery—or to have resurrected the ornery streak he'd had in his boyhood. While in the service, he notes, he was busted a couple of times for various infractions, such as drinking too much.

On their first date, Jimmy invited Marian out to lunch. After they finished eating, he realized he didn't have any money on him and asked her to loan him some. She concluded that he definitely was *not* like most men she had known, but an attraction developed. There was a certain twinkle in his eyes (partly due to his drinking, she later decided; he acknowledges that he was half-loaded throughout their courtship). When she complained about the piano she had to work with, he managed to obtain a requisition and appropriate one from a Nazi collaborator's home. Getting her a good piano was the best gift he could think of.

Shortly after they met, Jimmy proposed, but Marian figured it was liquor talking. He persisted, however, and she finally accepted. As he tells it: "After a few weeks, I got permission to get married, and we got married in Achen, Germany, February 3, 1945." She was seventeen years younger than he was and interested in more contemporary jazz. Still, she learned to love all of the older jazz that he loved and to play it with him. He helped teach her to swing, to feel the beat more. She had the technical facilities, but she wasn't what he considered a full-fledged swinger when he first met her. He, in turn, came to appreciate some of the more modern sounds. (In a 1952 *Down Beat* blindfold test, for example, they both agreed that Woody Herman's cooly modern "Early Autumn" was gorgeous.)

When this shot of the Wolverines was taken at Riverview Park in Des Moines, Iowa, in 1926, the bank was composed entirely of Austin High Gang members. Left to right: Frank Teschemacher, Jim Lanigan, Bud Freeman, Jimmy McPartland (who also led the band), Dave Tough, Floyd O'Brien, Dave North, Dick McPartland. (Author's collection. Courtesy of the Institute of Jazz Studies.)

Jimmy McPartland's band, circa 1940. Left to right: Joe Sullivan, Hank Isaacs, George Brunies, Jimmy McPartland, Eddie Condon, and Pee Wee Russell. (Author's collection. Courtesy of the Institute of Jazz Studies.)

Marian and Jimmy McPartland, with Billie Holiday, at the Blue Note club in Chicago, 1948. (Author's collection. Courtesy of Marian McPartland.)

Jimmy McPartland mugging with his buddies, Louis Armstrong and Muggsy Spanier. (Author's collection. Courtesy of Marian McPartland.)

Jimmy McPartland and Dizzy Gillespie duel in a "Battle of Jazz" for a 1953 MGM album in which McPartland's traditional jazz group, with Vic Dickenson and Edmond Hall, and Gillespie's modern jazz group, with Max Roach and Buddy De Franco, played the same four tunes, including "Muskrat Ramble" and "How High the Moon." The mood at this photo session may have been jocular, but the idea—prevalent in that period—that there was a "battle" between old and new styles (with some critics arguing loudly that only the new style was valid) hurt a lot of older jazzmen. (Author's collection. Courtesy of Marian McPartland.)

McPartland and Gillespie, older and grayer, re-create their "Battle of Jazz" pose. Nowadays, it's more common to find jazz fans with eclectic tastes who see no conflict in finding good in older as well as newer styles. (Author's collection. Courtesy of Marian McPartland.)

Jimmy McPartland (cornet), Marian McPartland, and friends at the final night of Eddie Condon's Club in New York City, July 31, 1985. (Photo by Chip Deffaa.)

Jimmy and Marian McPartland today. They were divorced in the 1970s (neither remembers the exact year) but, as they both put it, "the divorce didn't take" and they remain extremely close, both personally and professionally. (Author's collection. Courtesy of Marian McPartland.)

Right after the war, McPartland got an offer from Eddie Condon to play regularly at Condon's club in New York. It could have been a terrific break for him, but he said he wanted to take a little rest, visit with relatives and old friends in Chicago. He did just that, not worrying about anything, until one day the McPartlands realized they had no money.

Jimmy and Marian began working together in a quartet in Chicago. At first he didn't want to rehearse; he liked the idea of rehearsing on the job and getting paid for it. And there were occasions when his drinking left him incapable of working. But Marian helped to bring out the best in him. She got him to reach his potential more often and to expand his repertoire. They opened, he recalls, at "a little bar on the corner of Dearborn and Randolph. And we just were a tremendous hit."

Down Beat took notice of the new McPartland quartet in February 1947, under the headline "McPARTLAND BLOWS BETTER THAN EVER—NOT ALL DIXIE":

> A one-time great among trumpeters, McPartland was last heard here leading a dixie crew that included Pee Wee Russell, Eddie Condon and George Brunis among others and will admit, himself, that during this time he was struggling to maintain his place in the jazz spotlight. During the late '30s and early '40s, a fast pace had worn his powerful style thin—to the point where clinkers came as often as the strong, true notes of his earlier days. His lip was gone.
>
> Now, six years later, McPartland is back in town and the night caught was playing some of the greatest trumpet he had in the last ten years. And, this has an unusual slant. The present McPartland is not limiting himself to Dixieland. Many are still in the book, of course, but he is also taking advantage of worthy pops. And, he is playing the pops with the same verve and taste that marked his earlier jazz efforts.

Favorable reviews followed in *Time* and other publications. McPartland was being rediscovered. His career was on the upswing. "We got on the Dave Garroway radio show," he recalls. "I did 'Singin' the Blues,' I think it was, very pretty, with a symphonic orchestra, marvelous background."

The McPartlands played together, steadily, for the next four years or so. Marian became so good that eventually, when Jimmy got too sick to fulfill an engagement, his quartet—which became the Marian

McPartland Trio by default—went on without him. Not long afterward, Marian was working regularly under her own name.

> Marian started getting things and we decided to come to New York. Oh, I got a job at Nick's, down in Greenwich Village—Eddie Condon sent for me—so we came, and away we went. Marian proved herself, being able to sit in with different jazz bands in any idiom, whether it be modern or Dixieland or—she's an all-around musician. I didn't know that she played classical music, could play a concerto—the Grieg, for instance, or "Rhapsody in Blue." I was knocked out. She didn't tell me she could play that kind of stuff.
>
> From now on—go! I had plenty of jobs. I never had any problem finding work. The Metropole was a tremendous success in New York City, on Seventh Avenue around Forty-eighth, Forty-ninth [Street], crowds lined up the street. We got a nice apartment on the Upper West Side, and Marian got a job at the Hickory House with a trio. . . . she was there for a couple of years. I just kept going. And I was getting a fairly good reputation. So was Marian, by leaps and bounds. Everyone used to come over and hear her. Duke Ellington—she was one of his favorites.

McPartland was in good form then. He had outlasted many of his contemporaries and was recording steadily, usually as the leader of small bands. Except for a couple of V-discs he had cut in Belgium in 1945, nothing by Jimmy McPartland had been released from 1939 through 1948. Then came an explosion of jazz record dates: in 1949, 1950, 1952, 1953, 1954, 1955, 1956, 1957, 1958, 1959, and 1960. He got to work with guys like Pee Wee Russell, Edmund Hall, Vic Dickenson, Bud Freeman, George Wettling, Pops Foster, Cutty Cutshall, Eddie Condon, and Tyree Glenn. Not only did he re-record many of the old favorites, including a highly successful album in tribute to Bix Beiderbecke, but he recorded plenty of new things as well, such as a big band album of the music from Broadway's *The Music Man.*

Writers have often referred to McPartland's music as Dixieland, but he generally refers to it as swing. He likes music played with four beats to a bar rather than two. For many years now, standard Dixieland numbers have been only a portion of his working repertoire.

Even back in the old days, McPartland says, the musicians he hung around with were experimenting with modern sounds and harmonies in their free time. He commented, during Leonard Feather's 1952 blindfold tests for *Down Beat,* that Lee Konitz and Miles Davis's recording of an ultra modern George Russell composition entitled "Odjenar" sounded "like the jam sessions we used to have twenty-three or twenty-four years ago with Teschemacher and Bud Freeman, Davey Tough, Dave North, and Jim Lanigan . . ." When Marian interrupted: "Oh, come, James! Did you used to play like—" he responded: "We used to listen to Gustav Holst and Stravinsky, and one of us would start a theme, the next guy would pick it up, and we'd be weaving in and out—it sounded just like that! All augmented fifths and stuff like that."[4]

Marian McPartland has recorded frequently under her own name since 1951, usually leading a trio, and from time to time she has also recorded with Jimmy. (She's always liked working with him, not just for the music they made together, but because he'd drink less when they were together.) Now, she works regularly on her own and also provides invigorating support for Jimmy's periodic appearances. In addition, she has composed music, written a number of magazine articles and one book (*All in Good Time*), narrated TV documentaries, and hosted a long-running PBS radio series, "Piano Jazz." Perhaps, Jimmy could have insisted that she stay a regular member of his group in the 1950s, but he gave her the freedom to pursue her own career. Today, she's probably better known to most jazz fans than Jimmy is.

In addition to his playing, McPartland notes that he's done some acting over the years: "On stage, in *Showboat* [in the summer of 1957]. I [did] a few little steps and played the cornet, played 'Sweet Georgia Brown' at the end of the first act, with the band, and the company all dancing. It was swingin.' And I did some acting on television [including "The Magic Horn" on NBC's "Alcoa Hour" in the late 1950s]. I've been offered other jobs by producer Lee Guber as an actor. 'No, thank you.' "

McPartland has recorded infrequently since 1960, but he has continued to tour in the United States and abroad. He's also enjoyed reunions with Bud Freeman and other survivors from the old days. On November 20, 1965, he took part in the concert celebrating the seventy-fifth anniversary of Austin High School. And in the late 1960s and early 1970s, he worked a good bit at Jimmy Ryan's Club in New York. In 1972 he played in South Africa, where he offered greetings in the Zulu language to the native listeners. More recently, he performed at the closing of Eddie Condon's Club in New York, on July 31, 1985. He comments: "Well, sure, might as well pay tribute to Eddie and the guys. Eddie was a nice guy, in there slugging for jazz and a livelihood, and he was deserving of it." He also lent a note of authenticity to a re-creation of the Wolverines in a memorable Chicago jazz concert at the 1986 JVC Jazz Festival in New York.

The McPartlands bought a house in Merrick, Long Island, in the late 1950s—Jimmy notes: "It's comfortable out here near the ocean. We used to fish and golf around here. Although their marriage has since ended in divorce, they have remained extremely close and supportive of one another, musically and personally. (Neither will say much about why they divorced. Marian says she tried seeing other men for awhile, but when she realized she was falling for men similar to Jimmy, she figured she was better off staying with him.)

The gigs that Jimmy takes these days, Marian tends to find for him. She prods him not to slough off. And she can quietly cue him from the piano bench, if need be, if he's not sure what he wants to play next or if he forgets that he's already played a particular tune (he has Alzheimer's). Once he starts in on a tune, however, the rest flows smoothly. He'll sing "I'm Gonna Sit Right Down and Write Myself a Letter" with an infectious, room-warming élan. And his fingers can automatically tap out the rapidly rising and descending notes of the catchy cornet solo on the number that he developed years ago. His tone may be darker than in his youth, but the choice of notes, the phrasing remains unmistakably his.

He says he still practices regularly. "I have to. Because if you lay off—forget it, man! You'll go back, you don't go forward. It's hard to keep up an embouchure. But I don't practice as much as I should. Well, Marian's out of town, now. Like today and yesterday I didn't practice. She gets in this afternoon. I'll have to practice because she gets on my tail and it's that simple!"[5]

McPartland prefers small groups to big band work. "There's more freedom," he says.

> . . . Take a melody. The cornet's got the lead, phrases the melody with a nice beat. The rhythm section's laying down a good beat. I like four horns: trombone, clarinet, cornet, and tenor saxophone. There's a lot of body there with the trombone and the tenor; gives a lot of foundation, with the clarinet up high above the cornet. The cornet's in the middle there, in the middle register with the melody. Phrase the melody with a nice beat, or whether it's a pretty song, phrase it with nice feelings. And then everybody follows you.
>
> I don't have to play any more, financially. But I do, once in a while. If a job is something that I want, and it pays enough money and it's worth it, I'll take it. We were out at Nice, France,

> a couple of weeks ago, with George Wein. We got our board and room and transportation, and I made a thousand dollars just for showing up three times doing an hour set. With a quartet and sextet.
>
> Frankly, I must say I'm enjoying life tremendously. Marian lives upstairs. And we swim practically every day in the summer—a big pool over in Baldwin, public pool. And I'm enjoying life. I have four cats here. The house is paid for. I'm still breathing.

He's glad if he gets to run into Bud Freeman or any of his cohorts from the old days. "But we don't particularly seek anyone." There's no Austin High Gang that he feels part of anymore. "No, no," Jimmy McPartland reflects. "The gang is right here. Marian and myself. And our four cats."

7

FREDDIE MOORE

Keep the Customers Happy

"Boy, I tell you, I'm a character! Anything to make the people laugh, keep 'em happy. If you can't get 'em on the drums, get 'em on the vocal. If you can't get 'em on the vocal, eyeball 'em. Yeah. Get 'em one way or the other!" So says Freddie Moore, who's been "getting 'em" for well over seventy years.

Born August 20, 1900, Moore began drumming around 1912. I wonder how many of the people who catch his work today realize that they are witnessing a style of performing with roots back in the traveling black tent shows of the teens. Moore will flip his drumsticks in the air, the way the first professional drummers he saw as a boy used to do. He's a master of the finger roll—which involves rolling the sticks in the fingers in a particular way while drumming on the snare; in fact, he's virtually the only one left who *does* finger rolls. He'll even blow into the back of a snare drum to suggest a tiger's roar when the band plays "Tiger Rag." The mugging that is an essential part of his act—the bulging eyes, the exaggerated expressions of mock fright or childish delight—dates back to the comics he saw in his youth. He remembers happily those old-time black performers who worked with their faces covered with burnt cork, their lips with white greasepaint, minstrel-style. He uses some lines he learned from them.

In his early years, Moore worked in carnivals, circuses, minstrel shows, and theater pit bands. Whether he played dance music, show music, or jazz didn't matter all that much to him. He's played with his share of jazz greats, including King Oliver, Art Hodes, and Sidney Bechet. But he has never thought of jazz as "art," the way, for example, Miles Davis would. And the idea of trying to separate jazz from entertainment—a distinction that was essential to many black jazz musicians of Davis's generation—has always been foreign to him.

To many young black jazzmen of the 1940s, mugging was Uncle Tom–ing. It meant playing a stereotypical role—the black as the non-threatening clown, the simpleton—to ingratiate oneself with whites. And it was important, for the sake of dignity, to set that role playing completely aside, to relegate it to the past along with the burnt cork of minstrel days. It was an advance when black musicians no longer felt they *had* to mug to go over. Miles Davis not only didn't mug for audiences, he turned his back to them when he played, forcing listeners to concentrate solely on his music. Whites, he said, just wanted blacks to smile.

Moore, coming from an earlier generation, always figured his job was to entertain, to play up to his audiences, to keep them happy. Of his mugging he says simply, "Everybody liked the expressions on my face when I'm playing, you know, all of them different expressions." And when he recorded an album recently for New York Jazz Records, the other musicians were surprised to note that he mugged the same as always during the recording sessions, even though he had no audience. Mugging is an automatic component of his work. Onstage, he'll do whatever he believes it takes to hold an audience's interest—even donning a fright wig or a pair of large white glasses or waving a pair of gloves in one hand. He says simply that he likes making people laugh, making people happy.

Art Hodes, the Chicago blues piano giant, has observed: "If you've ever seen Freddie Moore roll his eyes, go into his act, you book him; get him on stage and no one's goin' to steal a scene when he's around. He's funny."[1] And that he is. He's a great crowd pleaser. To this critic, though, there are times when his routines can be a bit embarrassing. Moore will declaim lines from "Old Man Mose," which was a hit for Louis Armstrong in 1936. When he tells you how frightened he was to see the dead man lying flat on his back—giving an exaggerated shudder of fear as he does so—you're aware that the song fits in with a popular stereotype of that era, reinforced in films and in songs, of the easily frightened black man. Moore seems blithely unaware of such connotations. He is simply happy doing his schtick. He tells me that to create that shuddering effect, "you relax your lips and shake them." He'll end his patter with a peppy "That's all, that's all, you-all." He's a holdover from an almost-vanished style of performing.

Moore enjoys singing some songs that virtually no one else does anymore, such as "(You're Sure Some) Ugly Child" and "Snowball." "I got what you call one of them loud voices," he says in his usual extroverted way. "No voice—just open your mouth and sing." He also plays washboard, a skill he picked up in 1925. It is Moore's washboard, for example, that you hear on the recording of "Sweet Georgia Brown" played whenever the Harlem Globetrotters come onto a basketball court.

But mainly—and most important to Moore—he drums. You can see him at the Red Blazer Too in New York City, with bass player John Williams, who is eighty, and some other, younger musicians (who, for the most part, are playing songs that were popular well before their time). When the band goes into something like "St. James Infirmary" or "Jelly Roll," you realize that Moore is handling the drums in the way that was customary when those numbers were new. He keeps time on the bass drum, which gives a satisfying solidarity to the band. (Nearly all drummers today keep time in a much lighter fashion on the cymbals, and have done so since the late 1940s. That lighter sound is appropriate on modern jazz, but it has a way of undercutting traditional jazz.) Cymbals aren't so important to Moore—for that matter, the high-hat cymbal hadn't yet been invented when he mastered his craft. He'd rather you hear his *drums.* He keeps alive the dying art of the press roll (building in intensity), which in his youth was a key element in the drummer's repertoire.

Moore's drumwork sounds so good, so honest on these old numbers, that you wonder who will continue this style of playing after he's gone. Yes, some of his mugging, with its Uncle Tom overtones, can be a little unsettling. But, that point noted, his work as a whole still is mighty intriguing. To watch him perform is to peer back into time—to the era of the tent shows.

Many white musicians of Moore's generation grew up in homes where their parents hoped they'd attend college and then go into business or a profession. The parents of Bix Beiderbecke and Jimmy McPartland, for example, held such hopes. But Moore's mother, Hattie, who became a widow just nine weeks after his birth, could hardly afford the luxury of such dreams. She bore him in Little Washington, North Carolina, and raised him, as best she could, in New Bern, about forty miles to the south. Back then, society was not interested in providing much formal education to blacks in the rural South. They were expected to become farmhands or laborers. Moore figures he got about four years of schooling.

Moore picked up odd jobs, like being a delivery boy, when he could, but drumming held the promise of a more appealing life than working on a farm or in a factory. He says simply, "I fooled around on the drums, and I decided I should play." Much to the distraction of his mother, he'd drum on chairs and boxes and table legs. He learned by watching how other drummers played; he never took lessons.

"I used to give the drummer [at one local dance spot] twenty-five cents to let me sit on the drums," Moore recalls. "During intermission I'd sit on drums, hit 'em, I didn't know what I was doing. Rap-rap-rap-brrap, all that different thing. Then finally I turned out to be pretty fair, so they give me two nights a week at the place called the Livery Stable Ballroom. That was one flight upstairs, piano and drums. I was getting three dollars a night. That was big money then. I must have been about—in my teens."

Were they calling the music jazz then? "No. They called it swing. We didn't know nothing about no Dixieland or different names. All we know was swing," he replies. Today, of course, the term "swing" refers to the type of music that emerged in and became popular during the big band era, so it's possible that Moore didn't hear the term until later. But it may be that the term "swing" was used for hot music in the South long before it entered the general public's vocabulary in the 1930s. It should be noted, too, that jazz pioneer Jelly Roll Morton wrote "Georgia Swing," perhaps the earliest reference to "swing" in a song title, in 1907.

Moore continues: "Then after about a couple months, I got chances to get out of my hometown." Around fourteen when he ran away from home, he considered himself to be grown, capable of living on his own. He did what he had to, to get by. At one point, for example, he got a job with a carnival. Touted as "Hickory Bill from Bungus Hill, the African Dodger," Moore would stick his head through a hole in a mattress and stand there while people threw balls at him—which he'd try to dodge. One hit won you a cigar; two hits won you fifty cents; three hits won you $1.50.

By any standards, it was a degrading way to earn a living. Some of the hostility-filled racist youths who played the game no doubt believed that beaning a "nigger" was just good sport. Moore makes light of it, minimizing the pain he must have felt. He was, after all, earning real money. "I could make $15, $20, $25 a day," he maintains. "They used to throw baseballs. Hit me once in a while. But that wasn't so good because I had a hard head anyway. This was down south, in North Carolina or somewhere down there. The reason I gave it up? Someone threw a cueball at me. Bam! I think I still got the knot somewheres up there."

Eventually (he may have been sixteen), Moore joined a minstrel show: *Old Kentucky Minstrels.* "I used to walk by the side of the other drummer. His name was Joe White. He was one of the greatest drummers I ever saw in my life—then and now, if he'd been living. He was a street drummer, played drums in the street. And of course played for the shows at night." The thing that awed him was that White used as many as fifteen sticks when he drummed. He had them down his boots, under his arms, between his teeth; he'd switch from stick to stick as he drummed, without losing a beat—catching a stick in his teeth, flipping it from his teeth to one hand and then to an armpit or into his boots. The effect was tremendous. At that point, Moore barely knew how to use two sticks properly; he eventually wound up using nine. Even today he'll sometimes use four sticks, a technique that remains a crowd pleaser.

As Moore tells it, the minstrel troupe would pull into town at around nine or ten in the morning, set up the tent, and then at 12:30 the whole company would parade through town. The boss would ride in a rented car, along with a fellow touting the worth of the show they'd be putting on that night; the others would march alongside and behind the car. When they reached a prime spot downtown, the band would form a circle and give a concert. They wore long red coats.

Moore was a kind of band boy, as well as an apprentice drummer in the troupe. "I was what you called the Walking Gent: I'd take care of the coats when the band'd go on parade, about three miles downtown and three miles back. And when the band'd get through with the parade, they'd pull their coats off and hang them up—they'd be wringing wet, you know. Hang 'em up on the bushes, let 'em dry out. When they'd dry out, I'd put 'em on the coat hanger and put 'em in the locker-room." Starched collars and dickeys could get limp pretty quickly in the hot southern sun.

"We had one great big pullman car; we eat and sleep on this car. They had tables where you pull down, you know, you eat on the tables. You get ready to go to bed, the bed had a mattress you put on down on this. Then we had the tent; we'd fold that up and put it under the bottom of the car. They'd call that possum belly." (The roustabouts who set up the canvas tent slept in the possum belly.) The men all brought their wives and girlfriends along on the train with them, Moore says. "We went to places like Alabama, Mississippi, Georgia, South Carolina, Chicago. This was a minstrel show with all black performers. During that time, there was no mixing, you know, down south. Of course we did play for a lot of white people, you know. Most of them was whites. I stayed with the minstrel show about four months."

King Oliver's band, in New York City, March 1931. Oliver is fourth from the left; Freddie Moore is third from the right. (Courtesy of Duncan P. Schiedt.)

Freddie Moore, circa 1950, at the Stuyvesant Casino, New York City. (Courtesy of Duncan P. Schiedt.)

Freddie Moore, mugging as always, at the washboard in his New York apartmant, 1985. (Photo by Chip Deffaa.)

Freddie Moore during a concert at Ben Franklin Junior High School, Ridgewood, New Jersey, 1985. (Photo by Chip Deffaa.)

* * *

Moore tired of life on the road and found a job in the pit orchestra of a theater in Birmingham, Alabama. That's where he got his real musical experience, he feels. Over a seven-year period, he drummed for great stars of the black entertainment circuit.

> Way back in the teens, I played for all of them: Sarah Martin, Butterbeans and Susie, Ida Cox, Ma Rainey—she's the oldest one—Bessie Smith, all the old-timers. In the Gaiety Theater, Fourteenth Street and Third Avenue in Birmingham.
>
> The best blues singer was Bessie Smith. She could really sing the blues. The rest of them sang, but not like Bessie Smith. She had her own style. And she was one of the popularest blues singers there was, living. Of course the others was popular, but not like Bessie Smith. She was on her own. Sarah Martin, she had her style, but she wasn't what you call a blues singer. Ida Cox, Ma Rainey—she'd sing the blues too, but she had her own style of singing.

Ma Rainey, he notes, struck him as rather ugly, even if she did enhance her looks with a diamond in one tooth and a twenty-dollar gold piece as a pendant.

The acts would come into Birmingham on Sunday night, often exhausted from traveling. They'd rehearse at the theater that night and then again on Monday morning. If an act brought along its own drummer, Moore would work at a movie house. He'd get there before it opened for the day and watch the movie while studying the musician's cue sheet; that way, when the audience arrived he'd be ready. He'd do a roll on the bass drum for thunder, a rim shot for gunfire, and so on. He'd also watch the entertainers touring on the Theater Owners' Booking Association circuit and pick up their dance steps.[2]

William Benbow's touring show, *Charleston Dandies,* played Birmingham, and Moore left with it. The show toured southern cities and then hit Havana, Cuba, where Moore felt he was at a disadvantage because he was following in the wake of an exceptionally fast showman drummer named Rastus. After the tour ended, Moore gigged for a bit with Charlie Creath's band in St. Louis. Then, in Detroit, he became a leader for the first time: Buddy Moore and His Carolina Stompers, a seven-man band (Buddy had been his nickname since the minstrel show, nearly a decade earlier). By now he was good enough on drums that everyone was telling him he should be in New York, where, he was assured, money grew on trees. "Yeah, I was kind of fly on drums. I mean, I was fast; I think fast, you know."

Finally, in 1928, he went to New York by himself. He recalls: "I had an old, raggedy, beat-up set of drums, but I liked them. The kind of drums we have now, with the tom-toms and the cymbals and all that—I didn't have nothing like that at all. I went around to see the different drummers. The first one I met was Chick Webb. And the next drummer was Cozy Cole. And Big Sid Catlett." Was there any drummer Moore was particularly trying to sound like back then, or that he felt greatly inspired by? "No, I had my own style when I come to New York, and I didn't want to change it. A lot of different drummers want to play my style. But my style is kind of complicated like, although everybody said I had a good beat and my tempo was all right."

Moore remembers that his first big job was with Eubie Blake and a fourteen-piece band. Blake had separated from Noble Sissle, his former partner, and was leading his own band.

> I played at the Lafayette Theater, Seventh Avenue and 132nd Street, around 1929. Then we went to Washington, D.C., played there for weeks, Philadelphia and Baltimore, then came back here to New York, where the band broke up.
>
> We played "I'm Just Wild about Harry," "Love Will Find a Way" [hits written by Sissle and Blake]. We did about five, six numbers; I've forgotten the names of the others.
>
> We were part of a show; we had to play for a show. During that time, they had six chorus girls and a comedian and a soubrette—what you call a separate dancer—and a singer. There was about eight people in the cast and he had a fourteen-piece band—say about twenty-five people in all.

Other jobs followed, from backing Wilbur Sweatman in his specialty of playing three clarinets at once, to working in a dancing school, where Moore played no small number of tangos.

Sometime between 1929 and 1932, Moore states, he played drums in King Oliver's band.[3] He was filling the spot that had belonged to Baby Dodds in the early 1920s and to Paul Barbarin in 1926–27. "If King Oliver called rehearsal at three o'clock," Moore recalls, "he wanted you there at three o'clock. Don't come in at quarter after three or three-thirty." It seems that Oliver made his wishes quite clear. He'd walk into the rehearsal room packing his pistol, look his musicians over, set his sheet music down, hold his gun up—and then ask if everybody was there. When he noted all were present, he'd set the gun down on the table and start rehearsing. Moore was responsible for rounding up the band members; it was never a difficult task.

Oliver, who composed such famed jazz numbers as "Dipper Mouth Blues," "Chimes Blues," "Canal Street Blues," "Dr. Jazz," "Snag It," and "West End Blues," had enjoyed his greatest success as a bandleader in the mid-1920s. He peaked around 1923, when Louis Armstrong was the second cornet in his band and their teamwork was the talk of Chicago musicians, but he led organized bands almost continuously through late 1927. Then, suffering from dental problems that often made playing difficult for him, he and his musicians disbanded. He continued making records, however—his popular recording of "Snag It," for example, was made in 1928—and putting together occasional bands for specific dates.

Now, in 1930, Oliver was taking an organized band on tour, "trying to make a comeback," Moore notes. Although the band was formed in New York, it was billed as King Oliver and His New Orleans Creole Jazz Band. Moore recalls: "We rehearsed the band about three months before we recorded, here in New York; then we went on the road. We played in Texas, Alabama, Georgia, Mississippi, Fort Worth, Texas—all down through there, doing one-night stands."[4] Louis Armstrong, now a major attraction, was touring on the same circuit, and Moore claims that Oliver's band commanded a higher fee than Armstrong's. (In an April 1945 *Jazz Record* article, Moore offered the more plausible recollection that people paid $1.25 admission to hear Armstrong and $1.00 to hear Oliver.[5])

Those who came expecting to hear the numbers that had made Oliver's reputation were often disappointed. "He was playing the same sort of music he'd played back in the twenties," Moore recalls. "But he wasn't playing too much stuff from the period when Louis Armstrong had been with him, because the band was mostly built around Louis during that time, in Chicago." In addition, Oliver, now forty-five, simply couldn't play as well as he had eight years earlier. How did he sound? Moore equivocates: "Ah, he was sounding all right. . . . He had the pyorrhea in his gums. And his teeth wasn't so good, you know. He couldn't go so good. But there were three trumpets in the band. First, second, and King Oliver played some numbers."

According to Moore, Oliver seemed bothered by the fact that he wasn't as big as when he was younger: "Yeah, you could see it when he was playing—he wasn't like he wanted to be. You know, he'd try, but his teeth, pyorrhea was in his mouth, you know. And he couldn't make them notes. Couldn't hit them notes like he should." Still, Oliver continued to play, pacing himself on the bandstand. Some of the band's big numbers in that period, Moore says, were "Struggle Buggy," "Laura," "Edna," "That's a-Plenty," and "St. James Infirmary"; and Oliver might feature himself on "Snag It" and another number. A three-month booking in the Eltorian Ballroom in Wichita, Kansas, ended after three weeks, however, when Oliver wouldn't play his older, famous recorded numbers.

Oliver's limitations were also apparent in the recording studio, Moore recalls. He would try a solo on the first take of a number and maybe the second and third takes as well. But at some point a recording engineer would come out and say that Oliver had missed a note, and the solo would be reassigned to one of the other trumpeters, such as Dave Nelson, Ward Pinkett, or Henry "Red" Allen, who didn't tour with the band but was brought in for some recording sessions. Even if Oliver was no longer always able to cut it as a trumpeter, RCA knew that his name would sell some records. During Moore's tenure in the band, Oliver's records included: "Boogie Woogie," "Rhythm Club Stomp," "You're Just My Type," "I Must Have It," "Edna," "Mule Face Blues," "Struggle Buggy," "Don't You Think I Love You?" "Olga," "Shake It and Break It," "Stingaree Blues," "What's the Use of Living without Love?" "You Were Only Passing Time with Me," "Stealing Love," and "Nelson Stomp."

Oliver had difficulty accepting the fact that, at least to band bookers, his reign as king was history. On one occasion, he was asked to cover a date in New Orleans that Louis Armstrong couldn't make, but when he demanded more money from the bookers than Armstrong had been offered, the deal feel through.[6] Moore comments on a similar incident: "We went to Chicago to play at the Grand Terrace Ballroom. But King Oliver wanted too much money. They got Earl Hines instead. Hines had a twenty-two-piece band, but he broke it down to fifteen-piece." Touring in the South also brought the band its share of racial prejudice. "Yeah, we got a lot of it. Some places we couldn't play. But if it played, they wouldn't allow no black people in there, or whites, you know. It was tough, boy." Still, they did manage to play some white ballrooms that had not previously booked black bands.

Trombonist Clyde Bernhardt, a member of Oliver's band for eight months in 1931, wrote in his autobiography: "One thing that made the band cook was Freddie Moore's push-drumming." Bernhardt also recalled Moore's onstage antics when the band played "Sing You Sinners." Moore would be "shouting and praying, like he found religion. Suddenly, he [would] start to weave and hold his head" and then pretend to fall into a faint, as another band member would run to catch him at the last minute, all to the audience's amusement. One night, Bernhardt wrote, the other musician failed to catch him and "Freddie fell back off the bandstand, behind the drums. Oliver almost died laughing. The audience thought it was part of the act and wanted more. Cheered for five minutes."[7]

Moore remembers Oliver not only as "a nice fellow to work with" but as someone with an extraordinary appetite. Oliver seemed to eat and drink double portions or more of everything—a whole loaf of bread, a quart of milk at a single sitting; he also loved hot dogs and baked beans. Privately, his musicians called him "google-eye," because one of his eyes, which had been injured in an accident, bulged out.

Plagued by bad luck and the aftermath of the Depression, Oliver struggled to keep the band together. A couple of times they got stranded in places with no dates lined up—Moore recalls doing gigs in Kansas City, one time, until the band was able to resume touring—and at one point Oliver got sick and couldn't work. Finally, Moore says, "the band broke up in St. Louis. And everybody come back to New York, all but King Oliver." The band's library of 150 arrangements went with trumpeter and arranger Dave Nelson when Oliver was unable to pay for them.[8]

Band work wasn't plentiful in those days, but Moore managed to stay afloat. "My first time working with Sidney Bechet," he recalls, "*he* worked with me, in my own band. I had a five-piece band down at the Circle Ballroom, a taxi dance hall at Fifty-eighth Street and Broadway. And I had Bechet down there with me. We wasn't making no money; it was just a job during the depression time. I think the scale was $25 a week for the musicians and $30 for the leader. Out of that extra $5, I had to buy music—stocks—every week, because the manager wanted me to keep up with all the new numbers. That was after I worked with King Oliver."

Around 1933–36, Moore formed a trio, with Pete Brown on alto sax and Don Frye on piano, which he led for several years at the Victoria Cafe, on 141st Street and Seventh Avenue; they moved in January 1937 to the nearby Brittwood Club. Their group, he says, was popular in Harlem.

> During that time, musicians wasn't making much money, but they was happy. Like at the Victoria, I was supposed to play from nine to three in the morning. Do you know what time we come out of there sometimes? Nine, ten, eleven o'clock in the morning. Gene Krupa, Tommy Dorsey, Artie Shaw,

> Buddy Rich—he must have been about seventeen, eighteen years old—and oh, come up there and jam. There was a dance floor, it wasn't half big as this room. Sometimes we had a fifteen-piece band down there, jamming. We had three pieces on the bandstand, and the other guys'd come in, sit down on the dance floor. Oh boy!

He remembers with pride the night that Louis Armstrong dropped in and how he carried on, pleased to be entertaining royalty. Moore mugged, flipped his sticks, did "Darktown Strutters Ball" and the other old-time numbers, and—at Armstrong's request—sang Armstrong's theme, "When It's Sleepy Time Down South."

Bass player John Kirby hired Moore's group, along with some other musicians, to work under his leadership. They opened in May 1937 at the Onyx Club on Fifty-second Street, and Moore recalls that "during that time, Stuff Smith, the violin player, was right down the street from us at the Three Deuces, and Count Basie was at the Famous Door." Initially, he didn't mind Kirby taking over the group because business hadn't been good at the Brittwood and it was excellent at the Onyx. But Kirby had definite ideas about how he wanted the band to sound—he was developing a unique, subtle brand of small band swing—and eventually he made some personnel changes, including replacing Moore with O'Neill Spencer. For a brief time, Moore found work elsewhere on Fifty-second Street; after that he took whatever club dates came his way.

The mid-1940s found him working with trumpeter Max Kaminsky and pianist Art Hodes at the Village Vanguard. That was where Moore began featuring his singing and washboard playing. Hodes encouraged him to play washboard, noting later: "Moore was willing but he needed thimbles. And in the '40s they weren't the easiest thing to procure. The war had made such items a bit rare. But that was solved when my dad, a tinsmith by trade, made a set for Freddie. It was really something to hear Moore take off on that washboard. He made beats like you thought he was a dancer." Moore's eye-rolling and drumstick-tossing routines also went over well, as did his singing. Hodes remembered a number they created together, "Blues 'n' Booze," with a line by Moore that goes, "Mama, mama, mama, why do you snore so loud?" Moore would repeat the line, in classic blues fashion, then zing in with, "You may be a little woman but you sound just like a big crowd."[9]

Moore offers an old newspaper clipping—undated, and he doesn't remember the year—to show the kind of company he kept. It's an ad for a star-studded Town Hall jazz concert: "Farewell Party for Billie

Holiday prior to European Tour. Eddie Condon. Jo Jones. J. C. Higginbotham. Buck Clayton. Conrad Janis. Max Kaminsky. Freddie Moore. Bobby Hackett." He also talks of a Carnegie Hall concert featuring a drum contest in which he shared the stage with Gene Krupa and Cozy Cole. "I used four sticks—the most showmanship. But I was the second. You know they ain't going to give me the first prize. The first prize was Gene Krupa."

In 1945 and 1947, Moore worked under the leadership of Sidney Bechet; Bunk Johnson joined the band briefly in 1945. Moore recalls that Bechet had mixed feeling about his drumming. "If Bechet liked it, he liked it. If he didn't like it, he'd give you a hard way. When I first started working he didn't like me so well, because I was a little bit too loud." Moore's drumming, reminiscent of tent shows, street parades, and old-time vaudeville, probably was too heavy and blatant for many jazz musicians by the mid-1940s. The modern jazz drummers who were emerging were taking a subtler, more painterly approach.

Moore finally found his niche in the traditional jazz revival. It would be impossible for him to ever play drums with someone like Miles Davis—they inhabited different musical worlds—but he was just right for many musicians who favored older styles. By the late forties, when the spotlight of critical and public attention shifted mostly to the modernists, Moore found a steady stream of work by sticking with the music he liked. "I worked at the old Jimmy Ryan's, Fifty-second Street, about three years, with Wilbur de Paris. Then later, I come up to the new Jimmy Ryan's on Fifty-fourth Street and worked with Tony Parenti."

In 1948 Moore played briefly with young Bob Wilber, who idolized Bechet and was probably intrigued by using a drummer with whom Bechet had worked and recorded. Moore also worked with Art Hodes at the Blue Note in Chicago in 1950 and then with Conrad Janis in New York in 1951. He became the house drummer at the Stuyvesant Casino jam sessions and was with de Paris again in 1952–54. He went to Europe for the first time with Mezz Mezzrow in 1954, then again with Sammy Price in 1955. He also worked with the Nicholas Brothers in Paris.

In 1957 Moore got back together again, very briefly, with Art Hodes. An agent had booked them as a team for a nightspot on Chicago's South Side. Although the room was half empty, the patrons who were there were enthusiastic. After the first show, the bartender told Hodes the boss wanted to see him. Hodes was stunned when the boss, who was burning mad, swore he never would have hired the team if he'd known they were racially mixed. He ordered them to get out. Running up against such racism, particularly in a northern city, hurt both men, but what could they do? Hodes took Moore around the corner to buy him a drink, and after they were served without incident, they told their story to the bartender. They were surprised to learn that both joints were owned by the same man. Apparently, he had no objection to taking their money or to their drinking together, only to hiring them.

Steady jobs weren't always easy to come by, and in the 1960s, Moore even played one rock 'n' roll gig in Manhasset, on Long Island—something he never did again. Occasionally, he gave some lessons, although there wasn't much money in that. From 1968 to 1970, he worked with Tony Parenti, and then with Roy Eldridge in the summer of 1971 at Jimmy Ryan's. He also worked a good bit with singer Cathy Chamberlain. In the years since, he's gigged around New York, working one night a week throughout most of the eighties, first at the old Red Blazer and then at the new Red Blazer Too. He's willing to take other odd jobs, too, but at his age, he says he doesn't want to overdo things. He's glad he's no longer lugging his drums to clubs, setting them up, playing, and breaking them down again, every night.

During his career, Moore reflects, he has recorded with King Oliver, Hot Lips Page, Roy Eldridge, Wild Bill Davison, Art Hodes, Pops Foster, Jimmy Archey, and many others, but it wasn't until 1981 that he finally recorded an album under his own name. Banjo player Eddy Davis, a great admirer of Moore's work (and a believer that Moore could have been a star with proper management), got him to record *The Great Freddie Moore* (New York Jazz J-001). The album is a first-rate sampler of Moore's work and uses such well-known sidemen as Warren Vache, Jr., Kenny Davern, Milt Hinton, and Joe Muranyi. Wisely, producer Davis has included, in addition to instrumental and vocal numbers, some of Moore's spoken recollections.

Saturday night patrons of the Red Blazer Too can still see Moore roll and pop his eyes. They can laugh at his outrageous mugging, done with an innocence that is utterly disarming—as when he holds a large comb up to his bald head each time he gets to that line referring to "a fine-toothed comb" in "Won't You Come Home, Bill Bailey." They can also appreciate his amazingly brisk drum solo, considering that he's well into his eighties, on "Flying Home."[10]

Of course, Moore hasn't been immune to the aging process. His energies flag at times, and there are younger drummers who maintain faster tempos, sustain a steady beat with greater stamina. But none of them can play in the style Moore plays. He hits four even beats to the bar on the bass drum, and you hear every resounding beat, really pushing the band along. (Very few drummers are left who keep time on the bass drum. Panama Francis is one of them, but he plays the bass drum much softer than Moore does, so the pulse is felt more than heard, and he occasionally accents a beat.)

Ask Moore to sing the blues, and as the piano player vamps, he'll come up with verse after verse of earthy, age-old favorites, pulling lines from his memory that can surprise listeners and musicians alike. "The reason my grandmammy so crazy about my grandpappy—he got the same jelly roll I have," Moore will sing, with a casual wave of one hand toward his crotch. He'll add—as if forgetting that he's in his eighties—that his grandpappy's jelly roll is seventy-five years old: "That's sure some old jelly roll!" With surprising vigor he'll call out: "Shoot the juice to me, Lucy! Shoot it to me all night long." There are no records or videotapes of Moore singing the blues, and that's a pity. He draws upon old-time show business traditions, and he's irreplaceable.

And when he sings in that rough-edged, gravelly, sometimes raucous voice of his—lines like, "Who the hell was your pappy? You sure some ugly child"—you can't help but respond. Freddie Moore is a survivor from an era that's now almost completely gone.

8

JABBO SMITH

Elusive Genius

"The sound is still in my ears, you know, the way he sounded on trumpet," said master bassist Milt Hinton of Jabbo Smith. "I always considered him one of the greatest trumpet players I ever heard in my life."[1]

Hinton is fortunate that he can still summon up the memory of how Smith sounded in his prime, for precious little of Smith was ever captured on record. Smith made nineteen sides under his own name in 1929, a handful of which—among the most impressive of all jazz age recordings—show us what it was that so dazzled musicians of that day. In the late 1920s, Smith turned up, too, on a recording of "Black and Tan Fantasy" with Duke Ellington, on four numbers with the "Louisiana Sugar Babes" (Fats Waller, James P. Johnson, Garvin Bushell), and a smattering of less-important sides. In the 1930s, he made a few recordings with Claude Hopkins, as well as four more under his own name, before vanishing from jazz history, not resurfacing again until the mid-1970s. There is no other jazz star of the 1920s and 1930s who was praised anywhere nearly as highly by other musicians yet who left us so few recordings by which to judge his work. And those who actually remember Smith from his glory years are growing few.

Trumpeter Doc Cheatham claimed, "Jabbo Smith was Louis Armstrong's greatest rival back in those days; he was a wonderful player." In fact, when Cheatham first heard Smith in 1928, he found him to be a faster and, in his opinion, an even greater player than Armstrong. Drummer Tommy Benford declared that Smith "had Chicago on its head in 1929 with his trumpet playing." Roy Eldridge recalled a jazz battle in Milwaukee in 1930 when "Jabbo Smith caught me one night and turned me every way but loose. . . . He wore me out before that night was through. He knew a lot of music, and he knew changes. . . . Jabbo Smith didn't have Louis' sound, but he was faster." French critic Hugues Panassie wrote of Smith in 1936: "I have heard records on which he exhibited exceptional fertility of melodic invention. He has astonishing force and a positive attack of great beauty. Many very competent critics rate him as the greatest trumpeter since Louis." Milt Hinton, who worked with Smith back in 1930, maintained: "Jabbo was as good as Louis then. He was the Dizzy Gillespie of that era. He played rapid-fire passages while Louis was melodic and beautiful."[2]

One might question whether Smith was ever quite Armstrong's equal, for there is a towering grandeur to the best of Armstrong's performances that rivals would have been hard-pressed to match. And as Roy Eldridge noted: "Louis gave me something I couldn't get off Jabbo—continuity, which makes all the sense. Louis introduces the piece and sticks around the melody, but when he has it out, you know it's out, and you know he's going to finish a whole."[3] Armstrong had a natural feeling for structure.

Smith's recorded performances are more disorganized, more chaotic than Armstrong's. Yet that very element of erraticism, that streak of unpredictability in Smith's work, winds up at times—for me, anyway—contributing to its appeal. His sides may not have Armstrong's perfect symmetry, but they have a touch of divine madness that excites the listener in a way that is different from the more logically organized music of Armstrong.

Listen to Smith's "Decatur Street Tutti" (April 4, 1929)—the ecstatic yearning he conveys, that Dionysian sense of abandon. Joyous! Yes, but with a hint of plaintiveness. The essence of jazz is to be found in this recording. Smith is breaking loose, projecting that fervor to be free that has been central to the appeal of jazz from the beginning. His trumpeting is high, clear, and slightly wild. George James follows Smith's trumpet playing with an alto sax passage that is smooth and creamy (he no doubt took pride in his tone)—but wholly ordinary, uninspired, earthbound. And then Smith comes in to offer a fiercely urgent scat vocal. As I listen to this once again, my jaw drops. It's fantastic stuff. The record company was having Smith scat because that's what Armstrong had been doing on many of his well-received sides. And yet here, briefly, Smith actually is beating Armstrong at his own game. A record like "Decatur Street Tutti" makes you wonder if maybe the old-timers who insist that around 1929 Smith was Armstrong's equal weren't exaggerating—or certainly weren't exaggerating too much. This record—which, incidentally, enjoyed minimal sales when it was released—is absolutely first-rate jazz.

And then you put on a side like "Sweet and Low Blues" (February 23, 1929). It's a much less intense affair, and consequently, at first, seems much less impressive. But pay attention when Omer Simeon takes his clarinet solo. If you're not listening carefully, you could miss Smith's muted trumpet obligato in the background. The recording balance is hardly ideal; nearly all of the attention here is focused on Simeon. But Smith's casually brilliant obligato is offered in double-time. That is, he's playing at twice the tempo that Simeon and the others are playing. He's running on that horn now. This is the sort of thing you might expect from Dizzy Gillespie in the 1940s. But *nobody* was doing this on records in the 1920s.

Smith was a real jazz original. He could excite you, the way few in jazz could. Yet he faded into obscurity. By the late 1930s he was a forgotten man, unknown except to jazz record collectors. Then, nearly forty years later, he was "rediscovered," hailed as a "legend." But his trumpet playing had become a shadow of its earlier self, his constitution no longer strong enough to withstand the grind of nightly performing.

What accounts for the mystery of Jabbo Smith? Why did he fade from view so quickly, after flaring so brilliantly in the late 1920s? And how did that wild, astonishing talent develop?

Jabbo Smith and I meet at the Greenwich Village apartment of Lorraine Gordon (wife of Village Vanguard owner Max Gordon), who, as a close friend and de facto manager, looks after Smith's interests. She first met Smith when she was just a teenager in Newark, New Jersey, before the start of World War II. She would go to hear him play in a local club then; she even owned his old records. But she lost track of him during the war, and they met again only in the late 1970s, after his "rediscovery." On this evening, Smith has brought his friend a container of ice cream. She accepts the gift and advises him not to take out his false teeth while he is being interviewed. As soon as she slips out of the room, though, he removes them. It's a small, but telling, gesture of independence—or even, perhaps, of contrariness. He's never liked being told what to do.

Smith looks rather worn down. There is sadness in his eyes, and when he speaks, it is in a soft voice, the words often not easy to understand. Once in a great while a hint of the fierce pride that he must have had becomes evident—like when he reminds you, his eyes sparkling for a moment with remembered joy, that he didn't try to play like anybody else. And when he notes that he's never heard any other trumpeter play the way he did. Only his peak years seem to be in sharp focus, however; the long years of obscurity that followed run together in his memory, and his very early years are also somewhat hazy. He tells his story, haltingly, with some difficulty. Gordon picks up those threads that he leaves dangling.

His actual first name is not Jabbo but Cladys, which he has never liked. He had a cousin, born around the same time he was, who was named Gladys, and his mother invented the name Cladys as a kind of male equivalent. So where did the nickname Jabbo come from? It wasn't supposed to have been *his* nickname, he says. He recalls a boyhood incident involving his buddies from the orphanage they all grew up in. "Oh, we was in Washington, I guess, and we went to see a picture—cowboys and Indians—and there was an Indian there, getting ready to shoot William S. Hart. And somebody said, 'Look at old Jabbo. He's getting ready to shoot William S. Hart.' And this Indian was very homely, ugly. So my friend James Reddick was an ugly dude—[Smith laughs]—and we called *him* 'Jabbo,' you know, after the Indian."

Smith himself wasn't called Jabbo until some years later, when at age sixteen he got his first steady professional job, playing in a ballroom band in Philadelphia. The violinist asked him if he could recommend a trombone player, and Smith thought of his buddy James "Jabbo" Reddick. "And I say, 'Yeah, Jabbo.' The fiddle player says, 'Jabbo?!' Since my name is Cladys, you know, he didn't get it. So he starts calling *me* Jabbo. Of course, he has his cats. He'd say: 'Are any of you interested? Meet Jabbo.' So every one of the friends called me Jabbo." That nickname wound up sticking to Smith for the rest of his life.

Smith was born on Christmas Eve 1908 in Pembroke, Georgia—at least that's what he was told; there is no record of his birth. By the time he was old enough to begin registering memories—around age four—he was living in Savannah. His father apparently died when Smith was very young; his mother, Ida Smith, raised him by herself. When he was five or six, he was enrolled at a Catholic elementary school in Savannah, but he only attended for a few months. His mother worked cleaning Pullman cars, and since she wasn't always available to supervise him, he felt free to do as he pleased. He skipped school a lot. "She couldn't take care of my doing the school and everything," he says. "She couldn't take care of me —working, you know."

One day in 1914, an official named Mr. McIntyre came to the house and declared that, since Ida Smith was unable to look after her son properly, he should be placed in the Jenkins Orphan Home in

Charleston, South Carolina. She signed the legal papers to send him away and put him on the train by himself; someone from the orphanage would meet him when he got there. Smith wept bitterly upon his arrival at the home and for a few months afterward. He was hurt by the idea that his mother had dumped him, that he was now just one of hundreds of blacks, from infants to twenty-one-year-olds, staying at Jenkins. For about two years, he lived and worked on a large farm upstate, which supplied food for the orphanage, then he returned to Charleston, where he remained until he was sixteen.

Before the Jenkins Orphan Home was started, Rev. D. J. Jenkins had simply taken street children into his home. Then, as his operation expanded, he received a small amount of government funding and a good deal of private donations, allowing him to relocate to a former hospital. He also hit upon an unusual way to make the orphans help earn their upkeep: he organized five or six children's brass bands, each with perhaps a dozen members, which performed and raised money for the home—and enabled Jenkins and his wife to enjoy a fairly high standard of living. The orphanage thus became a kind of training ground for professional musicians, men like trumpeter Gus Aiken (born in 1902), who later played in Louis Armstrong's band; drummer Tommy Benford (born in 1905), who later played in Jelly Roll Morton's band; and trumpeter Cat Anderson (born in 1916), who later played in Duke Ellington's band. When Smith arrived, one of the orphanage's bands had just returned from a triumphant visit to England.

Smith recalls: "I was in the band at Jenkins. We'd go everywhere and travel. Like we'd come to New York here, and we'd go all up in Pennsylvania—everywhere. We'd play on the corners, you know, and pass the hat. And that's the way they had to raise the money for the orphanage." The band would play three or four tunes at a street corner before moving on to another location; and sometimes there would be indoor concerts, in which Smith and one of the other boys doubled as acrobats.

Kids of all ages, playing different instruments, got their lessons together in one room. They were taught to sing their parts first and then to play them. If they made mistakes, the older boy giving the lessons would stand behind them and hit them, wherever he chose, with a drumstick. Smith comments that everyone wound up being able to play all parts on all of the brass instruments.

When he was perhaps eight years old, Smith started on trombone; he also played alto horn and baritone horn before ultimately deciding that he preferred the cornet. He was around twelve, he says, when people started realizing he was good. The first tune he learned was "Nearer My God to Thee." The boys were taught sacred music first, then marches and overtures, and finally popular music—which drew the tips at street-corner performance. "Ja-Da," "Margie," "Wang Wang Blues," "Dardanella"—those were the sorts of tunes Smith recalls playing. Later, when he turned professional, many musicians who had learned their instruments under more conventional circumstances were amazed that he could play so many different tunes on so many different instruments.

The Jenkins Orphan Home bands were not jazz bands—indeed, the term "jazz" was not even in common usage when Smith moved to the orphanage. Eventually, as jazz began to catch on in the world outside, it also reached Jenkins—often via boys who had run away for a spell and found jobs in bands. Smith can remember, for example, when one boy who had run away returned with the very first saxophone at the orphanage. He can also remember kids who ran away and then came back with new tunes they had picked up while working in "real" bands. And he remembers the first time that Gus Aiken, six years his senior, came back and demonstrated how to *growl* on a trumpet. The boys at Jenkins had all been taught to play clear, well-rounded tones in classic brass band fashion. Then Aiken taught them how to flood their tones with rough, growling sounds. They had never heard anything like it before.

Smith got some of his early style from Aiken and more from a boy named Horace Holmes—but none from records. Kids didn't get to hear records at Jenkins.

Survival at Jenkins meant following strict rules, with miscreants subject to corporal punishment. Everyone awakened at six, to start the day with a prayer meeting; then came instruction in reading, writing, and arithmetic, as well as practical skills like farming, printing, and baking. Some boys had relatives nearby whom they could visit. Those who didn't, like Smith, were confined to the orphanage grounds, except when they went to church or toured with one of the bands. Music, quite literally, provided a means of escape from the strict atmosphere of Jenkins.

Smith says that the band he was in would head north to New York City in the summer, south to Florida in the winter, and perform everywhere in between. "If we'd go through Savannah, I'd stay at home, stay with my mom. And that was all right. Everywhere that we went, guys that were in the band stayed with their families." He missed his mother, of course, and tried to maintain some sense of connection via letters and all-too-infrequent visits. For a while, his mother had a job teaching young orphans at the Jenkins farm upstate.

Sometimes when the orphan bands toured, members were allowed to hear alumni who had made it as musicians in the real world. Smith recalls a stop in Toledo where they got to see Gus Aiken, by then out on his own and featured in Gonzelle White's touring show.

Smith recalls that he generally didn't get to hear jazz bands or dance bands, but once, while in St. Augustine, Florida, he and the others heard Arthur Pryor and His Million Dollar Band, a famous concert ensemble whose repertoire included popular music. And, more important, in 1920, when Smith went to Chicago for the first time, he got to hear King Oliver. The cornetist, who had relocated to Chicago from his native New Orleans just one year earlier, had not yet cut any records, though he had already made quite a name for himself. Reverend Walker, who was managing the Jenkins band that Smith belonged to, wanted to hear Oliver and took Smith with him. He figured that Smith, a good cornetist, might get better by hearing the man so many people were talking about. Smith remembers that Oliver, backed by just a pianist, played his own "Snag It."

When Smith was perhaps twelve or thirteen, which would have been around 1921–22, the stifling atmosphere of the Jenkins Orphan Home finally got to him. He knew he was good enough on cornet to play in a lot of professional bands on the outside, if he could just get away. So, while the orphan band was based for a stretch in Jacksonville, Florida, he carefully planned his escape. He split with one of his best buddies, trombone player James Reddick, and another guy whose sister lived in Jacksonville. They fell out of line and ran off as the band members marched down to the boat that was going to take them back to Charleston, knowing full well that the police would be looking for them and the orphanage staff would punish them if—or, probably, when—they got caught.

Smith landed a job with a band in a place called the Pink Carnation. Then, while walking down the street one day, he ran into a popular local pianist and bandleader, Eagle Eye Shields, who had heard him play in the orphan band. Shields was looking sharp, as usual—according to Smith, he owned a hundred different suits; he was *known* for his fabulous one hundred suits. Shields told Smith to forget the Pink Carnation, that from here on he was working in Shields's twelve-piece band. Smith, still in short pants, was thrilled to be treated like an adult.

Shields hired Reddick, too, and arranged for both boys to live at the apartment of the band's drummer. The two were delighted to have the opportunity to live rent-free, in exchange for working in the band. All went well for several months, until one night the police came into the club where the band was playing and jailed the boys until they could be put on a boat for Charleston. The people at the orphanage did not look kindly upon the runaways. Both boys were stripped naked and whipped with reins; Smith was treated especially harshly since he was believed to have been the ringleader of the escape.

No matter how hard they tried, the orphanage staff couldn't break his spirit. After having made some money and tasted freedom, Smith wasn't about to let them tie him down. He ran away from Jenkins every chance he could get, perhaps four or five times, always when he was in some distant city on tour with the orphan band. One time he worked with a bandleader in Newark, another time with a guy named Phillips in Philadelphia; they didn't care how old he was, as long as he could play.

In the fall of 1924, while still under the jurisdiction of the orphanage, Smith enrolled at South Carolina State Normal School, in Orangeburg, where several of his friends from Jenkins were students. He was soon expelled, however, after shooting himself in the leg—the school didn't want to have anything to do with someone who messed with firearms. Smith tried to return to the orphanage, but Reverend Jenkins now considered him to be incorrigible and washed his hands of him.

According to Smith, "They sent me home and said I was too bad, you know." Still, he feels that "they did everything they could for me." Reverend Jenkins gave him nine dollars so that he could travel to his mother's. "But instead of me going to Savannah, I had a [half] sister in Philadelphia, and that's where I went, to my sister's. Up north. We were southerners coming up north, you know." He wrote his mother that he was going to be a big success as a musician and would earn the huge sum of $100 a week.

Smith's half sister, Ethel, had no way of knowing that within a few short years Cladys Smith would be one of the outstanding jazz musicians in the nation. Not that it would have meant much to her, even if she could have imagined it. Jazz just didn't interest her. She was willing to do her duty, however, and take in this brother she hardly knew, at least until he could support himself. No doubt, he must have appeared to her to be something of a ne'er-do-well, arriving in Philadelphia on crutches as a result of his self-inflicted leg wound.

He sat in one night with Phillips, the local bandleader he had worked for as a runaway. He was heard by a more important bandleader, drummer Harry Marsh, who hired him on the spot. He was soon being featured in Marsh's ten-piece band at Philadelphia's Waltz Dream, a large, beautiful ballroom for black dancers, which had two bands on weeknights and three on weekends. (This was the band in which Smith picked up the nickname Jabbo.) He recalls asking for—and getting—$100 per week, at a time when the other sidemen were getting $65.

Playing opposite Marsh's band was a seven- or eight-piece outfit led by trombonist Wilbur de Paris, featuring his younger brother Sidney on trumpet. Sidney de Paris, who was then no more than twenty but seemed significantly older and more experienced, became Smith's favorite trumpeter. (In later years, Smith would recognize Louis Armstrong's brilliance; but at that point, he had not yet heard Armstrong.) Smith remembers with enthusiasm: "Sidney de Paris. Yeah, he was something else. I mean, he was using derbies and tin cans. He had all these mutes and tin cans. Yeah . . . I liked the way he used derbies. Sidney was my man. I liked the way he played. I liked the way he pulled the horn. He *pulled* it. I liked that." Smith sat under de Paris, watching how he played, but he never tried to play like de Paris: "Uh-uh," he declares flatly. He was on his own track now and wasn't about to copy anybody.[4]

For several months, Smith played trumpet in Marsh's band. (He had played cornet at Jenkins, but he preferred the more piercing tone of the trumpet.) Then Marsh left, and the sideman who took over as leader balked at the notion of Smith getting $100 a week. So Smith took off for Atlantic City to see what work he could find there. He went around, as was the custom among jazzmen then, sitting in with different musicians, such as Bernard Addison and Kid Norfolk.[5] Eventually, he ran into Gus Aiken, "who used to be in the Jenkins band. So I went with him. He was working with Drake and Walker [a touring show]. So I was working with him, and I stayed with him about a month." Smith next got a job in Roy Johnson's small band on the recommendation of Sidney de Paris, who had formerly worked for Johnson.

Smith knew he had arrived, though, when he was asked to join Charlie Johnson's Paradise Ten, which was working in Atlantic City in the summer of 1925.[6] The band was based in New York, at Smalls's Paradise in Harlem, and it was "big time." He was the youngest member of the Paradise Ten and a most promising hot soloist who played pocket cornet, coach horn, euphonium, trombone, and xylophone—and even occasionally beat a tambourine—in addition to trumpet. Sidney de Paris was the featured trumpeter, but he left when the band went to New York in the fall and Smith took over that spot. Others in the band when Smith joined included George Stafford (drums), Bobby Johnson (banjo), and Benny Waters (alto sax). Benny Carter and Edgar Sampson, both of whom played sax and wrote arrangements, were hired on a bit after Smith was. For a while, Smith lived at a boarding-house run by the widow of Scott Joplin.

Johnson's band didn't carry its own vocalists but provided music for shows at both the Harlem and Atlantic City venues. Such entertainers as Mary Stafford (a big name at that time), Mattie Hite (known for her risqué songs), and a man named Jazzbo would go from table to table, singing and collecting tips, which they split with the band. (Smith also remembers Ethel Waters among those who entertained at one time.) Johnson initially proposed paying Smith $65 a week, like the others in the band, adding that the young trumpeter would most likely make another $35 a week in tips. Instead, Smith agreed to work for $100 a week (which was eventually upped to $150), with Johnson keeping his share of the tips.

Johnson's band had a greater importance, in its day, than might be inferred from the relatively small number of records it made. Johnson was not a good businessman, and he didn't get the band the amount of exposure, on records or on radio, that he should have. Like King Oliver and Sam Wooding, he reportedly turned down an opportunity to go into the Cotton Club, an offer that Duke Ellington eventually accepted. Still, Johnson was an established big band leader whose group of musicians reigned supreme at one of the most desirable locations in New York City. Plenty of fans considered Johnson's their favorite band, and Smith couldn't have asked for a better spot in the mid-1920s than to be its featured trumpeter.[7] He reiterates that Charlie Johnson and Fletcher Henderson had the two top bands then, that at the time Ellington wasn't even in their league.

Smith recalls: "I joined up with Charlie Johnson in '25. We were in Atlantic City, and we came to New York. We worked in the Paradise in Atlantic City, and we worked in the Paradise in New York, Smalls's Paradise. So every year, we'd just go for one and go for the other, you know." The Paradise in Atlantic City, which was run by whites, and Smalls's Paradise in Harlem, run by Ed Smalls, who was black, were not connected. In the parlance of the day, the clubs were "black and tans." Both had racially mixed audiences, although whites predominated; and both were located in black neighborhoods, although they were geared toward the white trade.

Smalls's, a large place with tables and booths as well as a dance floor, was one of *the* places to go in New York. Audiences came for the shows and the overall atmosphere, not just to dance or listen to the band. But it was the band that drew so many musicians to the club. They'd sit in whenever they could, trying to make an impression, to "cut" in. Smith remembers, for example, Chick Webb's whole band coming in—not booked to play there, mind you, but simply coming in and getting up to play—in an attempt to cut Johnson's band. Various trumpet greats of the day, including Tommy Ladnier, came to challenge Smith—who feels he cut all challengers. Smith was particularly pleased when kids from the Jenkins orphan bands, performing in and around New York, would come to hear him at Smalls's. They were proud of his success, the way the boys in his crowd had been proud of Gus Aiken.

Johnson's first recording session was for the Emerson label, early in 1925 (before Smith joined); he didn't record again until February 25, 1927, when he made "Paradise Wobble," "Birmingham Black Bottom" (both of which include Smith solos), and "Don't You Leave Me Here" for Victor. A vocalist named Monette Moore was used on those sides, but she wasn't a regular with the band. (Smith doesn't remember any black bands that had female singers on their payrolls in those days.) Smith also recorded with Johnson's band at its next Victor session on January 24, 1928, which produced "Hot Tempered Blues," "Charleston Is the Best Dance After All," and "You Ain't the One" (with Monette Moore on vocals), the last two arranged by Benny Carter.

Because Johnson concentrated on the music and shows at Smalls's Paradise, we have far less recorded documentation of how Smith sounded than we should have. However, Smith also managed to do a bit of free-lance recording. He recalls that he was one of Clarence Williams's Blue Five, backing Eva Taylor when she sang "I Wish You Would Love Me Like I'm Loving You" and "If I Could Be with You" (February 10, 1927). Brian Rust lists him as one of the Georgia Strutters, along with singer Perry Bradford and musicians Willie "The Lion" Smith and Jimmy Harrison, among others, who recorded in 1926 (though Smith doesn't remember ever having recorded with Perry Bradford).[8] Most significant, however, is his appearance on a Duke Ellington recording of "Black and Tan Fantasy" on November 3, 1927. Two minor numbers, "What Can a Poor Fellow Do" and "Chicago Stomp Down," were also recorded at that session.

"I was with Charlie Johnson when I made 'Black and Tan Fantasy,' " Smith comments. "I don't know what happened with Bubber [Miley, Ellington's regular trumpeter, who had played on a version of the number recorded the previous month]. Anyway, I went and did it. I just made those records with Duke Ellington. Duke wanted me to join his band, but he wouldn't pay enough. Because at that time I was making a hundred and a half, and he offered ninety-five. I couldn't. I mean, Charlie Johnson . . . and me were like brothers." In fact, he felt all the members of that band were like brothers and notes: "I was the youngest guy there. . . . So they'd look after me." He got other offers to leave Johnson's band, but he turned them down. He was happy being there.

Never good at accepting authority, Smith was soon straining the patience of the other musicians. He knew his playing was outstanding—and getting better all the time—and he behaved, at times, more like a prima donna than a member of the band. He had a defiant streak, an urge toward freedom; it gave character and life to his trumpet playing but caused interpersonal difficulties.

At Smalls's, the band went on at nine and played until six the next morning. Smith was frequently two or three hours late. Ed Smalls made allowances for him, not just because he was a good player, but because Smalls liked him. Smith thinks it may have been because Smalls had grown up in Charleston, too, as had all twenty-one of the waiters at the club. Smalls "was crazy about everybody from Charleston," Smith says.

Smalls and Smith also hung out together after hours. From Smith's point of view, it was Smalls's fault if he got to work late because Smalls sometimes kept him out all night. Others in the band may have been jealous of their friendship. "Smalls was a big shot there in Harlem," Smith explains. "I was a kid—just seventeen—but I was with Smalls." When Smalls assured him it was okay if he got to the bandstand late, so long as he was there by midnight, Smith didn't argue. Needless to say, this didn't endear him to the other band members, some of whom became resentful. Sure he was good, but they no doubt believed they were just as good. In his autobiography, Benny Waters offered the opinion that "Jabbo didn't make Charlie Johnson, Charlie Johnson made Jabbo! He didn't influence the band. He was no asset to the band; we had trumpet players in the band that played as well or better. Sidney de Paris was a better jazzman for many people than Jabbo. But Jabbo was young and ambitious . . . ."[9]

No one doubted that Smith was a great trumpeter, but Johnson had to wonder whether having him in the Paradise Ten was worth the aggravation. He finally called a band meeting—the main purpose of which, or so it seemed to Smith, was to chew him out—and told Smith that if he didn't shape up he would be replaced. (Sidney de Paris was in town, Johnson noted; he had been excellent in the band before and could be excellent in it again.) Smith, who had thought the members of this band were brothers, smarted at being chastised. He quit the Paradise Ten and was replaced by Sidney de Paris.

* * *

Pianists Fats Waller and James P. Johnson had been after Smith to join them in the pit orchestra of *Keep Shufflin',* an all-black musical being prepared for Broadway as a follow-up to *Shuffle Along,* which had been such a smash earlier in the decade. Smith decided to accept the invitation; he would get $150 per week for playing in the orchestra plus $75 per week for accompanying singer Jean Starr in a featured spot. The cast included comedians Flournoy Miller and Aubrey Lyles (who had written the book), Juanita Hall, and dancer Johnny Hudgins (from *Chocolate Kiddies* with Sam Wooding). Con Conrad, composer of "Margie," had written the score.

Waller and Johnson, who were famous by then, frequently were hired to entertain as a team at hotels, for dinners and the like, and occasionally Smith got to work with them. The trio, along with one other member of the *Keep Shufflin'* pit band, Garvin Bushell (the multireed player long associated with Sam Wooding), even recorded together—"Willow Tree" (featuring some muted eloquence from Smith), "Thou Swell," "Persian Rug," and " 'Sippi" —on March 27, 1928. The four sides, released under the billing of the Louisiana Sugar Babes, had Waller on organ and Bushell on clarinet, alto sax, and bassoon.

Keep Shufflin' fell far short of matching the success of *Shuffle Along.* Still, after a rather brief Broadway run it headed out on tour, thanks to the financial backing of Arnold Rothstein. "He was a big gambler," Smith recalls, which is putting it mildly. Best known as the man who fixed the 1919 World Series, Rothstein was once described by Stanley Walker of the *New York Herald Tribune* as "the walking bank, the pawnbroker of the underworld."[10] With his murder in November 1928, outside of New York's Park Central Hotel, *Keep Shufflin'* lost its "angel" and was forced to close. It had been running for about a half a year. According to Smith: "When we got to Chicago—we had been there maybe two weeks—Rothstein died, and the show closed. Everybody went back to New York. But I liked Chicago. So I stayed there."

Smith wasted no time getting his name around in the Windy City. He started out at a speakeasy known as the Bookstore, where he jammed with anyone who showed up. The house combo was just three or four pieces, with a girl singer named Irene Eaddy (who later married Teddy Wilson). But musicians from Louis Armstrong—who was then based in Chicago—on down often congregated there early in the morning, after finishing their regular jobs. One mob-connected fellow who heard Smith play said he was going to take over Chicago's popular Sunset Cafe and he wanted Smith to lead the band there. But the musicians' union said that Smith would have to be in Chicago a year before he could have the job.

According to Smith, a succession of bands came into the Sunset—Tiny Parham, Jimmy Bell, Carroll Dickerson, Sammy Stewart, and others—and he appeared as a featured trumpeter with all of them. He was paid directly by the man who had taken over the club, not by the bandleaders. The idea was that, after a year's time, Smith would become leader of his own big band. But he kept getting into hot water with bandleaders because he wouldn't do what they wanted. They complained about him to the union, and word got around that he was "difficult."

The union president began to pressure Smith to fill in for absent musicians in other bands whenever he was free. Smith, who had never been good about having people tell him what to do, was hardly thrilled at being told to substitute for lesser trumpeters in boring bands.

It was almost by chance that Smith made his celebrated series of Brunswick records in 1929. In January of that year, he recalls, a banjo player named Ikey Robinson "asked me to record with him. And I made these records with him." For the first time—inspired, no doubt, by Louis Armstrong—Smith sang on record, in addition to playing trumpet. "This guy, Mayo Williams, heard me. . . . So he had me get a band under my name. So I did that. I just used the same guys that Ikey had," Smith says. Pioneering black record producer J. Mayo Williams, of Brunswick Records, was a key figure in the field of "race records." He wanted to build Smith up as a possible competitor to Armstrong, whose Hot Five sides and related recordings had been doing so well for the rival OKeh label since 1925.

The nineteen sides that Jabbo Smith and His Rhythm Aces recorded in 1929 were done with a casualness that makes the end results even more impressive. Smith would make up the tunes perhaps the night before the date, but he wouldn't write them down; in fact, he made no effort to copyright his compositions. The other musicians would learn the tunes only when he ran them down at the recording studio. He'd teach them the melodies, they'd rehearse for maybe a half hour, then they'd record. On "Lina Blues," recorded on April 17, 1929, Smith also plays trombone because the trombonist was drunk at the time. Some numbers, such as the dashing, intricate "Jazz Battle" (January 29, 1929) and "Take Your Time" (February 23, 1929), are instrumentals; others, such as "Take Me to the River" (March 1, 1929), "Let's Get Together" (March 1, 1929), and the memorable "Till Times

Get Better" (April 4, 1929), have lyrics. Smith's hot stomps are overflowing with energy; his playing, as cornetist Peter Ecklund aptly put it, "is frequently right on the edge of being out of control."[11] Titles were created casually: "Michigander Blues," named for nearby Lake Michigan; "Decatur Street Tutti," because his sister lived on Decatur Street in Philadelphia.

These records, which contain moments of absolute brilliance, did not do well commercially, and certainly never equaled the commercial success of Armstrong's recordings. Why not? In *Early Jazz,* Gunther Schuller wrote that in all of Smith's Brunswick recordings, his "extraordinary virtuosity, relentless energy, exemplary musicianship can be heard. He was above all an astonishingly consistent player and musician—a musician's musician, which I am sure is the reason Jabbo Smith was never a great public success. Every one of the arts is full of examples of great technicians and intelligent artists who do not quite catch on because their work is too advanced or sophisticated technically."[12] But Schuller's explanation falls short of being complete. In terms of his technique, Smith was, as Schuller suggests, "ahead of his time." He was running on his horn with a freedom that anticipated later players. But it's at least as significant that, in terms of format, Smith was a bit *behind* the times.

Brunswick, playing catch-up ball, was trying to copy Armstrong's successful Hot Five—without noticing that in 1929 Armstrong, sensitive to public tastes, had already begun making the transition from the small-group jazz he had been favoring on records for the past four years to the more pop-oriented big band music he would emphasize in the 1930s. When Armstrong made his recording debut as a leader in 1925, his Hot Five actually consisted of just five musicians, and they played pure hot jazz. He continued recording under Hot Five and Hot Seven billings into 1928, but by 1929 he was using more sidemen and playing more commercially oriented material, which was easier for the general public to take.[13]

Armstrong also had a more attractive sound; his tone was richer and fuller than Smith's. And his performances tended to be more carefully thought out than Smith's. (Smith could have benefited from the services of an arranger who knew how best to showcase him.) Armstrong—who was seven years Smith's senior—also had an advantage in that he got established earlier. He made over seventy recordings under his own name before the stock market crash of 1929. By then he was a star—strong enough to keep going through the Depression, when most people were listening to the radio, not buying records.

After the crash, as public tastes shifted increasingly toward sweet, rather than hot, music, Armstrong adapted, recording more and more pop tunes rather than the hot stomps he had favored a few years earlier. (The preference for sweet music continued into the early 1930s, until Benny Goodman's swing band broke through so spectacularly in 1935; in the early 1930s, conventional wisdom among jazzmen was that hot music didn't sell.)

Smith never had a chance to get a toehold in the record business, partly because of timing. He did not begin recording under his own name until 1929. He was then twenty, approaching the peak of his powers. By the time he got his next chance to record, in 1938, he would be well past his prime. In boom years, record companies could afford to take chances. But in the depths of the Great Depression, when even established stars were selling very few records, no company was eager to chance recording someone—like Smith—whose records had not enjoyed significant sales.

In 1929, though, Smith had no complaints. He was living well, a hot-shot jazz trumpeter who impressed fellow musicians in Chicago, the fans at the club, and—not unimportant to him—the ladies. "Lina Blues" was named after a girl he was dating from the Sunset Cafe, and at one point, he dated Alice Whitman of the famed black vaudeville sister act. He also used to go bike riding with May Alix, the cabaret singer who had recorded with Louis Armstrong, among others.

Smith was a local celebrity, best known within the black community and among musicians. (Veteran Chicago pianist Art Hodes told me Smith was no better known than—if as well known as—such jazz sidemen as Baby Dodds and Johnny Dodds.) Louis Armstrong's records were beginning to win him mass audiences. Within a few years, Armstrong would be a household name, nationwide.

Armstrong—already being promoted as the world's greatest trumpeter—was featured with Carroll Dickerson's big band at Chicago's Savoy Ballroom around the time Smith got into town. It was inevitable that the two would "battle." Smith recalls:

> Louis Armstrong was there in Chicago, and I was. They asked me to [battle him]. . . . A guy named Teddy Bunn—he played guitar; he was great—he was in the band. . . . So he went down there [to where Armstrong was playing]. He came back and said, . . . "Man, get your horn. You come down here. This cat thinks he can blow." Heh-heh-heh. You know, the cat was jiving.

> So I got up and went with him, down to the matinee. And the guys tried to stick me. They'd stick you—you know, like you come in a place and they put music up in front of you.
>
> So they found out that I could read and all that stuff. Found out that I *could,* you know.

That was the first test, Smith says, just being able to sit in with the orchestra and sight-read a challenging arrangement of "China Boy."

> So after [Armstrong] found out that I could read and all that I said, "Well let me play with you." . . . They had two bands in there, Clarence Black and Carroll Dickerson. And so Carroll got me to play with him on the stand . . . the *battle.*
>
> So everybody said that I was a young Louis. They hadn't heard nobody that sounded like Louis, you know. . . . They called it a battle.

Smith speaks humbly when asked which trumpeter came out on top: "I mean, you know, Louis played the 'West End Blues.' And he locked it up with the 'West End Blues.' . . . So I played the 'West End Blues.' He was his own man, you know." Pianist Sammy Price witnessed the battle, and his recollection is that Armstrong won: "Louis played about 110 high Cs, and sheet, that was it; and Jabbo could play."[14] Was that the only time the two battled in public? "Yeah, you know—or we would go down to the Bookstore. He would play, I would play, you know," Smith says in a vague way. "There's a lot of things that people say, you know, between him and I, that they remember, that I don't remember." (Lorraine Gordon adds that some felt Smith triumphed over Armstrong but that Smith is too modest to make such a claim for himself.)

Rex Stewart wrote in *Down Beat* magazine that he once saw Smith and Armstrong face off at a breakfast dance at the Rockland Palace in Harlem.[15] His recollection was that Smith was playing with Charlie Johnson's band at the time and Armstrong was playing with a band led by Don Redman, and that perhaps a hundred musicians turned out to witness the battle between the trumpet stars. "Jabbo was standing out in front, and I'll say this, he was *blowing*—really coming like the angel Gabriel himself." Smith was fanning his brass derby as he hit high Fs and Gs (in an era when high C was a high note), while a friend of his from Smalls's Paradise shouted things like, "Play it Jabbo," "Who needs Louis? You can blow him down anytime," and "Go ahead Rice" ("Rice" being a nickname that many Charleston friends called each other). Stewart remembered Smith "soaring above the rhythm and the crowd noise," and he was sure, from the way Smith beamed at the end, that Smith felt he had proven he was king.

But Armstrong, who was up next, was not to be cut. "I can still see the scene in my mind's eye," Stewart wrote. "I've forgotten the tune, but I'll never forget the note. He blew a searing, soaring, *altissimo,* fantastic high note and held it long enough for every one of us musicians to gasp. Benny Carter, who has perfect pitch, said: 'Damn! That's high F.' Just about that time, Louis went into a series of cadenzas and continued into his first number." Plenty of trumpeters in that era ruined their lips straining to hit those impossibly high notes, but Armstrong hit climax after climax as women rushed toward the stage, begging for his autograph.

To Jabbo Smith, battling "the world's greatest trumpeter" was probably just another high point in a booming career. He may not have had Armstrong's majestic sense of construction, but then he wasn't trying to be a carbon copy of Armstrong. He had his own statements to make, with multinoted work that in retrospect seems a forerunner of Roy Eldridge's and Dizzy Gillespie's. It is doubtful that Smith had any inkling at the time that his career was just about to crest.

The big decisions, the ones that shape careers, so often don't seem big at the time they are made. In 1930 Jabbo Smith began gigging in Milwaukee. At first he was just picking up jobs there on weekends and then returning to Chicago—glad to escape, however briefly, from being hassled by the Chicago musicians' union president. As time passed, he continued to alternate between the two cities, but he increasingly thought of Milwaukee as his home. He was comfortable there, and he had a woman in Milwaukee who was important to him. So he began to withdraw from the fray.

In jazz, reputations were made in Chicago and New York. They were not made in Milwaukee. Smith was a big fish in a small pond now, easily the best trumpet player in town. Yet, he could have been the best trumpeter in Chicago, had he made that city his base, for by mid-1929 Armstrong had left for New York. Smith would have been a natural to fill the void. Even in Milwaukee, though, his daring trumpeting attracted challengers, musicians like Roy Eldridge and Henry "Red" Allen. "All the guys took me on," Smith says. "Everybody took me on, because they knew I was the best. This was 1930, like that." Did Smith like Allen's playing? "I liked everybody, you know. I liked them all. But I was the best." He laughs happily at the memory.

Smith continued to work periodically in Chicago, although there were fewer jazz venues in the city than there had been in the 1920s. The Depression had hurt, as had a city crackdown on vice, which affected the mob-controlled joints. Still, Smith was knocking out those who heard him play. Around 1931, for example, Nat King Cole (then thirteen or fourteen years old) climbed the fire escape of Chicago's Indiana Theater to hear Smith play with Burns Campbell's band. Smith recalls Cole telling him about it when the two ran into each other in Newark around a decade later.

Louis Armstrong played Chicago again, briefly, in 1931. By then he was on top of the jazz world—and a favorite, as well, of many Americans who had no particular interest in jazz. When he left town, the attention again focused on Smith. "They wanted somebody to take Louis's place, down to My Cellar. So they went and got me, and that's where I followed, you know, My Cellar, in Chicago, there." Smith's band included Milt Hinton on bass and Cassino Simpson on piano. He was proud to have been booked to succeed Armstrong.

The next year, however, Smith returned to Milwaukee. "When I left My Cellar, I left the band there and I went out and got the job, leading a band at the Wisconsin Roof." That became his base for the next few years. His band played for dancing and a floor show; it also broadcast regionally and did occasional one-nighters elsewhere in the state. Did Smith prefer working with big bands or with small groups? "Well, it doesn't make no difference, you know. It's all right with me. I just work," he says.

Smith stayed in touch with both his mother and his half sister, although he rarely saw them. His mother did visit him once when he was living in Milwaukee and seemed to enjoy his playing, but she was hardly a connoisseur of jazz. Lorraine Gordon interjects: "They were out of it, completely, as far as Jabbo's history as a performer was [concerned]. They just didn't think in those terms. You know, it's not as if you had a little prodigy in your house and you fostered him and you helped him. They dumped him at a very early age. . . . I'm sure she [Smith's mother] loved him, but they were not in a position to know what a musician was."

As the 1930s wore on, Smith took whatever work he could get, not always as a band leader. He appeared in Harriet Calloway's show *Dixie Parade,* and in 1935 he led his own band for a spell at a Chicago cafe. There was a recording session with Charles Lavere and His Chicagoans on March 11, 1935; the sides they made went unreleased until the LP era. Smith also toured with Eli Rice and worked for a spell with Jesse Stone, whose band included string instruments and people hitting bottles with spoons.

Smith's difficulty in dealing with authority figures and his refusal to let anyone manage his career no doubt limited his commercial success. He felt put-upon by union officials and had no love for or trust in agents. Proper management could well have made the difference, for there were those who saw in Smith the potential of another Louis Armstrong. But Smith was headstrong and suspicious. He recalls, in an offhand fashion: "In Chicago, this guy, he managed me for a while—Joe Glaser"—the same Joe Glaser who managed Louis Armstrong throughout most of Armstrong's spectacular career.[16]

> What happened here was . . . he'd sit me down. I'd go down to his office to get some money, and he wouldn't be there. He'd be gone, you know. But when I needed the money, I had to go down, when I wasn't working. He put me with Jesse Stone, people like that.
>
> So Eli Rice came through Chicago, and stayed with the guy that was playing piano with me. He come up and . . . I say, "Joe Glaser." He says, "He ain't doing nothing. Well come and go, you know, to Milwaukee."

Lorraine Gordon interrupts: "Joe Glaser was managing Louis Armstrong, and Joe Glaser managed Louis's money. And he wanted to take over Jabbo. And he was going to run Jabbo's money. But Jabbo says, 'Nobody's going to manage my money; I want it.' But Joe Glaser . . . he's used to handling all Louis's things, and Louis was agreeable to the way Joe Glaser did it, but Jabbo was not agreeable to that kind of a format. So he eventually cut out from Joe Glaser." She turns to her friend and notes realistically, "It could have been a mistake, Jabbo."

"It wasn't no mistake," he declares firmly. "Ain't nothing a mistake. Because there's no mistake until you die. You'll never know until you die." Smith laughs, as if to soften the degree of his disagreement with her. Then he continues: "Later, Joe Glaser come to Washington when I was with Claude Hopkins and he told Claude Hopkins that I was the greatest, but he couldn't handle me. He said, 'There's nobody that can handle him.' "

So Smith free-lanced—and remained an unknown as far as the general public was concerned. He took odd jobs in the music world as they came along, winding up in Toledo for a stretch in the mid-1930s, in a band led by Gene Revels, and then for a few months in Detroit, with pianist Sammy Price's combo. A period of stability followed his meeting in Detroit with Claude Hopkins, whose big band he joined (1936–38). The band was based at the Roseland Ballroom in New York. Smith recalls: "I was there with Claude Hopkins at Roseland Ballroom for a couple of years. Joe Thomas, Vic Dickenson, Fred Norman—the trombone player, did all the arrangements for *everybody*—were in the band then." As for whether he enjoyed being in Hopkins's band, he gives his stock, noncommittal answer: "Yeah, it was all right."

Smith was the jazz trumpet soloist for Hopkins, but we can't judge how he was playing then because the band recorded only six sides during his tenure and all but one featured Beverley White, its undistinguished vocalist. J. Mayo Williams, who had recorded Smith for Brunswick in 1929, remembered him, however, and had him record four of his compositions for Decca on February 1, 1938. Using an octet assembled for the session, Smith cut "Rhythm in Spain," "Absolutely," "More Rain, More Rest," and "How Can Cupid Be So Stupid?" The records didn't go anywhere.

Relative obscurity wasn't Smith's only problem. He had developed a corn on his lip that he would have to shave periodically in order to get a satisfactory tone. He was resigned to the situation, however, feeling that it went with being a jazz trumpeter. He figures the corn came from playing with a lot of pressure, as the great trumpeters did in those days; the pressure was needed to create the excitement, the tension. Smith doesn't believe that today's trumpeters, who play without much pressure, can put across the same effect or convey the same intensity of feeling.

At the 1939–40 World's Fair in New York, Smith took over a band Sidney Bechet had organized and led it at the Midway Inn for about a year. "I rehearsed with Sidney Bechet," he says, "but he had to go to France or something. So I took the band, five pieces . . . stayed at the fair. Then after that, I went to Newark," where he worked from 1940 to 1945. For three or four years he was with a small group in a Newark joint called the Alcazar. Stride pianist Don Lambert worked with him during that period; most of the others were minor players.

Smith remembers one not-yet-famous singer, a native of Newark, then about seventeen years old, whom he encouraged during his Alcazar days: "I had the band down there. And Sarah Vaughan used to come down there and sing; she used to come to the place all the time. And I used to go to her house; she'd play piano and sing." Smith, who was living in New York, urged Vaughan to enter "the amateur night at the Apollo Theater. And I asked the people at the Apollo to give her a chance. If you won, they'd give you a week's booking. She sang with the band that was there. So Earl Hines was there at the time, you know . . . and that was that." After being "discovered" at the Apollo, Vaughan went on to considerable success, singing with Hines's band and then on her own.

(Lorraine Gordon recalls that Sarah Vaughan chanced to drop into the Village Vanguard one night in the mid-1980s when Smith happened to be sitting at the bar. "She looked over and almost dropped her teeth—*'Jabbo Smith.'* " The two hadn't seen each other since the 1940s.)

Although Smith was never a big name in Newark, he did have some white teenage fans, members of "the Hot Club of Newark," who collected jazz 78s and knew the brilliant recordings he had made in the 1920s. Lorraine Gordon—then Lorraine Stein—was one of them; her brother, Phil, was another. Phil used to go to Smith's apartment sometimes and was surprised to learn that Smith made sketches of people in his spare time.

In 1945 Smith returned to Milwaukee, intending to make the move permanent. In 1948 he married a woman named Vi who had two children from a previous marriage, and they bought a house in Milwaukee. Smith no longer entertained hopes of being a star in the jazz world. His goal now was simply to pay his bills, to get by. He got a job at a place called the Moon Glow, in a combo led by piano player Tim White. Later he worked at the Flame, in pianist Loretta Wright's small band; he stayed there five or six years.

Music was changing rapidly, and in the 1950s Smith wound up working in what he considered to be a rock 'n' roll group. The instrumentation, in his recollection, consisted of two electric guitars, piano, drums, and tenor sax. He was now just another sideman, playing sporadically at a club whose patrons would never have imagined he was once someone famous. Fights in the joint were not unusual. To help meet expenses, he also took day jobs, working for four or five years in a drugstore while his wife drove a cab. Then he got a job with Avis car rentals, where Vi Smith later joined him. "I was with Avis for about thirteen years," he notes. Only one of his co-workers was aware that he had a musical past.

Tired of scrapping for jobs as a musician, and hampered by problems with his teeth, Smith gave up playing entirely around 1957 or 1958. "I just put it down, you know. There was no work there. Maybe three nights here, three nights there. I was looking for something stronger." How did he feel about setting his trumpet aside? "I felt all right," he maintains, with a laugh. Did he ever take the horn out, perhaps when no one was around, and play it just for his own satisfaction? "No," he insists, then adds after a bit: "My teeth went bad, you know."

By 1960 Smith's name meant nothing to most younger jazz musicians and fans, while those old enough to remember the splash he had made in his youth didn't know whether he was even alive. Still, a few jazz musicians and fans in his area, those with a special interest in the hot jazz of the twenties, remembered Jabbo Smith and got him to record two sessions in 1961 at an auditorium belonging to the University of Illinois at Chicago. "We were just rehearsing," says Smith of those sessions; there were no plans to release the recordings commercially.

Guitarist Marty Grosz organized the sessions, which included Frank Chace on clarinet and some less-experienced musicians on piano, drums, and bass sax. The thirteen tunes were all from the 1920s, and the tapes of those sessions remained in the possession of record collector (and sometimes producer) John Steiner for the next twenty-two years. Acquired by Lorraine Gordon in 1983, they were released by her in 1985 as *Jabbo Smith, Hidden Treasure: Volumes One and Two* (Jazz Art Productions). The albums include some incomplete takes, which can be frustrating to listen to, and not all the performances are impressive. But since Smith made so few recordings in his lifetime, it seems important to preserve all of them.

What did Smith sound like in 1961? His tone was darker, heavier than in his youth. Not surprisingly, he no longer soared as high nor played as flexibly. Yet he made it clear on certain numbers that he had lost none of his power to fascinate. The dramatic brashness of his youth may have vanished, but his gift for improvising was intact. He turned "Love Me or Leave Me"—with suggestions of uncertainty, of poignance not found in his 1920s recordings—into an ineffably moving statement, a compelling, unforgettable rendering spun out of simple, but beautifully hewn, phrases. He dug into "Sunday" with zest and sang "Sweet Georgia Brown" in that loose, free, barely audible way of his—casual, unassuming, wholly appealing jazz.

After leaving this reminder for posterity, Smith was allowed to slip back into obscurity, returning to his day job at the car rental agency and an occasional, trivial job in music. An appearance at a Milwaukee Jazz Society concert in 1961 prompted Don DeMichael to report in *Down Beat:* "Embarrassed by his fluffs, Jabbo nevertheless played beautifully constructed solos, his low register often taking on the quality of dark gold." But the time simply wasn't right for the rediscovery of a jazz age survivor.

The trumpet section of Claude Hopkins's orchestra, 1937: Lincoln Mills, Shirley Clay, and Jabbo Smith. Hopkins's arrangements frequently featured this trumpet trio. (Courtesy of Duncan P. Schiedt.)

In 1937 Jabbo Smith (far left) was playing trumpet in Claude Hopkins's big band. Hopkins and vocalist Beverley White are seated at the pianos. (Courtesy of Lorraine Gordon.)

Jabbo Smith (at left), circa 1940, at the Alcazar in Newark, New Jersey. Musicians pictured here include Carl McIntyre on sax, Willie Johnson on guitar, and possibly Don Lambert on piano. (Courtesy of Lorraine Gordon.)

By the late 1940s, one of the most individualistic jazz artists of the twenties was reduced to playing in a minor band in Milwaukee, Wisconsin. Left to right: Loretta White, Bobby Burdette, Buster Washington, Pal Williams, Jabbo Smith, P. G. Wash. (Courtesy of Lorraine Gordon.)

Jabbo Smith with the Hot Antic Jazz Band of France, led by cornetist Michel Bastide, 1982. The band plays with great gusto numbers that Smith composed and recorded at his peak. (Author's collection. Courtesy of Michel Bastide.)

Jabbo Smith on Trumpet, with his euphonium at his side, 1982. (Photo by Nancy Miller Elliott. Courtesy of Nancy Miller Elliott.)

The dignity as well as the sadness of Jabbo Smith is captured in this striking portrait by jazz photographer Nancy Miller Elliott. (Courtesy of Lorraine Gordon.)

Wynton Marsalis and Jabbo Smith at the Greenwich Village (New York) Jazz Festival, August 1983. (Photo by Sam Siegel. Courtesy of Lorraine Gordon.)

In 1966 Smith resurfaced, briefly, to play piano and valve trombone at a place in Milwaukee called Tina's Lounge. In 1971 he was invited to the traditional jazz festival in Breda, Holland, where he met enthusiastic amateur European musicians who knew of his recordings from long ago. During the festival, he played trombone only, saying he was not in good enough shape to play trumpet.

Then, in 1975 George Wein reintroduced Smith to audiences in New York by including him in a program at Lincoln Center (part of the Newport Jazz Festival–New York) honoring the legends of jazz. Wein, who had not forgotten Smith's early recorded triumphs, presented him as one of the greatest of all living jazzmen. Smith stood onstage with such peers as Earl Hines, Milt Hinton, Teddy Wilson, Bobby Hackett, and Jo Jones. Still photos of Smith were projected on a large screen while his 1929 recording of "Jazz Battle" resonated throughout the concert hall. Although he didn't play that night—his lip wasn't in good shape—it was clear that the growing interest in jazz's past would mean a new beginning for Smith.

A return to Breda the next year was followed by the recording of *The Hot Dogs Meet Jabbo Smith,* with a group of amateur Dutch musicians. In 1977 Smith played London; he also worked around Chicago with a new Wolverines Band that consisted of young musicians re-creating performances they had transcribed from vintage recordings by Charlie Johnson, Chick Webb, and Fletcher Henderson. Smith was honored in Milwaukee, given a day at the arts center; and he appeared on local TV a number of times. He also worked in New Orleans, where tourists expect to find veteran jazzmen. After so many years of obscurity, he says, it was rewarding to be treated once again with some respect.

The full rediscovery of Jabbo Smith came when creator-director Vernel Bagneris gave him a small, but vital, role in the stage show *One Mo' Time.* Smith played in the band and was also featured, singing and playing, on two numbers he composed. The show itself was not great, yet audiences responded enthusiastically to its evocation of the world of black entertainment in the 1920s. Smith, of course, provided a crucial note of authenticity. The other performers portrayed characters suggested by real persons of that era, such as Ma Rainey and Bessie Smith; the other musicians, including a couple of Europeans, were re-creating hot jazz sounds of the twenties. But Smith wasn't imitating or re-creating anybody; he was just being himself. Audiences were fascinated.

One Mo' Time, in New York and then on tour, occupied Smith from 1979 to 1982 and revived interest in him. Reviewers and commentators focused attention on Smith. Although others in the show had far more to do, he was the star in terms of drawing power. Lorraine Gordon notes:

> And I, who had lost track of Jabbo for many years of life, sat here—I'll never forget—one Sunday, reading the Sunday *Times,* and I see "*One Mo' Time* at the Village Gate, Guest Artist Jabbo Smith." And I almost jumped out of my seat. I called my brother, I called my husband, called everybody. My brother and I ran down to see Jabbo.
>
> And, well, I must tell you, to see Jabbo sitting up on that stage, with the band, mysterious, charismatic, and [he] gets up and blows that horn—that huge room at the Village Gate in the basement was just filled with his trumpet—and he gets up and sings two songs. "Love" in the first act—it brings down the house—then "Yes, Yes, Yes, Yes" in the second act. Well, we just sat there, you know, with our tears. We couldn't believe we're seeing—he's alive again; there he is!
>
> So we grabbed him. We went backstage. They wouldn't let us in, but we kept saying, "Oh we know him, we know him." Finally he came out. And we said, "Jabbo, you don't remember us. We're the little kids from Newark. We live so close by. Would you like to come over for dinner?" So he put on his coat. And he didn't know where he was going; he kind of followed us. And we made dinner and we talked. We couldn't believe it was Jabbo.
>
> . . . You know, all these years had gone by. You don't think about it, really. You go on with your life. And there's Jabbo. Well, you know, our hearts were beating. And he was *playing* just fantastic. And the audiences just screamed for him, every performance.
>
> Eventually, we became friends again. And he came up here for many dinners with Vernel Bagneris and the whole cast. And I must have sat through every performance down there.

Unfortunately, the rediscovery, the reappreciation, of Jabbo Smith came too late. Now past seventy, he didn't have the stamina to perform nightly, to become—once again—a jazz star. During the run of *One Mo' Time,* he suffered his first stroke. Gordon recalls that night:

> At the end of act one, the band went into their dressing room. Act two starts and they all go out to play. They're sitting

> on the bandstand, playing, and Orange Kellin, the Swedish clarinet player, looks and sees this empty chair.
>
> Jabbo had the stroke in the dressing room. He went completely blind. He got up and he walked into a wall, he walked into a closet. But Jabbo heard the music on the bandstand—it's very close to the dressing room and he somehow sat in a chair in the dressing room, he played his music. And Orange, who's sitting out there, hears Jabbo playing, from way back. He gets off the stand, runs into the dressing room, sees Jabbo, his eyes glazed, playing. He says, "My God, something's happened to this man." He calls an ambulance and they take him to Saint Vincent's Hospital. The man had a stroke. But he's still playing his music, that's how tough he is.
>
> He was in Saint Vincent's Hospital, blind, a week maybe. His eyesight came back except for the peripheral vision.

About a week after his release, Smith returned to the show. When it went on tour, Gordon became, in effect, his manager, negotiating for him with the producers. "I got on the phone and said: 'Well, if you want him to go on the road, he *is* the star, you're going to have to pay him more.' Which they were angry about. But they did come around to it. Jabbo was on the road for a year. Philadelphia, Chicago, Los Angeles, San Francisco, and Washington. And I'd go to all these places with him, set him up, you know, and then come back."

Smith was the focus of attention wherever the production went. Gordon recalls: "They did a whole big TV show on him, 'Sunday Morning,' when he was playing *One Mo' Time* in Philadelphia. We went to the zoo with his half sister, Ethel, who's eleven years older than Jabbo, and we went to her house. We were sitting on her little porch there, in Philadelphia, and the reporters asked her, 'What do you think of your brother's music?' She said, 'I don't approve of it. It's the Devil's music,' or something. She's a church lady now."

After the show finally closed, Smith returned to New York and Gordon got him some bookings at the West End Cafe and other jazz venues, paying euphonium as well as trumpet. In 1982 he played ten concerts in France, Italy, and Switzerland with the Hot Antic Jazz Band, a French group that was already featuring re-creations of Smith's classic recordings. Leader Michael Bastide recalls: "It was for us a great shock: Jabbo was playing with a fire, enthusiasm, inventivity, technical possibilities, so far from what we heard in the recordings he did in the '70s. Of course he was not the Jabbo of 1929, but he was not the tired old man who he was said to be."[17]

Just after Smith returned from this tour, he suffered a second stroke—Gordon tells Smith affectionately, "You messed me up with that one"—which affected the motor control of his voice and some facial muscles. The stroke occurred on a night when he was scheduled to perform at St. Peter's Church. He also had a gig coming up at the jazz club Lush Life, to be followed by an appearance at the Spoleto Festival in Charleston, South Carolina. A nerve in Smith's cheek had been affected, so Gordon took him to exercise classes, to see if he could regain his ability to play. He did, returning yet again to the West End. ("He can do it, given the job and his interest to do it. He can do it," Gordon insists.)

Smith played trumpet for the last time, with the Hot Antic Jazz Band, at the 1983 Breda Festival. Bastide recalls: "Jabbo was still singing beautifully but was very much affected by his impossibility to control his lips for blowing the trumpet. He was perfectly aware of his physical possibilities and of what he was doing. At the end of the last concert in Breda, he talked to me a long time and told me, 'I shall not play anymore the trumpet.' It was a very sad moment."[18]

Today, Smith makes occasional appearances as a vocalist but not as a trumpeter. Around 1983 Buck Clayton arranged three of Smith's originals for the Mel Lewis Jazz Orchestra at the Vanguard and Smith sang every night for a week with the big band. Sometimes Gordon takes him to clubs, to hear different musicians, and he's sure she'll push him up on stage one night to sing. When I ask if he still practices the trumpet, Gordon answers for him, promptly: "He tells me he practices—I don't believe it. I say, 'You practice, you liar, you know you don't practice!' Sometimes he gets so mad and says, 'Oh, I'm practicing today.' I say, 'Oh, great.' He's lying. Musicians like him never practice. They just have it. The man is made out of iron. I say he's going to outlive us all."

Is Smith still writing songs? "Yeah, every now and then," he answers. And at Gordon's insistence he sings—so soft and low that he's barely audible—a sentimental number he has written, "I Took My Little Daughter to the Zoo." It is to be included—along with sixteen other old and new numbers by Smith—in a proposed Broadway musical version of "Amos and Andy," to be called *Fresh Air Taxi,* written by Stephen M. Silverman, the author of several film biographies. Silverman, who believes that "Amos and Andy" has timeless appeal and that Smith's score is "great," originally sought to mount the musical in 1981 but has been delayed by prolonged legal disputes.[19]

Smith now lives in Greenwich Village, in a single room at a hotel that has been converted into co-op apartments. He rents out the Milwaukee house in which he lived with his late wife, Vi, saying that he has adjusted, more or less, to living in New York. A frail, elderly man who has lost most of his vision and is understandably wary of muggers, he passes most days quietly, by himself, listening to the radio or TV. His 1929 Brunswick recordings have been reissued on various albums, but he says he never listens to them.

A few years ago, Gordon learned that Smith owned land in Baxley, Georgia, that had belonged to his mother and grandfather. She decided to see to it that Smith earned a fair income from it, for the land had just been lying there, fallow. She went to Georgia and arranged for someone to cut lumber on Smith's land, bringing him some money. Smith refused to make the trip with her, however, as he still carries in his head the racial programming of his youth that said a black man can't travel with a white woman in the South. In a similar vein, Gordon notes, when Smith went to Boston recently he asked passersby, upon his arrival, "Where's the colored section?" since, in his mind, that's where a black man would go to find lodging. He wound up staying at a YMCA. Gordon says it wouldn't have occurred to him that he could have stayed in any hotel in Boston.

In 1986 and 1987, Smith appeared a few times with Don Cherry's quintet, billed as Collaboration. The partnership may have seemed improbable at first, the pairing of a jazzman from the 1920s with a member of today's avant garde. But Cherry had enormous respect for Smith, and the team worked. First the band played the music that people expected of them, like Ornette Coleman tunes. Then Smith joined them and they slipped back six decades, with Smith and Cherry urging each other on in scat choruses of "Sweet Georgia Brown" that were pure magic. Audiences could feel the joy the musicians radiated.

The appearance of Collaboration at the Berlin Jazz Festival was reported in *Die Welt* on November 5, 1986 (translated from the original German):

> The breath of history at its most beautiful blew through the concert hall when the Don Cherry–Jabbo Smith "Collaboration" played. . . . [Smith] has now said good-bye to the trumpet, but he still can sing. And so he sits before the microphone and delivers the old standards ("Baby, I Love You") with a coquettish smile. When the tone wavered or the voice became

brittle, Jim Pepper was there with his soft saxophone to carry along the melody. At the end, as Smith scatted the duet with Cherry—without a doubt the most touching moment of the concert—the audience was still as a mouse.

Smith apparently suffered a ministroke just before his booking at the Village Vanguard in February 1987. The audience had no idea, when he stepped onto the floor, that he had just gotten out of the hospital and was now almost totally blind, that he was keeping the microphone pressed against his chin because he couldn't see it. The night I caught him during that week-long engagement—one of the most memorable nights I've spent in a jazz club in recent years—one of his doctors was in the audience, too.

In 1988 Don Cherry commented on television's "Joe Franklin Show" that he would never forget working with Smith:

> That was special for me, because Jabbo has always been one of the greats, and I can feel now that I've really studied with him. Because he's giving. And that's the thing about playing the music, is that it's something that you want to share and give. And Jabbo still has that quality. You know, it's something I remember that Jelly Roll Morton always said about jazz, is that it always has to have that Latin quality to it. And Jabbo, he always had that in his trumpet, and now as a composer. And his singing is so great. I'll never forget that night. The respect is there. And he can still push me into really what swing is about.[20]

Of course, it's not hard these days to find trumpet players who admire Smith. Clark Terry put it this way: "I feel extremely privileged and honored to be on the same planet with Jabbo Smith because he's the man who set down many of the standards that those of us who call ourselves jazz trumpet players follow today. He's a man of deep wit and humor and, of course, he's extremely talented . . . . he has never lost his yen for fun and indulgence in his craft. When I grow up I want to be just like Jabbo."[21]

And so Jabbo Smith hangs on. He may utter a small complaint once in a while that his eyes hurt, from his glaucoma, but for the most part he is rather stoic—and still capable, when the spirit moves him, of spinning out scat vocal phrases that are the very definition of swing.

Before I leave, I ask him if there's anything I haven't brought up, anything he'd like to talk about. He replies, simply and amiably, with a nod in Gordon's direction: "I don't know. There's nothing I can say.

She does all the talking." "Talk about today," Gordon says. "There's nothing happening today," he responds. "But would you like to be playing your horn a little bit, or singing a little bit?" she asks. "I'm all right," he says. (He rarely budges from that answer.) "How about when I take you down to the Vanguard?" Gordon asks. "He goes crazy," she says. "It's too far-out for both of us. Oh, God! Sometimes we have some good things to hear there. When Clark Terry plays there, you get your kicks."

The one thing Smith will talk about, more comfortably than if he's asked to talk about most other aspects of his life, is how he played trumpet. He reiterates that he admired Sidney de Paris, but he makes sure you understand he didn't try to copy de Paris, or Armstrong, or any of the greats of his day. And if you're foolish enough to ask who he did play like, you'll get a prompt answer:

> I didn't play like nobody. I was . . . an executionist. I would do all, you know, things on my horn. Just an executioner. I liked little things . . . . And anyway, I run over the horn. I say, I run over the horn.
>
> You know, some people they play like this: "ta-ta-tada, ta-ta-tada." You know, things like that. . . . Because everybody's trying to play like Louis, you know, he'd go "ta ta-ta, tada; ta ta-ta, ta." Things like that. I'd just run over the horn [here Smith scats a much freer run of notes]. . . . Anything—things like that. . . . So that's what was happening there. The rest of them—I was so different from everybody.

You can't resist asking if Smith thought, back then, that he was the best trumpet player of them all. "Yeah, I thought I was the best," he answers—and now he laughs a rich, full laugh, perhaps embarrassed at what he's saying. When Gordon brings up names like Clark Terry, Wynton Marsalis, and Miles Davis, Smith repeats his belief that "all of them sound the same to me. . . . I mean everybody sounds the same. Nobody plays like me. . . . Everybody do this [he scats a boppish-sounding run]. That's the way it sounds to me. Everybody looks like they got it from Dizzy Gillespie and Charlie Parker. You know, I guess they got it from them. So everybody is trying to do like them. But they don't sound like me." Gordon interjects: "Yeah, but you know a lot of people think that you were doing what Dizzy is doing today, and you were doing it way back then." Smith seems to accepts that notion, and with some pleasure. "I mean, everybody hears the records. I did these records . . . before anybody out there was doing anything. . . . There wasn't nobody out there doing nothing."

Notes

The clippings files of the Institute of Jazz Studies at Rutgers University in Newark, N.J., are a valuable source of vintage newspaper reviews and articles, programs, oral histories, and profiles of jazz musicians, not just from jazz magazines, but from general-interest magazines as well, ranging from the *New Yorker* to the *Nugget*.

INTRODUCTION

Information on the growth of the recording industry and radio is drawn principally from Eberly, *Music in the Air;* Sanjek, *From Print to Plastic;* and Allen, *Only Yesterday.*

1. Quoted in Stillman and Davidson, *American Heritage History of the 20's and 30's,* p. 136.

CHAPTER 1: **SAM WOODING**

An earlier, shorter version of this profile appeared in the *Mississippi Rag* (June-July 1986). I interviewed Wooding at St. Luke's Hospital in New York on April 5, 11, and 13, 1985. Rae Harrison Wooding supplied additional information, in July 1985 and after her husband's death in August of that year, as well as photographs. Wooding's oral history interview, conducted by Chris Albertson in 1975, is on file at the Institute of Jazz Studies and was used as a source of information but not quotations. Garvin Bushell's oral history interview, conducted by Mark Montgomery in 1977, is on file at the Institute of Jazz Studies and provided additional details but not quotations. Other sources of general biographical information include Richard Sudhalter (using the pseudonym Art Napoleon), "A Pioneer Looks Back," *Storyville* (London; Apr.-May, 1967); Chris Albertson, liner notes for *Sam Wooding and His Chocolate*

Dandies; and various clippings (including an interview by John S. Wilson) loaned to me by Sam Wooding. A number of articles, particularly several by James Lincoln Collier in Kernfield, ed., *New Grove Dictionary of Jazz,* were helpful in placing the development of Wooding (and others in this book) in proper historical context.

1. In 1920 Duke Ellington was still doing small-time gigs in Washington, D.C. His first—unsuccessful—visit to New York did not come until 1923.

2. Rust, *Jazz Records, 1897–1942,* p. 458.

3. In 1923 Duke Ellington worked for a bit as a pianist at Barron's Club.

4. Bjorn Englund, "Chocolate Kiddies," *Storyville* (London; Dec. 1975–Jan. 1976).

5. Music historian Mark Tucker says in a letter to the editor of the *Mississippi Rag* (Sept. 1986) that, Ellington's recollections notwithstanding, Ellington first used as many as ten players during his road engagements in the summers of 1926 and 1927, although he was still using six to eight players in New York City at that stage in his career.

6. Englund, "Chocolate Kiddies," p. 49.

7. All four recordings have been reissued on *Sam Wooding and His Chocolate Dandies* (Biograph 112025). By today's standards, these recordings don't seem particularly impressive—big band music simply had not gotten very far by 1925, the peppy saxes have a familiar 1920s dance band feel, and Wooding's band would take a noticeably looser, jazzier feel within the next few years—but they clearly impressed contemporary European listeners. Hot cornet solos add interest on "Shanghai Shuffle" and "Alabamy Bound," while "By the Waters of Minnetonka" is the sort of nonjazz, sweetly melodic number that Whiteman's band could have executed as least as well.

8. A number of other musicians played in both Wooding's and Henderson's bands at one time or another: trombonist Jimmy Harrison, bassist June Cole, reedman Jerry Blake, trumpeter Elmer Chambers, and banjo player Charlie Dixon. In fact, two of the first numbers that Wooding recorded, "Shanghai Shuffle" and "Alabamy Bound," had been recorded by Henderson a short time earlier; the two recordings are of about equal quality. Henderson's band of 1925 was, of course, greater overall than Wooding's, if only for the presence of giants Armstrong and Hawkins.

9. Smaller jazz combos had already made their marks. The five members of the Original Dixieland Jazz Band, for example, had been a smash in England in 1919–20.

10. Tucker wrote to the editor of the *Mississippi Rag* (Sept. 1986): "Although some might quibble with labeling Cook's group a 'jazz orchestra,' the important fact is that it introduced Europeans (conductor Ernest Ansermet, for example) to Afro-American performing styles and improvisation six years before Wooding crossed the Atlantic."

11. Ibid.

12. Chilton, in *Who's Who of Jazz,* states that Ladnier left Wooding in June 1926, in Berlin, to travel to Poland with the Louis Douglas Revue. He worked

with Henderson in New York from late 1926 through 1927, before rejoining Wooding in 1928–29 (p. 191).

13. Henry Miller wrote to Anais Nin in 1934, regarding the scene in Paris: "There's nothing more wonderful than to see a Negro handling a white woman carelessly. It thrills me." Quoted in Driggs and Lewine, *Black Beauty, White Heat,* p. 205.

CHAPTER 2: **BENNY WATERS**

An earlier, shorter version of this profile appeared in the *Mississippi Rag* (Sept. 1988). I interviewed Waters on June 1, 1987, in New York City. He gave me a copy of his zesty and candid memoir, *The Key to a Jazz Life*, self-published in France in 1985, which proved to be a valuable source of information, particularly on his personal life, but not of quotations. In subsequent telephone conversations, Waters vouchsafed the accuracy of his memoir.

1. Quoted in Charters and Kunstadt, *Jazz*, p. 194.

2. By the swing era, it would be expected that any name big band would be playing its own arrangements, in its own distinctive style. But in the mid-1920s, it was more accepted for big bands to play stock arrangements; indeed, you might hear the same arrangement of a popular dance tune played by any number of bands. Big band arranging was still in its infancy, and bandleaders were less concerned than they later would be about having an immediately recognizable style for their music.

3. Waters told me that there was a lot more he could have included but chose not to.

4. Given our culture's insistence upon equating "modern" with "good," it's understandable that Waters wants his playing to be described as modern; but for this critic, a key element of the charm of Water's work is its obvious roots in an earlier time. Listen to his extroverted playing on *Benny Waters and the Hot Antic Jazz Band*—the careening, skidding, and holding of notes suggest the reckless gaiety of the jazz age. Water's headlong playing is so infectious. He deserves to be much better known.

CHAPTER 3: **BIX BEIDERBECKE**

An earlier, shorter version of this profile accompanied *Sincerely, Bix Beiderbecke,* a collection of Beiderbecke's complete recorded works released by Sunbeam in 1988. Sudhalter and Evan's *Bix, Man and Legend,* easily the single most valuable source of Beiderbecke, provided the framework for this profile. I appreciate, too, Sudhalter's comments to me about Beiderbecke and jazz in general. I'm also grateful for Dan Morgenstern's comments and advice, particularly regarding Beiderbecke's place in jazz history and his influence on others. Wareing and Garlick's *Bugles for Beiderbecke* was particularly helpful in assessing Beiderbecke's influence, and Castelli, Kaleveld, and Pusateri's *The Bix Bands* provided useful information on records attributed to Beiderbecke but probably by others. My notes of jazz historian/radio host Phil Schaap's 1987 salute to Beiderbecke on WKCR-FM in New York were the source of the reminiscences of Charlie Davis and Jess Stacy.

I first wrote about Beiderbecke in "The Sons of Bix Keep Blowing," *Princeton Alumni Weekly* (May 2, 1984). I appreciate the information on him and the jazz scene circa 1926–31 provided in letters and/or orally by Princeton alumni Bill Priestley, Charles Smith, Avery Sherry, Rudy Leuthauser, Jack Howe, and Herb Sanford, and additional help provided by Matt Reese. I gained valuable information from the November 1980 *Princeton Recollector,* edited by Tari Miller, who also gave me some good research leads.

Ralph Berton's *Remembering Bix,* rich in the flavor of the times, was the source of all material in this profile pertaining to the Berton family. In a telephone conversation with me on March 2, 1989, he spoke of Beiderbecke's open personality and general willingness to try anything, and confirmed having attended a drag party with his brother Gene and Beiderbecke and having learned from Gene, in a kitchen conversation shortly after Beiderbecke's death, that Gene had had a brief homosexual involvement with Beiderbecke.

In 1988 record collector/producer Stan Hester provided me with copies of Beiderbecke's 1931 letters, whose contents are summarized in print for the first time. (Additional confirmation of the letters' authenticity was provided by Beiderbecke's great-niece, Liz Beiderbecke.) Hester also gave me copies of various newspaper clippings and the register of guests at Beiderbecke's memorial service.

1. Kaminsky, *My Life in Jazz,* p. 23.

2. In the New York area, it's actually not all that unusual for artists to salute Beiderbecke, whether with a single number or an entire program. During the period in which I wrote this profile, for example, I heard Beiderbecke's music played by such conscientious musicians as Randy Sandke and Randy Reinhart (both with Vince Giordano's Nighthawks), Jimmy McPartland, Bucky Pizzarelli, Dick Hyman, Warren Vache, and Richard Sudhalter. Sudhalter, using original arrangements, does an excellent job of suggesting Beiderbecke without copying him note for note, thus retaining an air of spontaneity and avoiding the studied quality sometimes found in players directly copying Beiderbecke. Bill Challis told me it was his opinion, and the opinion of others he knew who had known Beiderbecke, that cornetist Tom Pletcher today comes closest to sounding like Beiderbecke.

3. Stewart, *Jazz Masters of the Thirties,* p. 18.

4. Quoted by Marshall Stearns in "Beiderbecke," a clipping of unknown origin, apparently from 1936, in the files of the Institute of Jazz Studies.

5. Quoted in Sudhalter and Evans, *Bix,* p. 27.

6. Bismark Beiderbecke must have possessed a sizable ego. Not only was his younger son given his nickname, but elder son Charles Burnette was also called Bix in his youth. Mae Steffen, a childhood acquaintance of the Beiderbecke children, remembers, "We called the brothers 'Bix' and 'Bix 2.' " Steffen is quoted by Jim Arpy in his laudable feature "Remembering Bix," *Quad-City Times* (Davenport, Iowa), July 24, 1988.

7. Quoted in ibid.

8. Werentin and Von Maur are quoted in ibid.

9. The Original Dixieland Jazz Band (ODJB), organized in May 1916, was comprised of five white musicians who approximated the vigorous sounds they had heard being played by black bands in their native New Orleans. That June, during their first engagement in Chicago, they were heard by Al Jolson, then America's pre-eminent entertainer. Jolson was so taken with their exciting style that he insisted they be booked into New York. Promoted as a novelty act, they opened at Reisenweber's Restaurant in January 1917—and took New York by storm.

In the next few years, the ODJB made the nation jazz conscious. Without benefit of commercial radio, which was still in the future, their spunky early recordings—"Indiana," "Livery Stable Blues," "Ostrich Walk," "Tiger Rag," "Fidgety Feet," "Sensation Rag," "Clarinet Marmelade," "At the Jazz Band Ball," "Jazz Me Blues"—nonetheless found their way into even hick towns from coast to coast. An America that emerged from World War I feeling self-confident, and maybe a little giddy, found its mood reflected well in the rambunctious sounds of the ODJB.

10. The same notes may be produced via a variety of fingerings on the cornet or trumpet, although those produced using alternate (nontraditional) fingerings will sound slightly different. Some passages can even be executed more easily using alternate fingerings.

11. Quoted in Sudhalter and Evans, *Bix,* p. 39.

12. Quoted in Arpy, "Remembering Bix."

13. Quoted in ibid.

14. Quoted in ibid.

15. Quoted in Shapiro and Hentoff, *Hear Me Talkin' to Ya,* p. 141.

16. Quoted in ibid., p. 158,

17. Quoted in Arpy, "Remembering Bix."

18. Carmichael, *Stardust Road,* p. 54.

19. Berton's observations are consistent with comments Beiderbecke made to others over the years. Late in his life, for example, he told a former high school sweetheart that he hadn't accomplished anything worthwhile in music. And trumpeter Sylvester Ahola, who met Beiderbecke at the peak of his success, when he was the idol of so many up-and-coming trumpeters, was surprised to hear Beiderbecke dismiss himself as a "musical degenerate." By various accounts, he was barely aware of solos he had recorded, and as he grew older he looked down on his earlier work. Although he loved playing jazz, part of him believed the bourgeois judgment of his parents—that it was an inferior form of music. Ahola is quoted in Sudhalter and Evans, *Bix,* p. 211.

20. Quoted in ibid., p. 148.

21. Quoted in ibid., p. 274. Nichols was influenced by Beiderbecke—no doubt more so than he cared to acknowledge—but it is an injustice to write him off as a mere imitator. The careful listener would never mistake Nichols for Beiderbecke, or vice versa. There were certain things that Nichols would

do—the jaunty, self-confident way he would take a trumpet section suddenly upward, for example—that were characteristic of him and no one else. His playing, with its sometimes martial feel, is easily recognizable. The numerous, spritely Five Pennies sides he made from 1926 on were pacesetters, popular with many jazzmen no less than with the general public. By contrast, Beiderbecke often projected a poignancy that simply wasn't found in Nichols's work. Bandleader Charlie Davis, who wrote "Copenhagen," one of the Wolverines big hits, claimed that Beiderbecke's playing could make you cry. That's the sort of comment you often hear about Beiderbecke but never about Nichols, whose work was clean, precise, pure-toned, but without the depth of feeling that Beiderbecke had.

22. Mezzrow, *Really the Blues,* p. 80.

23. Quoted in Sudhalter and Evans, *Bix,* p. 350.

24. Author interview with Jimmy McPartland, Aug. 15, 1985.

25. Quoted in Shapiro and Hentoff, *Hear Me Talkin' to Ya,* p. 153.

26. For further information on Schaffner's affair with Beiderbecke, see Sudhalter and Evans, *Bix,* chap. 10.

27. Condon and Sugrue, *We Called It Music,* p. 102.

28. Riskin's recollections are in Simon, *Simon Says,* p. 330.

29. Oral history, on file at the Institute of Jazz Studies.

30. Oral history, on file at the Institute of Jazz Studies.

31. Quoted in Sudhalter and Evans, *Bix,* p. 186.

32. Stewart, *Jazz Masters of the Thirties,* p. 11.

33. Author interview with Bill Challis, Sept. 19, 1985.

34. Some of the later pure-jazz small-group instrumentals by Bix and His Gang, so well known and well liked by many jazz fans today, didn't go anywhere in terms of sales when they were first released. "Ol' Man River" and "Wa Da Da," for example, sold a scant 2,900 copies; "Rhythm King" and "Louisiana" sold about 2,225 copies. Far more copies of those 1928 sides exist on LP reissues than on the original 78s.

35. Stewart, *Jazz Masters of the Thirties,* p. 17.

36. Ibid., p. 18.

37. Oral history, on file at the Institute of Jazz Studies.

38. Author interview with Artie Shaw, Aug. 15, 1985.

39. The labels on many of the 78s that were pressed credited only Frankie Trumbauer and His Orchestra, with no identification of the cornetist who really made the number what it was. Some 78s were pressed with an added line, either "with Bix" or "with Bix and Lang." Trumbauer had a bigger name than Beiderbecke in the late 1920s; however, he was not the improviser Beiderbecke was. He joined with Beiderbecke and Eddie Lang on some trio recordings, such as "For No Reason at All in C" and "Wringin' and Twistin'." Beiderbecke played piano on those sides, but without the distinction he brought to his best cornet recordings.

40. Kaminsky, *My Life in Jazz,* p. 23.

41. Ibid.

42. Quoted in Berton, *Remembering Bix,* p. 358.

43. Sudhalter and Evans, *Bix,* p. 227.

44. Rust, *Jazz Records, 1897–1942,* p. 174.

45. Most of the sides recorded by the Whiteman orchestra before Beiderbecke joined and after he left have only a fraction of the interest for jazz collectors. This is not to disparage the quality of the other musicians, for Whiteman employed the best players he could find (the best white players, that is, since racial segregation was still the order of the day in the music business). Challis continued to turn out some superb charts after Beiderbecke left, but it was Beiderbecke who provided the vital spark that makes the sides essential for collectors.

46. Hammond, "For the Record, the Bix Beiderbecke Story," clipping from *The Compass* (date uncertain), in the files of the Institute of Jazz Studies; Waters shared his recollections with me on June 1, 1987.

47. Quoted in the *Princeton Recollector* (Nov. 1980), p. 9.

48. The beauty is especially apparent when these charts are brought to life by today's orchestras; only then is it clear how much was not captured by the limited recording techniques of the late 1920s. The Victor sides were generally better recorded, getting a warmer, fuller sound; the Columbia sides have a certain coldness to them. But the sound on all the sides has been vastly improved by the remastering of John R. T. Davies in the 1980s for the Sunbeam boxed collection. Beiderbecke comes through so vividly and boldly on those sides that the listener has a much easier time understanding why he wowed other musicians of his day.

49. Quoted in Shapiro and Hentoff, *Hear Me Talkin' to Ya,* p. 158.

50. Ibid., p. 159.

51. Author interview with Jimmy McPartland, Aug. 15, 1985.

52. Ibid.

53. Ibid.; author interview with Jack Howe, 1983; Freeman, *You Don't Look Like a Musician,* p. 19.

54. Author interview with Bud Freeman, Aug. 24, 1985.

55. Author interview with Jack Howe, 1983.

56. Author interview with Bill Challis, Sept. 19, 1985.

57. Sudhalter and Evans, *Bix,* p. 288.

58. Quoted in Balliett, *Jelly Roll, Jabbo and Fats,* p. 81.

59. Balliett has written in "Jazz Records: The Other Cheek," *New Yorker* (Sept. 23, 1961), that men such as Rex Stewart, Frankie Newton, Joe Thomas, and Roy Eldridge sounded to him as if they had listened to both Beiderbecke and Armstrong in their formative years (p. 100). Dan Morgenstern, director of the Institute of Jazz Studies at Rutgers University, told me that, in speaking with older musicians, he has heard Nichols's name volunteered much more frequently than Beiderbecke's when influences are cited. For example, when asked, Eldridge acknowledged that he had played in jam sessions with Beiderbecke, but he cited Nichols as a player who had influenced him. Die-hard Beiderbecke fans would argue that Nichols borrowed so much from Beiderbecke that any musicians claiming to have been influenced by Nichols were, indirectly, influenced by Beiderbecke. Doc Cheatham told me (on Nov. 8,

1988) that Nichols reached prominence before Beiderbecke did and seemed, at the time, to be outstanding. But Beiderbecke played so much more beautifully and with so many more advanced harmonies that he made Nichols seem corny by comparison. Of course, Cheatham added, once Armstrong reached full flower, he overshadowed both Nichols and Beiderbecke.

60. Quoted in Arpy, "Remembering Bix."

61. Ibid.

62. Author interview with Art Hodes, Dec. 5, 1988; Haymes's recollections are from Sudhalter and Evans, *Bix,* p. 298.

63. Shaw, *Trouble with Cinderella,* p. 233; author interview with Jimmy McPartland, Aug. 15, 1985.

64. Author interview with Bud Freeman, Aug. 24, 1985.

65. Quoted in Arpy, "Remembering Bix."

66. Condon and Sugrue, *We Called It Music,* p. 216.

67. Author interview with Bill Challis, Sept. 19, 1985.

68. Author interview with Charles Smith, 1983.

69. Quoted in the *Princeton Recollector* (Nov. 1980), p. 9.

70. Author interview with Bill Challis, Sept. 19, 1985.

71. Quoted in Simon, *Simon Says,* p. 332.

72. Quoted in ibid., p. 335.

73. The first important critical appreciation of Beiderbecke was Otis Ferguson's essay, "Young Man with a Horn," published in the July 29, 1936, *New Republic.* The title was later used by Dorothy Baker for her novel inspired by Beiderbecke and also for the subsequent film based upon that novel. Ferguson concluded his essay by citing Beiderbecke's solo work in "Riverboat Shuffle": "One hears it, and is moved and made strangely proud; or one does not, and misses one of the fine natural resources of this American country." Beiderbecke had never received a write-up like that during his lifetime.

74. Quoted in Simon, *Simon Says,* p. 329.

75. R. G. V. Venables, "Memorial," *Melody Maker* (Mar. 11, 1939).

76. Quoted in Bill Elliott and Rex Harris, "Collectors' Corner," *Melody Maker,* undated clipping (from the early 1940s?), supplied by Stan Hester.

77. Clipping of unknown origin, supplied by Stan Hester; Stearns is quoted in Venables, "Memorial," n.p., emphasis added.

78. Simon, *Big Bands,* p. 379.

79. Comparing Armstrong's and Beiderbecke's work is somewhat like comparing apples and oranges. They were two different talents, trying to do two different things, each in his own way. Beiderbecke had a fondness for whole-tone scales and the ability to create passages of crystalline elegance; he believed in the value of understatement. Armstrong's work is warm, expansive, embracing all of humanity. Interestingly, some beboppers who couldn't really get into Armstrong's work appreciated Beiderbecke. They could relate to the coolness he sometimes projected and to his interest in exploring modern harmonies.

80. Oral history, on file at the Institute of Jazz Studies.

81. Musicians' memories, like just about everyone else's, cannot always be trusted. For example, Marion McKay, the leader of an otherwise forgotten midwestern dance band, often told people that young Bix Beiderbecke had soloed on his Gennett recording of "Doo Wacka Doo." His story, told with much pride, was accepted by many. The cornet work does sound Beiderbeckean, and McKay no doubt enjoyed basking in the reflected glory, but the soloist has been conclusively identified as Leroy Morris.

82. Freeman, *You Don't Look Like a Musician.* p. 19.

83. Blesh, *Shining Trumpets,* p. 229; Hammond, "For the Record."

CHAPTER 4: **JOE TARTO**

An earlier, shorter version of this profile appeared in the *Mississippi Rag* (Feb. 1985). I interviewed Tarto at his home in Boonton, N.J., on September 8, 1984 (my gratitude to Vince Giordano for making the connection). Other sources consulted were Steve Hester's detailed liner notes for the album *Joe Tarto: Titan of the Tuba* (Broadway Intermission Records 108); and Warren Vache, Sr., "Joe Tarto: Titan of the Tuba," *Jersey Jazz* (Mar. 1982).

1. This particular recording date may have occurred during the period Tarto was with the Paul Specht Orchestra (1922–24), although his recollection is that it occurred almost immediately after he got out of the army, before he went to New York.

2. See Steve Hester's liner notes for the album *Joe Tarto: Titan of the Tuba* (Broadway Intermission Records 108).

3. Many of the greatest jazz records of the 1920s were made by musicians who were earning their livings playing commercial music—whether in pit bands, dance halls, or on the radio—not jazz. The commercial jobs allowed them the luxury of making jazz records for their own satisfaction, after hours.

CHAPTER 5: **BUD FREEMAN**

An earlier, shorter version of this profile appeared in the *Mississippi Rag* (Dec. 1986). I interviewed Freeman on August 24, 1985, at the Hotel Conneaut during the annual jazz festival in Conneaut Lake, Pennsylvania; additional conversations took place in subsequent days at that festival and at the following year's festival. Two of his volumes of recollections—*If You Know of a Better Life* and *You Don't Look Like a Musician*—were the source of additional information but not quotations. (Freeman fans will also want to check out his new autobiography, *Crazeology.*) Other sources include Ira Gitler, "Saga of a Saxophone Sage," *Down Beat* (May 24, 1962); and Dan Morgenstern's interview with Freeman in *Jazz* (Oct. 1963).

1. In the *Encyclopedia of Jazz* (1960), Leonard Feather, after consulting numerous players, listed the six most important and influential tenor saxists. In chronological order of emergence, they were: Coleman Hawkins, Bud Freeman, Lester Young, Illinois Jacquet, Stan Getz, and Sonny Rollins (p. 89).

2. It has often and accurately been suggested that Freeman's lighter

touch has more in common with Lester Young's approach than with Coleman Hawkins's, though Freeman was not influenced by Young. He and Young began playing sax at around the same time and probably drew upon common influences, but Young did not make his recording debut until 1936, eight years after Freeman made his, and was totally unknown to Freeman during Freeman's formative years. Freeman may have had an influence upon Young, though Young named Jimmy Dorsey and Frank Trumbauer as significant influences; and it was Young who influenced many later "cool" saxists. When I tell Freeman that his sound is "very unique," he answers, "Well, thank you, that's what I would rather hope."

3. Freeman also saw dancers more or less forgotten today, such as Brown and McGraw, who were at Chicago's Sunset Cafe when Louis Armstrong starred there in 1926–27, and Rector and Cooper. Freeman found so much music in the way they all danced. He says that their dancing was jazz to him.

4. For those who hold a stereotyped view that all jazz musicians chronically overindulge in drink and drugs, it should be noted that Freeman did neither. Chicago jazz pianist Art Hodes wrote in *Selections from the Gutter:* "[Freeman]'s a straight cat. In all the time I've known Bud I never knew him to indulge. Women? Yeh; he had 20-20 vision, but if he drank or smoked I never noticed it" (p. 164).

5. Hugues Panassie, "Bud Freeman, One of the Finest Hot Musicians," *Down Beat* (Aug. 1936).

6. In 1939 the Dorsey band dropped its Dixieland slant in favor of a Jimmie Lunceford–style smooth swing.

7. From a clipping of unknown origin in the files of the Institute of Jazz Studies.

8. Just as many of the young Turks wrote off the older jazz greats as passé and reactionary, some of the older jazz figures vehemently expressed their contempt for the rising new players who were attracting the favor of younger jazz fans. Eddie Condon dismissed bebop with the cynical quip that he and his crowd didn't flat their fifths, they drank them.

CHAPTER 6: **JIMMY McPARTLAND**

An earlier, shorter version of this profile appeared in the *Mississippi Rag* (July-Aug. 1987). I interviewed Jimmy McPartland at his home on Long Island, N.Y., on August 15, 1985. McPartland's oral history interview, conducted by Helen Armstead Johnson, is on file at the Institute of Jazz Studies and was a most valuable source of information but not quotations. I'm grateful, too, to Marian McPartland for her helpful comments and for supplying photos.

1. Feather, *Encyclopedia of Jazz,* p. 329.

2. Other Austin High Gang members included: Dick McPartland, born in 1905; Frank Teschemacher, 1906; Bud Freeman, 1906; Jim Lanigan, 1902.

3. In 1922–23, members of the Austin High Gang were not yet old enough to be permitted inside the Friars Inn, home of the Friars Society Orchestra, so they used to stand in the doorway to listen.

4. Quoted in Leonard Feather, "Blindfold Tests," *Down Beat* (Apr. 18, 1952), p. 12. The McPartlands were asked to listen to records without being informed who was playing on them and then offer their reactions.

5. Marian McPartland seems quite fond of her ex-husband. She notes that Benny Goodman once griped that the members of the Austin High Gang never grew up. She supposes that's true—but adds that they're certainly more fun to be around than Benny!

CHAPTER 7: **FREDDIE MOORE**

An earlier, shorter version of this profile appeared in the *Mississippi Rag* (Apr. 1988). I interviewed Moore at his New York City apartment on August 12, 1985. Additional information was gleaned from his spoken recollections on the album *The Great Freddie Moore* (New York Jazz J-0001) and from "King Oliver's Last Tour," an article by Moore in the *Jazz Record* (Apr. 1942).

1. Hodes and Hansen, *Selections from the Gutter,* p. 87.

2. The Theater Owners' Booking Association (T.O.B.A.) circuit booked black performers for black audiences, paying less than circuits for white performers did. Black performers said that T.O.B.A. really stood for "Tough on Black Actors" or "Tough on Black Asses."

3. Brian Rust, in *Jazz Records, 1897–1942,* confirms Moore's presence in Oliver's band in 1930 (p. 1170). Photos and the autobiography of trombonist Clyde Bernhardt establish that Moore was with Oliver in 1931 (see Bernhardt, *I Remember,* p. 93). Trumpeter Dave Nelson, Oliver's nephew and the arranger for the band, was the one who brought Moore to Oliver's attention. Oliver had long valued good drumming.

4. Brian Rust, in *Jazz Records, 1897–1942,* indicates that Moore's first recording session with Oliver took place on March 18, 1930, and that the band also included Hilton Jefferson on alto sax and Jimmy Archey on trombone (p. 1170). Moore recollects that the band consisted of fourteen musicians; Rust suggests that ten to thirteen musicians were used on Oliver's recording sessions in 1930–31 (pp. 1170–71).

5. See Moore's article, "King Oliver's Last Tour," in *Jazz Record* (Apr. 1945).

6. Ibid.

7. Bernhardt, *I Remember,* pp. 96, 97.

8. Oliver fought against all odds for the next few years. He made no recordings after 1931 but continued leading bands. He also continued his string of bad luck. An engine block on his band bus had to be replaced, at considerable expense, and shortly after that the bus was wrecked in an accident. He suffered from high blood pressure but was unable to afford medical treatment. At one point, he had trouble getting his money out of a Depression-damaged bank. In 1938, the year he died, Oliver was reduced to working as a poolroom attendant.

9. Hodes and Hansen, *Selections from the Gutter,* p. 87.

10. Since this profile was written, Moore has had to cut back on his

activities. As of 1989, he is limiting himself to a couple of appearances per set as a vocalist with a band. He has turned over regular drumming duties to a younger player, although he'll occasionally drum for a set. But when the spirit moves him—as he proved at a recent Highlights in Jazz concert at New York University, where he was a surprise guest—he's still fully capable of stealing a show with his drumming and singing.

CHAPTER 8: **JABBO SMITH**

An earlier, shorter version of this profile appeared in the *Mississippi Rag* (July-Aug. 1988). I interviewed Smith at the Manhattan apartment of Lorraine Gordon, who provided valuable commentary during the interview, on November 2, 1985; Smith and I met again at his apartment on November 27, 1988, to clarify various points. Smith's oral history interview, conducted by John Steiner and on file at the Institute of Jazz Studies, was a valuable source of information but not quotations.

1. Hinton is quoted in Eddie Cook, "Jabbo Smith," *Jazz Journal International* (Apr. 1984), p. 8.

2. Hinton in quoted in ibid., p. 8; Cheatham is quoted in ibid., p. 6; Panassie is quoted in ibid, p. 7; Benford is quoted in Balliett, *Jelly Roll, Jabbo and Fats,* p. 50; and Eldridge is quoted in Shapiro and Hentoff, *Jazz Makers,* p. 299.

3. Eldridge is quoted in Shapiro and Hentoff, *Jazz Makers,* p. 301.

4. De Paris has not received the general appreciation he may well have deserved. Samuel Charters and Leonard Kunstadt write in *Jazz:* "De Paris was easily the finest growl trumpet man of the twenties, perhaps the finest in jazz" (p. 205).

5. The practice of "sitting in" with a group, playing without getting paid, has largely vanished, although it was once a key means for musicians to gain extra experience, get their names around, keep their chops in shape, find work, and exchange musical ideas. After-hours jam sessions, which were so important in the development of jazz, have also just about vanished due to the union's insistence that musicians should only play in clubs if they are being paid to do so.

6. If Smith's recollection that he joined Johnson's band in 1925 is correct, he would not even have been seventeen years of age; conceivably, he may have joined the band in 1926, when he would have been seventeen. He thinks he was with Johnson for about two years, and it is certain that he left in 1928.

7. When Smith joined Johnson's ten-piece band, Ellington was still mostly leading a sextet; Ellington sometimes expanded it for gigs or for records but did not permanently expand it to big band status until December 1927. Chick Webb similarly led bands of five to eight men until December 1927, when he expanded to eleven.

8. Rust, *Jazz Records, 1897–1942,* p. 562.

9. Waters, *Key to a Jazzy Life,* p. 102.

10. Walker, *Night Club Era,* p. 10. A great deal could be written about the

importance of underworld money in the development of jazz. Plenty of jazz musicians, not to mention singers, dancers, and songwriters, earned their livings in clubs and shows that were financed with "dirty" money.

11. Ecklund is quoted in the album liner notes for *Peter Ecklund and the Melody Makers* (Stomp Off S.O.S. 1175); the album includes Ecklund's rendition of Smith's challenging, manic "Jazz Battle."

12. Schuller, *Early Jazz,* p. 210.

13. In 1929 Armstrong recorded his first popular tune, "I Can't Give You Anything But Love." Although the label on the 78 read "Louis Armstrong and His Savoy Ballroom Five," the orchestra actually consisted of ten musicians: a big band. Some other noteworthy Armstrong recordings of 1929, such as "Some of These Days," "When You're Smiling," "After You've Gone," and "I Ain't Got Nobody," used eleven musicians. These quality pop songs, recorded in big band formats, helped win Armstrong an ever larger audience. His professionally crafted songs were also superior melodically to the casually created numbers that Smith was offering.

14. Price is quoted in Pleasants, *Great American Popular Singers,* p. 104.

15. Rex Stewart is quoted in the album liner notes for *Jabbo Smith and His Rhythm Aces—Sweet 'N' Low Down* (Affinity AFS 1029).

16. Like many of his generation, Armstrong believed that, as a black man, it was essential that he have a white man (Glaser) deal with the white business world for him. Glaser may have taken advantage of Armstrong, but Armstrong knew he would never have made as much money as he did—or gotten the prime jobs—if he had used a black manager or tried to handle his career himself.

17. Undated letter, Michel Bastide to the author (ca. Nov. 1988).

18. Ibid.

19. The Columbia Broadcasting System, contending it owned exclusive rights to "Amos and Andy," sued to block production of Silverman's musical. A federal district court judge in Manhattan initially ruled in favor of CBS, but on February 7, 1989, the United States Court of Appeals for the Second Circuit ruled that the rights to all pre-1948 "Amos and Andy" radio scripts had passed into the public domain because CBS had not renewed the copyrights.

20. "Joe Franklin Show," WWOR-TV, Jan. 13, 1988, from the author's notes.

21. Liner notes, *Jabbo Smith, Hidden Treasure: Volume One* (Jazz Art Productions).

A Guide to Further Listening

The problem with recommending recordings of jazz reissues is that albums often go in and out of print so quickly that a discography is apt to be partially obsolete even before it is published. Throughout this book, noteworthy original recordings have been mentioned, and reissues of some of them are likely to remain available even if specific albums recommended here do go out of print. For example, Bud Freeman soloed on so many recordings with Tommy Dorsey's band from 1936 to 1938 that samples of his work with Dorsey always seem to be available, even though RCA periodically releases new albums of Dorsey reissues and deletes others. The contents of some albums that have recently gone out of print are also likely to eventually turn up in compact disc form. Addresses are provided for smaller companies mentioned here since you may not be able to find their records in local stores.

Bix Beiderbecke, Bud Freeman, and Jimmy McPartland are much better represented on albums than the other musicians discussed in this book. In 1988 Sunbeam Records (13821 Calvert Street, Van Nuys, CA 91401) released *Sincerely, Bix Beiderbecke,* a twenty-album boxed set containing every recording on which Beiderbecke is known to have played, as well as samples of work by players influenced by him, such as Red Nichols, Jimmy McPartland, and Sterling Bose. This set presents Beiderbecke in far better sound than did earlier reissues. Indeed, on some selections Beiderbecke flares up with a brilliance that made me feel, when I listened to the set, that I was hearing him for the first time.

Columbia has long kept in print a very good sampling of Beiderbecke's work on three albums: *The Bix Beiderbecke Story,* volumes 1 (CL 844), 2 (CL 845), and 3 (CL 846), which include such masterpieces as "Singin' the Blues," "I'm Comin' Virginia," and "In a Mist." In 1989 RCA Bluebird released (in cassette, album, and CD form) *Bix Lives* (6845-4-RB), which includes "Clementine," with Jean Goldkette, and "San," "Lonely Melody," and "Dardenella," with Paul Whiteman. *The Unheard Bix* (Broadway 102; Broadway Intermission Records, Box 100, Brighton, MI 48116) offers obscure sides, not always with very good fidelity.

Recordings of Bud Freeman and Jimmy McPartland are readily available. *The Chicagoans—The Austin High Gang (1928–1930)* (MCA-1350) gives a spirited sampling of late 1920s Chicago jazz, although most of it actually is not (despite the title) by Austin High Gang members per se. *Sounds of Chicago (1923–1940)* (Columbia 4CSP JSN-6042) contains classic Austin High Gang sides but has unfortunately been allowed to go out of print, as has *Swing Street* (Epic SN-6042), an important collection that includes the quintessential Freeman recording, "The Eel," plus "Home Cookin' " and "Tennessee Twilight," as well as a wide sampling of swing era recordings by various artists that help to put those sides into their musical context. These two sets are worth looking for in libraries or used record shops.

Early Freeman may also be heard on a few cuts on *Red Nichols and His Five Pennies, 1929–31, Featuring Benny Goodman* (Sunbeam SB-137). *Chicago/New York Dixieland ("At the Jazz Band Ball")* (RCA Bluebird 6752-2) offers Freeman in the company of Eddie Condon, Muggsy Spanier, and others. Freeman turns up repeatedly in volumes 2–7 of RCA's *Complete Tommy Dorsey* series, covering the years 1936–38, and assorted other Dorsey albums. Freeman participates in recordings on volumes 6 and 7 of RCA's *Complete Benny Goodman* series (which was recently repackaged into a boxed set, *Benny Goodman, The RCA Victor Years,* covering Goodman's entire RCA output from 1935 to 1939), although Goodman used Freeman much less than Dorsey did. Out of print at this time is *Jack Teagarden—King of the Blues Trombone* (Columbia Special Products JSN-6044), a superb three-album set that has sides including Freeman and McPartland. Then there is: *Bud Freeman, The Commodore Years* (Atlantic ATC 2-309); *Midnight at Eddie Condon's* (TRP 5529; Trip Records, distributed by Springboard Records, Inc., 947 U.S. Highway #1, Rahway, NJ 07065); *That Toddlin' Town: Chicago Jazz Revisited* (Atlantic 90461-1), with Condon, Freeman, and others; *Bud Freeman All-Stars Featuring Shorty Baker* (Fantasy/OJC-183); *World's Greatest Jazz Band of Yank Lawson and Bob Haggart Live* (Atlantic 90982-1/Jazzlore 47), including fine latter-day Freeman on "That D-Minor Thing"; *Bud Freeman and Buddy Tate—Two Beautiful* (Circle 69); and the particularly recommended *Compleat Bud Freeman* (Jazzology J-165; the last two are available from Collector's Record Club, GHB Jazz Foundation Building, 1206 Decatur St., New Orleans, LA 70116).

Early samples of Jimmy McPartland's work may be heard on *Benny Goodman with Ben Pollack (1926–31)* (Sunbeam SB-136). *A Jazz Holiday* (MCA 2-4018) includes recordings McPartland made with Benny Goodman in 1928, plus classic period recordings by Red Nichols, Adrian Rollini, Joe Venuti, and Eddie Lang, which evoke well the white jazz scene of the late twenties and early thirties. *Jimmy McPartland—Shades of Bix* (MCA 2-4110), a highly recommended sampling of McPartland's work, includes recordings he made in tribute to Beiderbecke in the 1950s, as well as other recordings he made in the 1930s. Halcyon Records (Box 4255 Grand Central Station, New York, NY 10017) offers Jimmy McPartland on such albums as *Marian and Jimmy McPartland—Going Back a Ways (1948–1949)* (Halcyon 116) and *The McPartlands Live at the Monticello* (Halcyon 107). Available by mail from the Collector's Record Club (GHB Jazz Foundation Building, 1206 Decatur St., New Orleans, LA 70116) are *Jimmy McPartland on Stage* (1967; Jazzology 16); *One Night Stand* (Jimmy and Marian McPartland, 1976; Jazzology 137); and *Bud Freeman and Jimmy McPartland Meet Ted Easton's Jazzband* (Circle 10). *Chicago Jazz Summit* (Atlantic 81844-1) includes a bit of Jimmy and Marian McPartland at the 1986 JVC Jazz Festival in New York.

Jabbo Smith, The Ace of Rhythm (1929) (MCA 1347) contains the best of Smith's recorded work from 1929, when he was at his peak. A larger sampling of Smith's work from that period is available on the harder-to-find *Jabbo Smith, Trumpet Ace of the '20s* (two records; Melodeon 7326/7; distributed by Waterfall Records, Box 109, Canaan, NY 12029). *Jabbo Smith—Sweet 'N' Low Down* (Affinity AFS 1029) contains, in addition to classic 1929 Rhythm Aces recordings, two 1927 Duke Ellington sides featuring Smith: "Black and Tan Fantasy" and "What Can a Poor Fellow Do?" (If you can't find this British import in a record store, write to Charly Records Ltd., 156/166 Ilderton Road, London SE15 INT, England). *Jabbo Smith, Hidden Treasure,* volumes 1 and 2, available from Jazz Art Productions (2 Charlton Street, New York, NY 10014) capture him in 1961. *Jabbo Smith and the Hot Antic Jazzband: European Concerts* (Memories ME 04) was recorded live in Europe in 1982. That album has not been widely distributed in America, but you could write to the producer, Jean-Pierre Daubresse (Amis du Jazz Traditional, 6 Villa Coeur de Vey, 75014 Paris, France) to learn how to obtain a copy.

Sam Wooding and His Chocolate Dandies (Biograph #112025; Biograph Records, Inc., P.O. Box 109, Canaan, NY 12029) contains recordings Wooding's band made in Germany in 1925 and in Spain in 1929. *Black and White Jazz in Europe, 1929* (Wolverine 5; Wolverine Records, 2919 Pine Grove, Chicago, IL 60657) contains six recordings Wooding's band made in France in 1929, as well as recordings of other bands in Europe at that time.

The only album recorded under Freddie Moore's name is *The Great Freddie Moore* (New York Jazz J-001; New York Jazz, a Micallef/Davis Co., Room 4D, 27 Washington Square North, New York, NY 10011). The sides Moore recorded with King Oliver are not in print at this time, although you might find a copy of the deleted RCA album in a library or used record store.

Benny Waters has recorded albums in a variety of European countries (including France, Belgium, Germany, Czechoslovakia, and Italy); however, most of those albums are not to be found in U.S. stores. *The True Side of Benny Waters* (KS 2041), released by Sweden's Kenneth Records, may show up in some larger stores, or you may write Kenneth Records (c/o Classic Jazz Productions, Ramgrand 1, s-175-47 Jarfalla, Sweden). *Benny Waters and the Hot Antic Jazz Band* (Memories ME 05) captures Waters at age eighty playing songs ranging from "Nagasaki" to "She's Funny That Way" and singing "When You're Smiling." Recordings Waters made with Clarence Williams may be heard on *Clarence Williams' Orchestra, 1927–1929* (Biograph BLP-12006) and *Clarence Williams, Volume 2, 1927–28* (Biograph BLP-12038). The sides Waters recorded with Charlie Johnson's orchestra are not in print in the United States at this time, except for "Hot Tempered Blues" and "The Boy in the Boat" on *Early Black Swing* (RCA 9583-2-RB). Waters was in Jimmie Lunceford's band for some of the period covered by the album *Jimmie Lunceford, The Last Sparks, 1941–44* (MCA 1321). Waters's 1928 arrangement of "Aunt Hagar's Blues" may be heard on the album *King Oliver and the Dixie Syncopaters—Papa Joe* (MCA 1309) and on *The Encyclopedia of Jazz on Records, Volumes 1 and 2* (MCA 2-4062), which include a variety of 1920s and 1930s recordings that are helpful in understanding the music of the period covered in this book. Waters commented in February 1989 that Muse Records had an unreleased album by him and that he expected Stomp Off Records to release an album by him.

Sellers of used and out-of-print jazz records advertise regularly in such publications as *Cadence, Coda,* and the *Mississippi Rag.* The Institute of Jazz Studies (Bradley Hall–Room 135, Rutgers University, Newark, NJ 07102) will, for a fee, make copies for research purposes of out-of-print jazz recordings from their extensive collection.

Selected Bibliography

Allen, Frederick Lewis. *Only Yesterday: An Informal History of the 1920s.* New York: Perennial Library/Harper and Row, 1964.

Armstrong, Louis. *Satchmo: My Life in New Orleans.* New York: Prentice Hall, 1954.

Balliett, Whitney. *Jelly Roll, Jabbo and Fats.* New York: Oxford University Press, 1983.

Basie, Count (as told to Albert Murray). *Good Morning Blues: The Autobiography of Count Basie.* New York: Random House, 1985.

Berger, Morroe, Edward Berger, and James Patrick. *Benny Carter: A Life in American Music.* Metuchen, N.J.: Scarecrow Press and the Institute of Jazz Studies, Rutgers University, 1982.

Bernhardt, Clyde E. B. (as told to Sheldon Harris). *I Remember: Eighty Years of Black Entertainment, Big Bands, and the Blues.* Philadelphia: University of Pennsylvania Press, 1986.

Berton, Ralph. *Remembering Bix.* New York: Harper and Row, 1974.

Blesh, Rudi. *Shining Trumpets: A History of Jazz.* New York: Alfred A. Knopf, 1946.

Bruyninckx, Walter. *Sixty Years of Recorded Jazz, 1917–1977.* Mechlin, Belgium: n.p., 1978.

Carmichael, Hoagy. *The Stardust Road.* New York: Greenwood Press, 1969.

Castelli, Vittorio, Evert (Ted) Kaleveld, and Liborio Pusateri. *The Bix Bands.* Milan: Raretone, 1972.

Charters, Samuel B., and Leonard Kunstadt. *Jazz: A History of the New York Scene.* New York: Da Capo Press, 1981.

Chilton, John. *Who's Who of Jazz.* 4th ed. New York: Da Capo Press, 1985.

Collier, James Lincoln. *Duke Ellington.* New York: Oxford University Press, 1987.

Condon, Eddie, and Hank O'Neal. *The Eddie Condon Scrapbook of Jazz.* New York: St. Martin's Press, 1973.

Condon, Eddie, and Thomas Sugrue. *We Called It Music.* New York: Henry Holt and Company, 1947.

Deffaa, Chip. "The Sons of Bix Keep Blowing," *Princeton Alumni Weekly,* May 2, 1984, pp. 30–35.

Deffaa, Chip. *Swing Legacy.* Metuchen, N.J.: Scarecrow Press and the Institute of Jazz Studies, Rutgers University, 1989.

DeLong, Thomas A. *Pops: Paul Whiteman, King of Jazz.* Piscataway, N.J.: New Century Publishers, 1983.

Driggs, Frank, and Harris Lewine. *Black Beauty, White Heat: A Pictorial History of Classic Jazz, 1920–1950.* New York: William Morrow and Co., 1982.

Eberly, Philip K. *Music in the Air.* New York: Hastings House, 1982.

Ellington, Duke. *Music Is My Mistress.* Garden City, N.Y.: Doubleday, 1973.

Feather, Leonard. *The Encyclopedia of Jazz.* New York: Da Capo Press, 1985.

Ferguson, Otis. *The Otis Ferguson Reader.* Ed. Dorothy Chamberlain and Robert Wilson. Highland Park, Ill.: December Press, 1983.

Freeman, Bud. *If You Know of a Better Life.* Dublin: Bashall Eves, 1976.

Freeman, Bud. *You Don't Look Like a Musician.* Detroit: Balamp Publishing, 1974.

Freeman, Bud, as told to Robert Wolf. *Crazeology: The Autobiography of a Chicago Jazzman.* Urbana: University of Illinois Press, 1989.

Giddins, Gary. *Satchmo.* New York: Dolphin Book/Doubleday, 1988.

Goodman, Benny, and Irving Kolodin. *The Kingdom of Swing.* New York: Frederick Ungar Publishing Co., 1961.

Hadlock, Richard. *Jazz Masters of the Twenties.* New York: Macmillan, 1965.

Haskins, Jim. *The Cotton Club.* New York: New American Library, 1984.

Hodes, Art, and Chadwick Hansen, eds. *Selections from the Gutter.* Berkeley: University of California Press, 1977.

Jewell, Derek. *A Portrait of Duke Ellington.* New York: W. W. Norton and Co., 1977.

Johnson, Grady. *The Five Pennies.* New York: Dell, 1959.

Kaminsky, Max, with V. E. Hughes. *My Life in Jazz.* New York: Harper and Row, 1963.

Keepnews, Orrin, and Bill Grauer, Jr. *A Pictorial History of Jazz.* New York: Bonanza Books, 1966.

Kernfeld, Barry, ed. *The New Grove Dictionary of Jazz.* New York: Grove's Dictionaries of Music, 1988.

Kimball, Robert, and William Bolcom. *Reminiscing with Sissle and Blake.* New York: Viking Press, 1973.

Lax, Roger, and Frederick Smith. *The Great Song Thesaurus.* New York: Oxford University Press, 1984.

Larkin, Philip. *All What Jazz.* New York: Farrar Straus Giroux, 1985.

McPartland, Marian. *All in Good Time.* New York: Oxford University Press, 1987.

Manone, Wingy, and Paul Vendervoort II. *Trumpet on the Wing*. Garden City, N.Y.: Doubleday, 1948.

Mezzrow, Milton "Mezz," and Bernard Wolfe. *Really the Blues*. New York: Random House, 1946.

Miller, Tari, ed. *The Princeton Recollector*. Princeton, N.J., 1980.

Pearson, Nathan W., Jr. *Goin' to Kansas City*. Urbana: University of Illinois Press, 1987.

Pleasants, Henry. *The Great American Popular Singers*. New York: Simon and Schuster, 1974.

Ramsey, Frederick, Jr., and Charles Edward Smith, eds. *Jazzmen*. New York: Limelight Editions, 1985.

Rust, Brian. *Jazz Records, 1897–1942*. Chigwell, England: Storyville Publications, 1982.

Sanford, Herb. *Tommy and Jimmy: The Dorsey Years*. New York: Da Capo Press, 1980.

Sanjek, Russell. *From Print to Plastic: Publishing and Promoting America's Popular Music (1900–1980)*. New York: Institute for Studies in American Music, Conservatory of Music, Brooklyn College of the City University of New York, 1983.

Schuller, Gunther. *Early Jazz*. New York: Oxford University Press, 1968.

Schuller, Gunther. *Musing*. New York: Oxford University Press, 1986.

Shapiro, Nat, and Nat Hentoff, eds. *Hear Me Talkin' to Ya*. New York: Dover Publications, 1966.

Shapiro, Nat, and Nat Hentoff, eds. *The Jazz Makers*. New York: Rinehart, 1957.

Shaw, Artie. *The Trouble with Cinderella*. New York: Da Capo Press, 1979.

Simon, George T. *The Big Bands*. New York: Schirmer Books, 1981.

Simon, George T. *Simon Says: The Sights and Sounds of the Swing Era, 1935–1955*. New York: Galahad Books, 1971.

Stearns, Marshall. *The Story of Jazz*. New York: Mentor Books, 1958.

Stearns, Marshall, and Jean Stearns. *Jazz Dance*. New York: Schirmer Books, 1968.

Stewart, Rex. *Jazz Masters of the Thirties*. New York: Macmillan, 1972.

Stillman, Edmund, and Marshall Davidson. *The American Heritage History of the 20's and 30's*. New York: American Heritage Publishing Co., 1970.

Sudhalter, Richard M., and Philip R. Evans, with William Dean-Myatt. *Bix: Man and Legend*. New Rochelle, N.Y., Arlington House, 1974.

Walker, Stanley. *The Night Club Era*. New York: Blue Ribbon Books, 1933.

Wareing, Charles H., and George Garlick. *Bugles for Beiderbecke*. London: Jazz Book Club, 1960.

Waters, Benny. *The Key to a Jazzy Life*. Privately printed in France, 1985.

Williams, Martin. *Jazz Masters of New Orleans*. New York: Macmillan, 1967.

Index

Index

Index

Index

Index

Index

Index

Index

Index

Index

Index

Index

Index

Index

A Note on the Author

CHIP DEFFAA, a jazz critic for the *New York Post,* has published jazz reviews and interviews in such publications as *Down Beat, Jazz Times,* the *Mississippi Rag,* and England's *Storyville* and *Crescendo.* A graduate of Princeton University, he has contributed to the landmark *New Grove Dictionary of Jazz,* authored the recently published *Swing Legacy* (Scarecrow Press and the Institute of Jazz Studies), and is at work on *A Jazz Portait Gallery.*

Books in the Series Music in American Life

Only a Miner: Studies in Recorded Coal-Mining Songs
Archie Green

Great Day Coming: Folk Music and the American Left
R. Serge Denisoff

John Philip Sousa: A Descriptive Catalog of His Works
Paul E. Bierley

The Hell-Bound Train: A Cowboy Songbook
Glenn Ohrlin

Oh, Didn't He Ramble: The Life Story of Lee Collins as Told to Mary Collins
Frank J. Gillis and John W. Miner, Editors

American Labor Songs of the Nineteenth Century
Philip S. Foner

Stars of Country Music: Uncle Dave Macon to Johnny Rodriguez
Bill C. Malone and Judith McCulloh, Editors

Git Along, Little Dogies: Songs and Songmakers of the American West
John I. White

A Texas-Mexican *Cancionero:* Folksongs of the Lower Border
Americo Paredes

San Antonio Rose: The Life and Music of Bob Wills
Charles R. Townsend

Early Downhome Blues: A Musical and Cultural Analysis
Jeff Todd Titon

An Ives Celebration: Papers and Panels of the Charles Ives Centennial Festival-Conference
H. Wiley Hitchcock and Vivian Perlis, Editors

Sinful Tunes and Spirituals: Black Folk Music to the Civil War
Dena J. Epstein

Joe Scott, the Woodsman-Songmaker
Edward D. Ives

Jimmie Rodgers: The Life and Times of America's Blue Yodeler
Nolan Porterfield

Early American Music Engraving and Printing: A History of Music Publishing in America from 1787 to 1825 with Commentary on Earlier and Later Practices
Richard J. Wolfe

Sing a Sad Song: The Life of Hank Williams
Roger M. Williams

Long Steel Rail: The Railroad in American Folksong
Norm Cohen

Resources of American Music History: A Directory of Source Materials from Colonial Times to World War II
D. W. Krummel, Jean Geil, Doris J. Dyen, and Deanne L. Root

Tenement Songs: The Popular Music of the Jewish Immigrants
Mark Slobin

Ozark Folksongs
Vance Randolph; Edited and Abridged by Norm Cohen

Oscar Sonneck and American Music
William Lichtenwanger, Editor

Bluegrass Breakdown: The Making of the Old Southern Sound
Robert Cantwell

Bluegrass: A History
Neil V. Rosenberg

Music at the White House: A History of the American Spirit
Elise K. Kirk

Red River Blues: The Blues Tradition in the Southeast
Bruce Bastin

Good Friends and Bad Enemies: Robert Winslow Gordon and the Study of American Folksong
Debora Kodish

Fiddlin' Georgia Crazy: Fiddlin' John Carson, His Real World, and the World of His Songs
Gene Wiggins

America's Music: From the Pilgrims to the Present
Revised Third Edition
Gilbert Chase

Secular Music in Colonial Annapolis: The Tuesday Club, 1745–56
John Barry Talley

Bibliographical Handbook of American Music
D. W. Krummel

Goin' to Kansas City
Nathan W. Pearson, Jr.

"Susanna," "Jeanie," and "The Old Folks at Home": The Songs of Stephen C. Foster from His Time to Ours
Second Edition
William W. Austin

Songprints: The Musical Experience of Five Shoshone Women
Judith Vander

"Happy in the Service of the Lord": Afro-American Gospel Quartets in Memphis
Kip Lornell

Paul Hindemith in the United States
Luther Noss

"My Song Is My Weapon": People's Songs, American Communism, and the Politics of Culture
Robbie Lieberman

Chosen Voices: The Story of the American Cantorate
Mark Slobin

Theodore Thomas: America's Conductor and Builder of Orchestras, 1835–1905
Ezra Schabas

"The Whorehouse Bells Were Ringing" and Other Songs Cowboys Sing
Guy Logsdon

Crazeology: The Autobiography of a Chicago Jazzman
Bud Freeman, as Told to Robert Wolf

Discoursing Sweet Music: Town Bands and Community Life in Turn-of-the-Century Pennsylvania
Kenneth Kreitner

Mormonism and Music: A History
Michael Hicks

Voices of the Jazz Age: Profiles of Eight Vintage Jazzmen
Chip Deffaa